The Fall into Eden

Other books in the series
ROBERT ZALLER: *The Cliffs of Solitude*
PETER CONN: *The Divided Mind*
PATRICIA CALDWELL: *The Puritan Conversion Narrative*
STEPHEN FREDMAN: *Poet's Prose*
CHARLES ALTIERI: *Self and Sensibility in Contemporary American Poetry*
JOHN McWILLIAMS: *Hawthorne, Melville, and the American Character*
BARTON ST. ARMAND: *Emily Dickinson and Her Culture*
ELIZABETH MCKINSEY: *Niagara Falls*
ALBERT J. VON FRANK: *The Sacred Game*
MARJORIE PERLOFF: *The Dance of the Intellect*
ALBERT GELPI: *Wallace Stevens*
ANN KIBBEY: *The Interpretation of Material Shapes in Puritanism*
SACVAN BERCOVITCH and MYRA JEHLEN: *Ideology and Classic American Literature*
KAREN ROWE: *Saint and Singer*
LAWRENCE BUELL: *New England Literary Culture*

Yosemite Valley. A wood engraving based upon a sketch by Thomas Ayres in 1855, "the first ever taken." From J. M. Hutchings's *Scenes of Wonder and Curiosity in California* (1870).

The Fall into Eden

Landscape and Imagination in California

DAVID WYATT

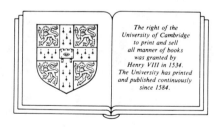

The right of the
University of Cambridge
to print and sell
all manner of books
was granted by
Henry VIII in 1534.
The University has printed
and published continuously
since 1584.

CAMBRIDGE UNIVERSITY PRESS

Cambridge

London   New York   New Rochelle

Melbourne   Sydney

Published by the Press Syndicate of the University of Cambridge
The Pitt Building, Trumpington Street, Cambridge CB2 1RP
32 East 57th Street, New York, NY 10022, USA
10 Stamford Road, Oakleigh, Melbourne 3166, Australia

First published 1986

Printed in the United States of America

Library of Congress Cataloging-in-Publication Data

Wyatt, David, 1953–

The fall into Eden.

(Cambridge studies in American literature and culture)

Bibliography: p.

Includes index.

1. American literature – California – History and
criticism.   2. California in literature.   3. Landscape
in literature.   4. Eden in literature.   I. Title.
II. Series.

PS283.C2W9 1986   810'.9'9794   86-1004

ISBN 0 521 32399 1

British Library Cataloguing in Publication applied for.

CREDITS

Frontispiece and cover: Yosemite Valley. From J. M. Hutchings's *Scenes of Wonder and Curiosity in California* (1870). Courtesy, Graphic Arts Collection, Princeton University. 1. Bonneville's map. Courtesy, Princeton University Library. 2. John C. Frémont. Courtesy, the Bancroft Library. 3. Hetch Hetchy Valley. Photograph by Taber. Courtesy, John Muir Papers, Holt-Atherton Pacific Center for Western Studies, University of the Pacific. Copyright 1984 Muir-Hanna Trust. 4. John Muir. Courtesy, the Bancroft Library. 5. California Geological Survey. Courtesy, U. S. Geological Survey. 6. "Winter Sunrise, the Sierra Nevada from Lone Pine, California, 1944." Photograph by Ansel Adams. Courtesy of the Trustees of the Ansel Adams Publishing Rights Trust. All rights reserved. 7. San Emigdio Ranch. Photograph by Carleton Watkins. Courtesy, the Library of Congress. 8. The basket woman. Courtesy, the Huntington Library. 9. Frank Norris. Courtesy, the Bancroft Library. 10. San Juan Bautista. Courtesy, the Bancroft Library. 11. "John's tree." Photograph by Ann Porotti. 12. John and Elaine Steinbeck. Courtesy, University of Virginia Library. 13. *True Confessions*. From the United Artists release *True Confessions* © 1981 United Artists Corporation. 14. *The Big Sleep*. From the United Artists release *The Big Sleep* © 1946 Warner Brothers Pictures Inc. Renewed 1973 United Artists Television, Inc. 15. Tor House and the Tower. Courtesy, Occidental College Library. 16. Gary Snyder and Masa Uehara. Photograph by Banyam Ashram. Courtesy, New Directions Publishing Company.

FOR MY FATHER

The extent to which certain places dominate the California imagination is apprehended, even by Californians, only dimly. Deriving not only from the landscape but from the claiming of it, from the romance of emigration, the radical abandonment of established attachments, this imagination remains obdurately symbolic, tending to locate lessons in what the rest of the country perceives only as scenery.

– Joan Didion

Contents

═══════════

List of illustrations   *page* ix

Acknowledgments   xi

Prologue: The mythology of the region   xv

1   Spectatorship and abandonment: Dana, Leonard, and
    Frémont   1

2   Muir and the possession of landscape   32

3   King and catastrophe   47

4   Mary Austin: nature and nurturance   67

5   Norris and the vertical   96

6   Steinbeck's lost gardens   124

7   Chandler, marriage, and "the Great Wrong Place"   158

8   Jeffers, Snyder, and the ended world   174

    Epilogue: Fictions of space   206

    Notes   211

    Bibliography   247

    Index   269

Illustrations

Yosemite Valley   Frontispiece
1. Bonneville's map   9
2. John C. Frémont   29
3. Hetch Hetchy Valley   40
4. John Muir   44
5. California Geological Survey   54
6. "Winter Sunrise, the Sierra Nevada from Lone Pine, California, 1944"   61
7. San Emigdio Ranch   77
8. The basket woman   85
9. Frank Norris   99
10. San Juan Bautista   110
11. "John's tree"   125
12. John and Elaine Steinbeck   156
13. *True Confessions*   159
14. *The Big Sleep*   167
15. Tor House and the Tower   177
16. Gary Snyder and Masa Uehara   201

Acknowledgments

===

This project began with my father, James Wyatt, who showed me the territory, and who never got lost. The book is dedicated to him as the most adaptive Californian I know.

The idea for this book came to me while reading John Muir. He gets the last word, because he provoked the first one.

Four people gave me essential support in the period of setting out. I remember a wonderful day on Solano Avenue when Robert Hawley began pulling books off the shelves in his Ross Valley Book Store. He gave me a bracing glimpse of the extent of the literature, and of one man's love for it. Kevin Starr provided me not only with a model of scholarship but with advice and encouragement as well. His willingness to believe persisted over five years, from the early letters in which he urged me to press on, to his reading of the final manuscript for the press. I hope that he recognizes in my book a spirit kindred to his own. James Hart gave me a warm reception at the Bancroft Library and read my prospectus with generous scrutiny. He supplied me with essential information on Richard Henry Dana, as well as giving us all *A Companion to California,* a book I seem to have opened daily since buying it. Robert Hass came to Charlottesville at a crucial stage in my work, and talked with me about California. He showed me how a mind full of a place could sublimate its learning into living metaphors. I hope he recognizes as not too misshapen the ideas I have stolen.

Bob Smith did yeoman service as a researcher in the early days. His map of the field was later filled in by John Leo, who exposed me to many odd corners of the West, both past and present. Donald Wesling and Robert Engberg kindly sent me the galleys of their book on Muir, and thereby offered up a text worth arguing with. Clarence King proved more fugitive, and I was aided in my unsuccessful attempt to track down his descendants by Thurman Wilkins, Fritioff Fryxell, and James Shebl. Peter Davison urged me to keep on the trail. Rae Ballard gave me key information on Mary Austin, as well as a careful reading of my Austin chapter. It was great fun to read Merril Greene's screenplay for a movie about Austin, *Lost Borders,* as well as to talk with her about ways to narrate and visualize the life. Jackson Benson came to my aid in a search for photographs of Steinbeck Country. I am also glad that his biography of Steinbeck appeared in time for me to test my theories against its meticulous research. Alfred Bush helped in the final round-up of my photographs.

In the matter of reconnaissance, three people were boon companions. Libby Ortiz remembers, I hope, as I do, the many happy days spent driving and camping up and down California. Frank Cebulski put me in touch with Bob Hawley as well as a host of other fascinating people and places in the Bay Area. Tim Coffin gave me the freedom to navigate and talk as we spent a special week doing a loop that took in a lynx at Point Reyes, a storm on Mount Dana, and freshly baked bread at Mission San Juan Bautista.

Those who volunteered to read this book likewise helped in the creation of it. David Levin, like Kevin Starr, was there at the beginning and the end. His readings of two early chapters helped me focus on the facts, and his final service as a reader for Cambridge ensured that my style as well as my scholarship was tested against his high standards. John Irwin gave the chapters on Muir and King the benefit of his usual gusto. Al Filreis helped me erect the argument of the Norris chapter, and gave the whole its first complete and sympathetic reading. Don Sheehy also went through the whole with his eagle eye. He helped me to make small and big changes, especially the addition of two key transitional passages. Bob Schultz came on board near the end, but his reading of the pages about Jeffers and Snyder strengthened me in the resolve that I still had a book worth finishing.

Norman Grabo was the man who made the first step in getting this book published. I thank him for this and many other favors. Albert Gelpi shepherded the manuscript through the acceptance process and gave valuable aid and counsel along the way. The editors and staff at Cambridge University Press have proven a model of courtesy and efficiency. My thanks especially to Andrew Brown, Jeanne Burke, Renée Gernand, Rhona Johnson, and Nancy Landau. Lewis Simpson, George Core, and Staige Blackford were kind enough to publish portions of this book in *The Southern Review, The Sewanee Review,* and *The Virginia Quarterly Review.* Permission to reprint those pages from "Muir and the Possession of Landscape," "Norris and the Vertical," and "Gary Snyder and the Curve of Return" is here gratefully acknowledged.

Support for this project came in the form of a summer stipend from the National Endowment for the Humanities, a summer grant and a

Sesquicentennial Fellowship from the University of Virginia, and two research fellowships from the Huntington Library. The Huntington was for me during a difficult time an oasis of hospitality and humane scholarship, and Virginia Renner and Martin Ridge made my days there happy ones. I would like to thank the Huntington for giving me permission to quote from the Clarence King and Mary Austin collections.

Ann Porotti helped me in all the ways that only the people we love can help. I am in her special debt for proving that one can swim in the Atlantic as well as the Pacific Ocean.

The final envoi goes to Luke Wyatt, who, even before he could swim, loved what he called the "big water," and with whom I hope to revisit all the good places.

January 1986
Charlottesville, Virginia

Prologue: The mythology of the region

As you drive south from Pasadena to Long Beach, the freeway follows the bed of the Los Angeles River. The river is paved. A trickle runs down the central cement aisle except during flash floods. Just after the freeway crosses the river there is an off-ramp for "Imperial Highway." Multicolored homes fan out in all directions below. There was a house here once, white stucco with palms out front and a good piece of land out back, shaded by persimmon trees. It was called "The Acre." Dairy farms surrounded it, and anything would grow there. You planted or bred whatever you could sell during the Depression: rhubarb, corn, dogs, worms. Fogs off the ocean checked the summer sun, and in the winter the heavy rains came. My father survived the quake of '33 there, and, after the war, the brothers brought their wives home. Soon grandchildren ran across the Bermuda grass, dodging the fallen, ripe persimmons. It was a favored spot of earth, a humanly nurtured landscape, and people came back to it. The Acre is now under the Long Beach Freeway.

This book comes out of that fact. The California I grew up in was a beautiful, now vanished garden. Little did the cousins playing under the trees know that their college friends would one day sneer at the landscapes we were to inherit, although they had never seen them. California has always been a place no sooner had than lost; every family has its paved garden. There is a recurring pattern in the experience of place in California that echoes our First Story. Commissioned to survey the state in the 1860s, William Brewer comes upon a lovely, unweeded garden. In the courtyard of the second oldest mission in California, geraniums flourish as "rank weeds," and, inside the ruined church, "a dead pig lay beneath the finely carved font for holy water." This land of broken cisterns evokes a biblical nostalgia. "I find it hard to realize that I am in America – in the *United States;* the young and vigorous republic as we call her – when I see these ruins. They carry me back to

xv

the Old World with its decline and decay." His is an experience of
simultaneous discovery and fall, and it is not unique. Perhaps Californians have been protected by the experience of a continually disappear-
ing landscape from some of the more stubborn nostalgias. Perpetual
expulsion from paradise ought to breed skepticism about its naive recovery. It is just as likely to leave its dispossessed survivors the stunned
occupants of a perpetual present. The way Californians live in time has
everything to do with the history of their experience of space. That,
however, is the story for another book. This one is for the landscapes
that have survived.

Wallace Stevens claims that "a mythology reflects its region." We
have masterly studies of the regional mythologies of New England and
the South, but few, if any, of the Pacific Coast. Perry Miller has celebrated a "New England Mind," and Lewis Simpson has begun a similar
project for the South. Can such legacies be claimed for California? The
answer, I think, has everything to do with landscape. In the literature of
the West, and of California in particular, the energies that had been
concentrated into convenant theology or the rationalization of southern
history are displaced into an unmediated encounter with landscape. In
California the history of these encounters usurps the function of ideology. The experience of landscape is understood to control, or validate,
human life. In graphing landscape, California writers also measure, in
indirect acts of autobiography, the power of the self in relation to the
world. The mythology of this region takes as its underlying premise
the apotheosis of the Pathetic Fallacy.

The American settlement of California marked the end of Western
man's Hesperian movement. So great was the beauty of the land that it
conferred on the completion of the quest the illusion of a return to a
privileged source. As the sense of an ending merged with the wonder of
beginnings, California as last chance merged with California as Eden. It
proves a garden but briefly held. The city that rises like an exhalation,
San Francisco, burns and rises again and again. For Bayard Taylor, this
panorama of "dissolving views" proves the type of all California landscape. Returning to California in the same year as Richard Henry Dana,
he discovers as well that California is the place that repudiates *déjà vu*.
Whole mountains have been hosed away. The moral of *New Pictures
from California* (1862), the chastened sequel to *El Dorado* (1850), is that
nothing gold can stay. The tonic and insidious effects of the perpetual
state of sudden wonder induced by California landscape stand behind
my title, *The Fall into Eden*. The sense of dispossession with which
imaginative careers in California usually end also evokes the Edenic
paradigm. Loss here becomes associated with some irrecoverable spot
of earth. It is not clear that the recompense for such loss is a paradise

within. My book will therefore conclude with some speculations on the
liabilities of operating within a literary tradition – one as national as it is
regional – that projects psychomachia into a space empty of other selves
and the institutions they create.

My focus will be on the unfolding of this mythology in imaginative
literature. I have divided my book into two central sections with two
introductory and two concluding chapters. The early naturalists see
landscape as validating human behavior; the later novelists see landscape
as controlling or restraining it. John Muir, Mary Austin, and Clarence
King each celebrate the spiritual liberation conferred by a particular
California region; Norris, Steinbeck, and Chandler map the advance of
human hopes against the steady encroachments of space. A penultimate
chapter on the poetry of Robinson Jeffers and Gary Snyder examines
their attempts to find hope in a place where history seems to be ending.
A meditation on our "Fictions of Space" then follows. To place these
classic encounters with landscape within the local tradition that gives
rise to them, I begin with a chapter on Richard Henry Dana, Zenas
Leonard, and John Charles Frémont. These three pioneers discover that
self-consciousness and its discontents will be the recurring melodrama
played out against and within California space.

Few other states have provoked more ambitious projects of self-
definition. Hubert Howe Bancroft's pioneering thirty-nine-volume
history finds its most recent descendant in a format usually reserved
for compendia about national literatures – James Hart's *A Companion to
California* (1978). Any student of the mythology of the region must
acknowledge a debt to the Big Four – Franklin Walker, Carey McWilliams, Kevin Starr, and William Everson. Walker's *San Francisco's Literary Frontier* (1939) eulogizes California's first literary renaissance
through an account of its representative lives, and *A Literary History of
Southern California* (1950) recovers for a region continually threatened
with amnesia a usable past. If the tradition thus disclosed is decidedly
minor, McWilliams restores an amplitude to the story by widening
the focus. *Southern California: An Island on the Land* (1946) celebrates
the process whereby this culture authenticates itself through complex
and quirky public images and rituals. Starr fuses literary criticism and
sociology in the first truly "cultural" history of California. *Americans
and the California Dream, 1850–1915* (1973) dignifies the history of the
state by discerning in its major fantasies and imaginative achievements
a unique and answerable style. *Inventing the Dream: California Through
the Progressive Era* (1985) extends Starr's narrative to Southern California and secures his place as the foremost interpreter of life in the Far
West. Where Starr envisions the story of California as the recurring
betrayal of a consciously articulated dream, Everson assumes an even

deeper unity of regional consciousness. In *Archetype West: The Pacific Coast as a Literary Region* (1976), he argues that the literature of the Pacific Slope fulfills itself in moments of apotheosized violence. His is the most ambitious attempt to refer the imaginative productions of the region to the workings of a collective mind.

There are many books about California addressed to Californians; these four authors claim a national audience. I hope this volume also presents a nonprovincial account of a profoundly provincial experience. All literature is in some way the artifact of a specific spot – as William Carlos Williams says, "The classic is the local fully realized, words marked by a place." As a practical critic, I focus on the language of specific texts as they are marked by a place. As a Californian and an American, I try to place these readings within our traditions of national self-characterization. This is an imaginative biography of a region, and I must apologize in advance for the brevity of the portraits that constitute it. This book is an essay – an attempt – at valorizing for a national audience those California texts that raise the local toward the level of the classic. George Wharton James included over forty figures in his *Heroes of California* (1910). I have settled for a more limited company: eleven writers who define the possibilities for a marriage of mind and place in the spot that *Las Sergas de Esplandián* (1510), the book that gave California its name, located "very close to . . . the Terrestrial Paradise."

Chapter 1

Spectatorship and abandonment: Dana, Leonard, and Frémont

First sightings have a way of foreclosing the future, and a book may one day be attempted on the way our vision of the West has been arrested by those original acts through which its landscape was given a character and a name. It would be a hard book to write; one of the most clearly defined frontiers in human history, the American West is also one of the most obscured by the rhetoric through which, from the beginning, it was packaged and sold. The West held out to its pioneers the chance to become primary, original namers, and yet when they came to write about it, these firstcomers often found response mediated not only by all the conventions of a language but by irrepressible myths of national and even human destiny. Even the man who had found the New World was preempted by the old thinking; Columbus tried to locate Paradise up the Orinoco.

The memorable western voices are those that somehow engage the felt tension between received forms and unprecedented experience. The tension is as old as the ur-document of western exploration, *The Journals of Lewis and Clark*. The drama of *The Journals* lies less in the shape they impose upon the West than in the tension between two kinds of voice. Clark's descriptive syntax seems at times overwhelmed by the shock of the new. Most moving here are those refrain sentences that register the sheer human need to keep track, sentences like "Deer scarce" and "Proceeded on." Lewis's more aggressive and analytical style keeps perhaps too safe a distance from the surround. The true subject of his narration seems to be the quality of his own response, and he is never more characteristic than when taking his own measure, especially on the occasion of his thirty-first birthday in the Rocky Mountains, when he resolves "in future, to life *for mankind,* as I have heretofore lived *for myself.*" When it comes to uncharted territory (geographic or psychological), Clark seems as naively open as Lewis seems self-consciously closed. Clark sees clearly what is before him, and prevents custom and introspection from mediating the emerging ground. Lewis saves *The Journals* from becoming a mere record of incongruity, and links the expedition to recurring human ambitions and concerns. Read together, their receptive and spectatorial accounts achieve a stance toward the West that is full, and human, and compelling.

In this chapter I tell the story of three California originals. Dana was the first writer to come by sea; Leonard, the first to enter California across the Sierra mountain wall. Their words render up a landscape just now coming into being, a world being named – in English – for the first time. But to the simple appeal of an aboriginal vision, Dana and Leonard add something more. For it was their good fortune to prove responsive to that drama of distance which lies at the center of their national literature and the work about California that follows them. California tested their capacity to give and to withhold, and in their contrary responses to the new land they embody the tension that would make or break – their heir is Frémont – so many California careers.

THE SAILOR AND THE TRAPPER

A Harvard undergraduate, suffering from a "weakness of the eyes," ships out for the western coast of North America on the brig *Pilgrim*. On October 1, 1834, he becomes a son of Neptune, without incident. At the watch off Cape Horn, he hears the slow breathing of whales. A friend falls overboard near Patagonia. One hundred and fifty days out of Boston his ship drops anchor south of Point Concepcion. The sailor rides breakers at Santa Barbara, chops wood on Angel Island, saves shipmates from robbery in San Diego. He sails hides seaward from atop the four-hundred-foot bluff that will one day bear his name. After sixteen months on this lonely coast, the *Alert* (now his ship), with forty thousand bullock hides in her hold, sails for home. Twenty-four years later the sailor, now a successful Boston lawyer, returns to find the one shack of Yerba Buena transformed into a city of 100,000: San Francisco.

Three years before the departure of the *Pilgrim,* a young Pennsylvanian rides westward from St. Louis in the fur trade. After months on the prairies south of the Platte, his band makes camp in the Wyoming Rockies. The harsh winter sees them eating beaver skins. A desperate venture to walk the eight hundred miles to Santa Fe fails. A year's continual skirmishing with the Blackfeet and the Rickarees leaves the trapper disposed "to do that which would not have been right." Weak from an arrow wound, he makes a rendezvous with Captain Joseph Walker on the Green River and joins him in his explo-

rations down the Humboldt. The river disappears; the party marches
westward. They come to water and high mountains. A granite defile
with shooting waterfalls interrupts their path. They descend the
range's western flank through trees eighteen fathoms around. Within
weeks the trapper will have passed into a region that baits bulls with
grizzly bears; three months later he crosses the Sierra again on his
eastward trek home.

Richard Henry Dana (1815–82) was nineteen in the year he sailed
westward; Zenas Leonard (1809–58), but twenty-one when his company headed overland on a trip that would end in Monterey. Dana
arrived on the windy coast eleven months after Leonard had started east
again. The two never met, though in San Diego, Dana's ship collided
with the *Lagoda,* the very trader on which Leonard had celebrated New
Year's, as a guest of the captain, the year before. Dana had little but
scorn for trappers (after months of toil they are "stripped of everything" by "amusements and dissipation" in Monterey), and might have
appreciated the irony in Leonard's elevation to a station on board a
sister ship that he, a common sailor, was never to enjoy. Leonard was
matter-of-fact about the ravaging effects of the hide trade on the region's vast cattle herds, whose abandoned carcasses littered the plains
while the cured leather sailed eastward. But the coincidence of their
fates (both men were after animal skins) is more than offset by the
divergence of their responses to the land. Theirs are the first fully
realized American encounters with the landscape of California. The
imaginative stances they adopt become paradigmatic for generations of
sojourners west. *Two Years before the Mast* (1840) is our first self-conscious classic about California, but the *Narrative of the Adventures of
Zenas Leonard* (1839) is the book that unwittingly maps out the land.

The meaning of Dana's California experience hinges on the possibility
of return. *Two Years before the Mast* must be read with its sequel,
Twenty-Four Years After (1869), if we are fully to understand the refusal
of this place to render up a continuity of impressions over time. Dana's
disappointment in return certainly has everything to do with his own
grasping imagination, which had so thoroughly appropriated every detail of the voyage and the coast as to fix it forever beyond the touch of
time. But his story points to a deeper contradiction, one in which the
human imagination is devastated by the sheer power of culture in California to overwhelm the simple permanence of nature.

When Dana returned to California in 1859, this is what he found:

Miles out at sea, on the desolate rocks of the Farallones, gleamed
the powerful rays of one of the most costly and effective light-

houses in the world. As we drew in through the Golden Gate, another light-house met our eyes, and in the clear moonlight of another unbroken California summer we saw, on the right, a large fortification protecting the narrow entrance, and just before us the little island of Alcatraz confronted us, – one entire fortress. We bore round the point toward the old anchoring-ground of the hide ships, and there, covering the sand-hills and the valleys, stretching from the water's edge to the base of the great hills, and from the old Presidio to the Mission, flickering all over with the lamps of its streets and houses, lay a city of one hundred thousand inhabitants.

But this is what he felt in 1835:

The first impression which California had made upon us was very disagreeable; – the open roadstead of Santa Barbara; anchoring three miles from the shore; running out to sea before every south-easter; landing in a high surf; with a little dark – looking town, a mile from the beach; and not a sound to be heard, nor anything to be seen, but Sandwich Islanders, hides, and tallow – bags.

The great bay into which he sailed in 1859 had been a mere "solitude," and the *Alert,* not the landscape surrounding it, had been the "spectacle." As the focus now shifts from ship to shore, Dana is drawn into a revaluation of all that he had once seen.

The unexpected element in Dana's second narrative is the tone of bewildered regret. In 1836, California had been a "hated coast," a land where fresh beef was cheaper than salt. The typical landscape had been San Pedro's:

The land was of a clayey consistency and, as far as the eye could reach, entirely bare of trees and even shrubs; and there was no sign of a town; – not even a house to be seen. What had brought us into such a place, we could not conceive.

Now, as Dana stands beside the pile of dry hides, what was "dreary" becomes "dear":

I was in a dream of San Diego, San Pedro, – with its hills so steep for taking up goods, and its stones so hard to our bare feet, – and the cliffs of San Juan! All this, too, is no more! The entire hide – business is of the past, and to the present inhabitants of California is a dim tradition. The gold discoveries drew off all men from the gathering or curing of hides, the inflowing population made an end of the great droves of cattle; and now not a vessel pursues the – I was about to say the dear – the dreary, once hated business of gathering hides upon the coast, and the beach of San Diego is abandoned and its hide-houses have disappeared.

Dana's second narrative achieves poignance through its discovery that California is the place that refuses *déjà vu*. If "California is a dim tradition" in 1859, what will it prove a generation hence? Any return to such a place is a return to a memory, not a place. "The old spots" are gone. The water where Dana had once beached his boat is now land. Even "the climate has altered" off Point Concepcion, and the winds that blew Cabrillo back no longer plague California shipping. In San Francisco, Dana experiences a profound sense of displacement: "When I saw all these things, and reflected on what I once was and saw here, and what now surrounded me, I could scarcely keep my hold on reality at all, or the genuineness of anything, and seemed to myself like one who had moved in 'worlds not realized.' " The allusion alerts us to Dana's doubts, finally unfounded, about his power to effect the Wordsworthian resolution in which the self is affirmed in proportion to its "obstinate questionings" of the permanence of "outward things."

Dana's meditations on the changingness of occupation and place will lead, gradually and indirectly, to intimations of the immortality of the self. In reenacting his first landing at Santa Barbara, he marvels that "I was somehow unaccountably a passenger." Where landscape had previously seemed an impoverished vacancy, it is now rich with the "softening" tints of memory. As Dana wanders about the harbor of San Diego, the awareness that only the changing self has survived comes upon him: "I alone was left of all, and how strangely was I here." If Dana feels himself to be haunting the site of his youth, it is in part because he only willingly situates himself in California on return.

As a sailor of nineteen, Dana had betrayed a marked ambivalence about locating himself on a specific spot of land, an ambivalence he submerged into a fascination with the vast anonymity of the sea:

> A man dies on shore; his body remains with his friends, and "the mourners go about the streets;" but when a man falls overboard at sea and is lost, there is a suddenness in the event, and a difficulty in realizing it, which give to it an air of awful mystery. A man dies on shore – you follow his body to the grave, and a stone marks the spot. You are often prepared for the event. There is always something which helps you to realize it when it happens, and to recall it when it has passed. A man is shot down by your side in battle, and the mangled body remains an *object* and a *real evidence;* but at sea, the man is near you – at your side – you hear his voice, and in an instant he is gone, and nothing but a *vacancy* shows his loss.

A man dies on shore: This is Dana's most powerfully sounded refrain.
There is a terrible freedom in not being able to "realize" one's mortality, an uncanny gift from the sea. "There is no scenery at sea" Dana
adds in 1869, no spot into which identity can be concentrated. What it
offers instead is a sublime lapsing out, as during sunrise on the water:

> There is something in the first grey streaks stretching along the
> eastern horizon and throwing an indistinct light along the face of
> the deep, which combines with the boundlessness and unknown
> depth of the sea around you, and gives one a feeling of loneliness,
> of dread, and of melancholy foreboding, which nothing else in
> nature can give.

The sheer activity of a sailor's life also keeps faces indistinct. Dana's is a
precise instruction manual in which the notation of every shift of wind
leaves no time for self-consciousness. On water Dana can lose himself
in communal routine. He seems happiest "when once more upon the
ocean, where sky and water meet."

Land for Dana is the place of specific location, of memorials, of *self.*
The "stillness" and "solitude" of California make it the perfect place for
Dana to play out his ambivalence about life ashore. It is a stillness he
can associate with the end of all motion: "Day after day, the sun shone
clear and bright upon the wide bay and the red roofs of the houses;
everything being as still as death, the people hardly seeming to earn
their sunlight." This human culture scarcely troubles the elements. The
landscape is almost completely free of the sense of being a humanly
defined space. Every venture ashore can be one into an anonymity
almost as vast as the sea's, but one that also challenges Dana to give its
locations a name. This is just what happens at Dana Point, near San
Juan Capistrano, "the only romantic spot in California." Dana has
landed in "a small cove, or 'bight,' which gave us, at high tide, a few
square feet of sand-beach between the sea and the bottom of the hill.
This was the only landing-place. Directly before us, rose the perpendicular height of four or five hundred feet." Dana separates himself
from the others, and seats himself on a stone that marks the spot:

> Compared with the plain, dull sand-beach of the rest of the coast,
> this grandeur was as refreshing as a great rock in a weary land. It
> was almost the first time that I had been positively alone – free
> from the sense that human beings were at my elbow, if not talk-
> ing with me – since I had left home. My better nature returned
> strong upon me. Everything was in accordance with my state of
> feeling, and I experienced a glow of pleasure at finding that what
> of poetry and romance I ever had in me had not been entirely
> deadened by the laborious and frittering life I had led.

Here Dana breaks through his reluctance to encounter the self as concentrated in a spot. Poetic selfhood is imaged as a lonely upright figure
in an empty landscape. Such self-definition can readily give way to a
sense of limitation, even mortality, and it is the peculiar luxury of
California landscape that it does not afford many spots in which such
encounters can occur. Dana locates only one other, the small island off
San Pedro where an Englishman lies buried:

> It was always a solemn and interesting spot to me. There it stood
> desolate, and in the midst of desolation; and there were the re-
> mains of one who died and was buried alone and friendless. Had it
> been a common burying-place, it would have been nothing. The
> single body corresponded well with the solitary character of
> everything around. It was the only thing in California from which
> I could ever extract anything like poetry.

This quotation allows us to complete the complex proportion that Dana
had set up between life at sea and life on land. Sea = motion = mystery =
community = life :: Land = stillness = location = self-hood = death.'
From the beginning, Dana sensed that his immortality lay in not identifying himself with a spot of earth. It is only on return that he revalues the
terms of the equation and comes to accept himself as situated, almost as
permanently as the Englishman, on a spot of California land.

As Dana wanders about the "broken bricks and bits of mortar" near
San Diego, his rage against the new California works a change in his
sense of the old: "The past was real. The present, all about me, was
unreal, unnatural, repellant." His sense of dislocation enjoins an act of
reverie in which he seems to see this place for the first time, and the once
ordinary landscape becomes the most privileged place he can recall:

> To rally myself by calling to mind my own better fortune and
> nobler lot, and cherished surroundings at home, was impossible.
> Borne down by depression, the day being yet at its noon, and the
> sun over the old point, – it is four miles to town, the Presidio; I
> have walked it often, and can do it once more, – I passed the
> familiar objects, and it seemed to me that I remembered them
> better than those of any other place I had ever been in; – the open-
> ing to the little cave; the low hills where we cut wood and killed
> rattlesnakes, and where our dogs chased the coyotes; and the black
> ground where so many of the ship's crew and beachcombers used
> to bring up on their return at the end of a liberty day, and spend
> the night *sub Jove*.

The depression is a symptom of imaginative strength, a measure of
Dana's fidelity to compacts he had never consciously sworn. He dis-

covers after all that much of the real drama of his voyage had been on shore, in those moments of stillness in a spot where his anonymity fell from him. If such moments threatened then to delimit the historical self he had hoped to flee, the ability to revive them now gives evidence of his power to transcend mere history. Dana can identify himself with a California spot on return precisely because the spot is no longer there.

If Dana returns only to loss, he returns also to authorship, to the public fact of his imaginative appropriation of a landscape whose worth he can only belatedly measure. For Californians, he is *the author,* as he discovers in conversation with an old acquaintance in San Francisco: "He professed at once to remember me, and spoke of my book. I found that almost – I might perhaps say quite – every American in California had read it; for when California 'broke out,' as the phrase is, in 1848, and so large a portion of the Anglo-Saxon race flocked to it, there was no book upon California but mine." His memorialization of a place has become his authentic memorial. He had succeeded in writing himself into California long before accepting it as his imaginative home. The cherished spot has expanded into an entire state that claims him as her own. Could this have happened anywhere? It might have, although it was the peculiar vacancy of the California coast, combined with its almost complete lack of historical associations, that encouraged Dana to become an exemplary type of that onlooker for whom landscape becomes visible only when memorialized by the memory of loss. In his eventual recognition that this was and continued to be the place where he had been most himself, Dana acts out the first American version of what will become a familiar story, the discovery of California as paradise only once it is lost.

Zenas Leonard fell into Eden. He never quite recovered the distance to know that he had. If Dana has the authority of knowledge, Leonard has the power of innocence. In moving west across the continent, he simply had no idea where he was going. His salvation was not in withholding himself from an experience of place, but in a thoroughly unplanned surrender.

In July 1833, Captain Walker was ordered to leave the Green River in Wyoming and "to steer through an unknown country, towards the Pacific." Zenas Leonard was appointed clerk of the expedition. His narrative now becomes an obligatory record of the party's movements; it is something for which he is being paid. But it is not a salary alone that draws Leonard to Walker; the untrapped streams of the Far West beckon with the chance to "restore our lost fortunes." Compensation is uppermost in Leonard's mind, and compensation is the experience his adventures in California will ask him to redefine.

1. Bonneville's map, based on Captain Joseph Walker's expedition of 1833, first printed in Irving's *The Adventures of Captain Bonneville* in 1837.

Walker and his party march southwest toward the Great Salt Lake.
On the advice of friendly Indians they proceed to the headwaters of the
Humboldt and across Nevada to Humboldt Lake. A day's march brings
them to Carson Lake, from which they begin the assault on "a large
mountain." The landscape behind had not been arresting:

> Our horses were reduced very much from the fatigues of our
> journey and light food, having travelled through a poor, sandy
> country extending from the buffaloe country of the Rocky Moun-
> tains, to our present encampment, a distance of about 1200 miles,
> without encountering a single hill of any consequence (with the
> exception of the one in which Barren river heads, and that we
> went around,) and so poor and bare that nothing can subsist on it
> with the exception of rabbits.

Only at the top of the range would Leonard judge the view of this
"unbroken level" to be "awfully sublime."

Now, at the base of the Sierra, unable to find any game, the party
begins slaughtering its horses. A scout stumbles across an Indian path
that leads upward. Traveling soon through deep snow (it is mid-
October), the horses grow "stupid and stiff." Their riders can scavenge
only gin berries. Five days are spent trying to find the summit of "this
inhospitable region." The situation grows "more distressing every
hour." They come to a major obstruction:

> Here we began to encounter in our path, many small streams
> which would shoot out from under these high snow-banks, and
> after running a short distance in deep chasms which they have
> through ages cut in the rocks, precipitate themselves from one
> lofty precipice to another, until they are exhausted in rain be-
> low. – Some of these precipices appeared to us to be more than a
> mile high. Some of the men thought that if we could succeed in
> descending one of these precipices to the bottom, we might thus
> work our way into the valley below – but on making several at-
> tempts we found it utterly impossible for a man to descend, to say
> nothing of our horses.

As they push westward on the "ridge between two of these chasms," a
lone hunter frightens an Indian into dropping a basket of acorns. This
first satisfying California meal proves "superior to any chestnuts I ever
eat." The party arrives at the "brink of the mountain" and another
striking prospect:

> In looking on the plain below with the naked eye, you have one
> of the most singular prospects in nature; from the great height of

the mountain the plain presents a dim yellow appearance; – but on taking a view with the spy glass we found it to be a beautiful plain stretched out towards the west until the horizon presents a barrier to sight.

During the descent to the valley a third phenomenon brushes by Leonard's now fully alerted attention: "In the last two days travelling we have found some trees of the Red-wood species, incredibly large – some of which would measure from 16 to 18 fathoms round the trunk at the height of a man's head from the ground." On October 30 – "having spent almost a month in crossing over" – the company reaches the base of the mountain. "It is quite romantic – the soil is very productive – the timber is immensely large and plenty, and game, such as deer, elk, grizzly bear and antelopes are remarkably plenty." The animals are "the fattest of the kind I ever had to eat." While wonders do not cease – the rapids of the Merced River will prove "the most remarkable of any other water course" – by the time Leonard reaches this unpromised land his crucial experience of landscape is over.

As Leonard moves west from St. Louis, the land he sees is just country, and the purpose of moving through it is to make money. The "two long years" spent before joining Walker leave him "destitute of everything except an old greasy blanket, a rifle and a few loads of ammunition." Immediately on striking out, Leonard recovers hope in his goal: "I sometimes thought that we were now on an expedition from which we would realize some profit." As Leonard nears the Sierra, the word "remarkable" begins cropping up. He starts spending time "gazing" at "curiosities." The relentless depletion of supplies and economic prospects as he traverses the mountains may leave him focused on his belly, but it also frees him for an unmediated encounter with California space. As Leonard crosses the summit the digressions and adjectives begin to mount: It is as if in California, country begins to be seen as *landscape*.

There is no chance for self-consciousness here; Leonard will continue to define the self by what it has earned, or, in his major revision of the concept of worth, by what it has seen. Unconcerned about wages, Dana knew that he carried his worth in his person, and his awareness of the unique selectivity of his vision is correspondingly acute. Leonard's discontinuous and ungrammatical style does not conceive of the act of writing as a memorialization of self. His attention is turned outward to what happens along the way; there is no attempt to impose a story on what he sees. (The one try at storytelling in the *Narrative,* "Adventures of Fitzpatrick," is invented by somebody else.) This makes him melodramatically unresponsive to the historical significance of his descriptions. As he crosses and descends the Sierra, his gathering tiers of response show him as scarcely aware that he has set out to penetrate a natural paradise. Leonard reveals that the commercial man, reduced to the surviving man, reluctantly turns aside: "We spent no time in idleness – scarcely stopping in our journey to view an occasional specimen of nature's handy-work." Leonard admits in principle what he cannot appreciate in fact: wonders remain obstacles until he reaches the valley floor. At the shores of the Pacific, Leonard's past experience of landscape finds its wonted relief: "Here was a smooth unbroken sheet of water stretched out far beyond the reach of the eye – altogether different from mountains, rocks, snows & the toilsome plains we had traversed." In this mood, the parts of the places through which he has traveled remain just parts, things to be toiled around. But Leonard's honest notation confers on the reader the luxury of being able to name what Leonard was only able to see: Yosemite, the San Joaquin, *Sequoia gigantea*. These are the great trophies the trapper has unwittingly ensnared, and his historical naiveté ensures for us the shock of recognition, even the illusion of discovery.

Leonard's lack of time to appreciate the land he moves through registers itself in the recurring impression of a prospect belatedly coming into focus. The first sighting of the *Lagoda* is exemplary: "About noon of the third day, after we arrived here, the attention of the company was directed to an object which could be dimly seen at a distance riding on the water, which was immediately judged to be a ship." In a similar fashion (he is now somewhere on the Merced River), the value of Leonard's landscape experience becomes apparent in retrospect, once he has passed beyond sight of it:

> This night it was decided that we should forthwith commence trapping for furs and make this expedition as profitable as possible, for, as yet we had spent much time and toil, and lost many horses, without realizing any profit whatever – although every man expressed himself fully compensated for his labour, by the many natural curiosities which we had discovered.

In the space of a dash, Leonard redefines his sense of the appropriate compensation for human labor. He begins to convert an experience of landscape into spiritual capital, a possession proof against any material loss. Leonard had reason enough to feel compensated, for he was very likely among the first explorers ever to look upon Yosemite and the Big Trees, the first to look down upon the Central Valley after crossing the Sierra from east to west. It is as if the awesomeness of his discoveries tardily works its spell upon him, in spite of his ignorance of their historical importance. What he does know is that he has reached a place worth gaining, a conviction brought home to him by the sound of ocean waves:

> The idea of being within hearing of the *end* of the *Far West* inspired the heart of every member of the company with a patriotic feeling for his country's honour, and all were eager to lose no time until they should behold what they had heard. We felt as if all our previous hardships and privations would be fully compensated, if we would be spared to return in safety to the homes of our kindred and have it to say that we had stood upon the extreme end of the great west.

The word "compensated" here achieves the status of a shifter, and the beneficiary is Leonard's sense of place. Although he still cannot get beyond an economic language in conveying the emotion of extremity, he discovers through it the more permanent ways in which an investment of time in natural space can achieve return. Simply having arrived at a place becomes self-substantiating. For a man standing at such a spot in California, having seen what he has seen, *location is compensation*.

Leonard's stay in the great West, given the plenitude of arrival, was bound for bathos. He was arrested by the apparent reversal of the seasons – "as there is no winter nor freezing weather here it may be said that August, September and October, is their only winter, (to substitute *warm* for *cold*) as, at the end of this period the face of nature assumes a new dress and vegetation shoots forth precisely in the manner that it does in Pennsylvania when the frost leaves the ground in the Spring of the year" – but found the human culture in California incommensurate with its natural beauties. So irksome are the feeble inroads of the Spanish – their adobe houses contain "no floor, partition, or work of any kind except the bare walls" – that Leonard even reverts to his notion of space as something best literally owned. The Manifest Destiny of the United States – "she should assert her claim by taking possession of the whole territory as soon as possible" – threatens to crowd out, in Leonard's disdainful assessments, his emerging conception of a more visionary possession. "Of a ferocious and wicked nature," the natives steal horses for sport and dispatch Indians "as if they were dogs." Even after he has enjoyed the "cold" California winter, Leonard's disgust with the "stupid Spanish" leaves him "bent upon never again returning to this region." So another prophetic script is acted out – rapture followed by expulsion. Generations of travelers were to find that if their toilsome journey to California was rewarded with delight, their sojourn in the Far West would end in disillusion.

However ill at ease Leonard eventually becomes in California, he does not find it easy to leave. California is as reluctant to grant exit as

she had been initially "inhospitable." On the way west, there had
been the Indian skirmishes along the Humboldt, the near starvation in
the Sierra. It took Walker's party almost a week just to cross the summit of the "Calafornia mountain." On descending into the Central
Valley, they were greeted by the roar of breakers, a sound they mis-
took for an earthquake. The ultimate greeting fell from the skies:
"Soon after dark the air appeared to be completely thickened with
meteors falling towards the earth, some of which would explode in
the air and others would be dashed to pieces on the ground, frighten-
ing our horses so much that it required the most active vigilance of
the whole company to keep them together." This was the meteor
shower of November 13, 1833. After such a welcome, Leonard's
eventual expulsion might have seemed just a matter of time. As he
tries to leave, the compensation of location diminishes into another
frustrated linear quest, this time toward home. It is as if paradise,
having nourished Leonard alike by beauty and by fear, now seeks to
prevent the ingratitude of departure. The recrossing of the Sierra (and
unremarked discovery of Walker Pass) goes easily enough. But once
they are on the far slope, the fear of "perishing for water in crossing
this extensive desert" forces the party to steer a course away from the
proper northeast. (The *Alert* had struck a sandbar on its homeward
tack out of San Diego, and Dana and his shipmates "felt as though we
were tied to California.") As the party marches up the range's eastern
flank, it, too, begins to feel tied to California: "Travelling along the
mountain foot, crossing one stream after another, was anything but
pleasant. Day after day we travelled in the hope of arriving at the
desired point when we would strike off in a homeward direction."
The endless fording of streams forces the march out onto the arid
plains of the land of little rain. When Leonard and his company finally
stumble across water, it is after having been fully weaned of attachment to a place that had threatened never to let them go.

The student who came by sea held the land at a distance, and possessed
it only in return. The trapper who came by land entered into this most
western landscape waywardly, abandoning himself to the wonders of
its unexpected supply. Dana's initial experience was of shipboard community and routine; Leonard's, of undiscovered and almost unnoticed
place. Leonard never went back, but what he saw "compensated" him
forever; Dana, the sojourner who pined for home, came belatedly to
feel that the once unappreciated place was the one "real" past he had
ever had. The sailor's California became a place fully internalized, one
that he alone contained. Leonard's California became a fact of the
imagination too, but one by which he also saw himself encompassed. If

we think of Dana as motionlessly incorporating a natural space, we think of Leonard as moving through one. Leonard experiences landscape as metonymy – what happens next. Only once in California does he begin to unify his story through the metaphor of the garden. Dana approaches the West with metaphors ready at hand, and organizes his experience not only into chapters but under the grand heading of a quest of the spirit. But however divergent the images their stories render up, the cultured spectator and the naive participant are one in their sense that encounter with California landscape has been the central event of their lives.

FIGURE AND GROUND

Accounts of the American imagination often fall into binary oppositions, and mine will be no exception. California was at once a spectacle and an experience, and the choice for any visitor might seem to be between competing intensities. Dana and Leonard embody a tension between spectatorship and abandonment. Dana founds the line of distanced spectators; Leonard becomes one of the first voluptuaries of California space. The cultivated sublime would find its champions in men like Bayard Taylor, Robert Louis Stevenson, and John Smeaton Chase. Enthusiastic autodidacts also followed: men like Edwin Bryant, William Manly, Joaquin Miller. The most distinguished California careers would aim for a balance between these two ways of giving oneself to the ground. Their story forms an important episode in the history of imagination in America.

Facing the mystery of a great continent, the self can be kept and asserted, or the self can be given and lost. This is the theme of William Carlos Williams's *In the American Grain* (1925), a profound and quirky meditation on the history of the human response to American space. Williams prizes a passionate relationship with the ground. But by "ground" he means not simply the American earth. *In the American Grain* unfolds as a complex pun on the meaning of the word "ground." For a culture to be grounded, it must at once react to place and maintain an account of that reaction. "Ground" begins for Williams as soil, landscape, territory, but becomes writing, history, literature. We are grounded not only in place but in the verbal record of our sense of place. Williams declares

That unless everything that is, proclaim a ground on which it stand, it has no worth; and that what has been morally, aesthetically worth while in America has rested on peculiar and discoverable ground. But they think they get it out of the air or the rivers, or from the Grand Banks or wherever it may be, instead of by word of mouth or from records contained for us in books – and that, aesthetically, morally we are deformed unless we read.

By deploying "ground" as his central metaphor for that on which a culture is founded, Williams reminds us of how much of American literature and history has turned upon our response to natural space. He also reminds us that we are latecomers, and that if our ancestors encountered the land without mediation, we accomplish our "descent . . . to the ground" through the humus of their texts.

"Withholding" and "surrendering": The terms are Frost's, but they sum up Williams's sense of the ways in which we have given ourselves to the land. His book outlines a psychomachia between the inner Puritan and the inner Spaniard. "The English appraised the New World too meanly. It was to them a carcass from which to tear pieces for their belly's sake, a colony, a place to despise a little. They gave to it parsimoniously, in a slender Puritan fashion. But the Spaniard gave magnificently, with a generous sweep, wherever he was able." Williams's is a book about heroes, figures like Daniel Boone and Sam Houston who stand out against the ground by virtue of having passionately embraced it. Unhappily, such heroes go against the American grain – the Puritan typically triumphs over the Spaniard, and our national story becomes one of withheld love: "Nearly all our national heroes have been driven back – and praised by reason of their shrewdness in making walls: not in bursting into flower." What stands between us and such giving? For the Puritan it is the primitive fear of the undiscovered. "The emptiness about them was sufficient terror for them not to look further." Fearful of an outer emptiness and possessed of an inner one, the Puritan invents the "soul." Now imagining himself full, he turns away from the "whole weight of the wild continent" and toward the lonely and impoverished life of the spirit.

Williams judges the Puritan inability to connect as a moral failure induced by the nature of American space. He might well have located the problem in the nature of consciousness itself. There is something spectatorial about any encounter with the natural world, a tension between figure and ground that can throw us back on an awareness of ourselves as separate, human, perceiving. This is the burden of Thoreau's famous passage on "thinking" in "Solitude":

> With thinking we may be beside ourselves in a sane sense. By a conscious effort of the mind we can stand aloof from actions and their consequences; and all things, good and bad, go by us like a torrent. We are not wholly involved in Nature. I may be either

the driftwood in the stream, or Indra in the sky looking down on it. I *may* be affected by a theatrical exhibition; on the other hand, I *may not* be affected by an actual event which appears to concern me much more. I only know myself as a human entity; the scene, so to speak, of thoughts and affections; and am sensible of a certain doubleness by which I can stand as remote from myself as from another. However intense my experience, I am conscious of the presence and criticism of a part of me, which, as it were, is not a part of me, but spectator, sharing no experience, but taking note of it; and that is no more I than it is you. When the play, it may be the tragedy, of life is over, the spectator goes his way. It was a kind of fiction, a work of the imagination only, so far as he was concerned. This doubleness may easily make us poor neighbors and friends sometimes.

The recurring figure in *Walden* is of a man looking at himself thinking, and it is made possible by Thoreau's withdrawal from society into nature. Landscape provides the site for such events because in its inhuman otherness it at once accepts and resists our projections. Ideally, the spectator and the participant accompany each other on such expeditions, although as the book proceeds Thoreau recenters the site of participation in the self rather than in the world. We have been patrons of the displaced quest:

What was the meaning of that South-Sea Exploring Expedition, with all its parade and expense, but an indirect recognition of the fact, that there are continents and seas in the moral world, to which every man is an isthmus or an inlet, yet unexplored by him, but that it is easier to sail many thousand miles through cold and storm and cannibals, in a government ship, with five hundred men and boys to assist one, than it is to explore the private sea, the Atlantic and Pacific of one's being alone.

Nature finally leads beyond nature as Thoreau argues that every human remains the spectator of an inner landscape for which any natural one is only a complex analogy.

Williams drives down toward ecstatic abandonment; Thoreau reaches up toward self-conscious spectatorship. Each acknowledges that as Americans or as perceivers, we live in the tension between. The "doubleness" Thoreau celebrates is a human bequest finally independent of the world into which we are thrust. But in America the charting of consciousness has often begun as an act of mapping a landscape. Thoreau can after all only get at the inner through metaphors borrowed from the outer – his book is an essay on the fact that if the self is the ever-present tenor, nature is the abiding vehicle. The literature of California everywhere explores the ways we express identity in terms of topography. For the contemporary of Thoreau's seeking to explore his "being alone," California was still virgin land. The man who would most dramatically find and lose himself in the conquest of its landscapes was John C. Frémont.

THE PRICE OF CONQUEST

Frémont (1813–90) directed the energies of his first expedition west in 1842 toward the ascent of – Frémont Peak. On the summit he happened to see a bumblebee: "It was a strange place, the icy rock and the highest peak of the Rocky Mountains, for a lover of warm sunshine and flowers, and we pleased ourselves with the idea that he was the first of his species to cross the mountain barrier, a solitary pioneer to foretell the advance of civilization." This is a touching example of Frémont's habit of authenticating the self through conquest in space. The bee becomes an emblem of the explorer's fulfilled ambitions, a gesture on the part of the wilderness that confirms the momentousness of the human gesture being made in it. By producing this "solitary pioneer," nature serves narrative designs. Frémont scarcely seems to wonder if design govern in a thing so small; his typical concern is to assimilate accident to "the course of the narrative." His place in history will in fact derive from his ability to convert adventitious experience into a text. In a gesture premonitory of the medium through which he would be preserved, Frémont closes off the anecdote by placing the bee "in at least a fit place, in the leaves of a large book."

Had Frémont not been a writer, he would scarcely be remembered as an explorer. His originality lay not in the trails he blazed – he had been preceded nearly everywhere by men like Smith, Bridger, Pattie, Bonneville, Walker, and Chiles. He rode often in the ruts of the Oregon Trail. His uniqueness lay rather in the skill with which he identified the written history of a private desire with a collective act of discovery. The text of his *Report of the Exploring Expedition to the Rocky Mountains and to Oregon and North California* (1845) was the most widely read official document to come out of the West, and it was read as epic. Joaquin Miller was propelled westward after hearing his father read the *Report* on his Ohio farm. "I never was so fascinated. I never grew so fast in my life. Every scene and circumstance in the narrative was painted in my mind to last and to last forever." An exuberant Jessie Benton Frémont wrote from Washington in 1846 that "You are ranked with DeFoe. They say that as *Robinson Crusoe* is the most natural and

interesting fiction of travel, so Frémont's report is the most romantically truthful." Josiah Royce's hard pun casts a more reductive light on
Frémont's achievement: "I fancy that this Report will be, in future
generations, General Frémont's only title, and a very good one, to
lasting and genuine fame." Writing in 1885, Royce proved prophetic;
the first printing of the *Report* was doubled to ten thousand by a Senate
request, and, as Frémont's biographer tells us, "from that day to this no
one in the United States has ever had any difficulty procuring it at little
cost."

Frémont led five expeditions west. The first three were the most
historically significant. In each, a public scientific purpose coincides
with a private narrative design. His orders as a member of the Army's
Topographical Corps were, in his own generalizing words, "to give a
connected survey of the interior of our continent." But as Frémont
probed westward his purpose became less to reveal the contours of the
landscape than to situate and memorialize himself in a privileged place.
The place becomes California; if the Great Basin (the term is Frémont's)
was the area he most sucessfully mapped, "to open California" was the
objective toward which all of his ambitions moved.

Frémont's expedition of 1842 (The Short Stab) took him up the Platte
to Fort Laramie, South Pass, and the Wind River Mountains. In 1843–4
(The Great Circuit) he pushed across the Rockies via Fort Laramie and
Fort Hall and down the Walla Walla and the Columbia to Fort Vancouver. At The Dalles, Frémont decided to march south past Klamath
Lake and into western Nevada. Near Pyramid Lake he made the decision to cross the Sierra to the valley of the Sacramento. The party
returned east through the parks of the Rockies after marching across the
deserts of southern Nevada and central Utah. The accounts of these
two expeditions were given separately but published in one volume as
the *Report*. The expedition that left Bent's Fort in 1845 (The Interrupted
Return) drove across Colorado and Utah to the Salt Lake, followed
Hastings's Cut-off, and crossed the Sierra through Donner Pass. In a
California on the brink of civil war, Frémont began a complex period
of maneuvering that eventually sent him up the valley of the Sacramento into southern Oregon. At this point the expedition was interrupted by news from Lieutenant Gillespie. When Frémont returned
south to the Bear Flag Revolt and the conquest of California, his career
as an explorer came, effectively, to an end.

Frémont structures each of these three expeditions toward a dramatic
but unofficial goal. Frémont Peak – the Valley of the Sacramento – the
governorship of California: In arriving at each of these destinations,
Frémont provided his audience with a sense of an ending. Resolved
narrative depends in each case on a liberal disregard for orders. Frémont

was a great disobeyer. He had never been instructed to proceed to
South Pass and the Wind River Mountains; in 1843 he had been ordered
to proceed to Oregon and return. And in 1845–6 it was, of course, the
interpretation of orders – especially those pertaining to his reentry of
California – that would come to overshadow, in Frémont's eventual
court-martial, the topographic aims of his mission. Whatever his actual
instructions, Frémont found a way to enlarge a destination into destiny.
The emerging goal of these expeditions – literal power over the Far
West – allows us to read the *Report* covering the first two and Frémont's *Memoirs* about the third as a continuous act of conquest.

 With Frémont's writings, the literature of California and the West
falls into self-consciousness. The figure they render up is a man looking
at himself at the center of a map of his own making. It was Emerson
who put down Frémont's *Report* as unable to "repress this eternal vanity of *how we must look*." The episode with the bee demonstrates
Frémont's skill at converting unattended moments into advertisements
for the self. He displays at the same time a willingness to abandon
himself to the field. Figure and ground continually vie for attention in
Frémont's work. In his verbal self-presentations, we can trace the ways
in which Frémont formalizes the dominant modes of imaginative encounter with the frontier.

 From the first, Frémont was seen by his colleagues as a voluptuary
scientist. As an assistant to Nicollet in the late 1830s, Frémont had
joined two expeditions toward the headwaters of the Mississippi. He
suggests his immersion in prairie life in an implied contrast with his
superior: "In all this stir of frontier life Mr. Nicollet felt no interest and
took no share; horse and dog were nothing to him. His manner of life
had never brought him into their companionship, and the congenial
work he now had in charge engrossed his attention and excited his
imagination. His mind dwelt continually upon the geography of the
country." Frémont identifies rather with the "reckless" Lorrison
Freniére, the first of many voyageurs and mountain men who would
become his willing tutors and passionate friends. (No other army officer was to win the unqualified love of such frontiersmen as Kit Carson
and Alexis Godey.) He suspends his scientific labors for a "royal hunt"
with an entire Indian village, fights off a prairie fire, and plunges so
violently into his first buffalo hunt as to get lost. Yet throughout this
time he takes astronomical observations, makes topographical notes,
fixes elevations. From the beginning, his is a complex fate; the landscape he is paid to abstract into pattern is a surround by which he loves
to be overcome. What arrests him about prairie life are the surprises
produced out of its vast distances. The appearance of any "object" on
the horizon creates an "always existing uncertainty." "There is always

the suspense of the interval needed to verify the strange object; and, long before the common man decides anything, the practised eye has reached certainty." Frémont here registers the tension between pleasures that would often be his: between the suspense of immersion in the unknown, and the assurance of the distancing, "practised eye."

Experience and spectacle are precisely the terms in which Frémont could have characterized the great set-pieces in the account of the first expedition—the two buffalo hunts. On first sighting buffalo, he "feels a strange emotion of grandeur." One can sense Frémont reaching here, in the sudden elevation of the language, toward a kind of prairie sublime. Boundaries are about to be transgressed and affirmed. In the first hunt, Frémont becomes utter participant. As he and Carson gallop toward the herd, "the chase became so engrossingly intense, that we were sensible to nothing else." Literal immersion in the herd soon follows. "We entered on the side, the mass giving way in every direction in their heedless course. Many of the bulls, less active and less fleet than the cows, paying no attention to the ground, and occupied solely with the hunter, were precipitated to the earth with great force, rolling over and over with the violence of the shock, and hardly distinguishable in the dust." Pursuit leads to a blurring of distinctions between hunter and hunted, and to a swift curtailment of the senses:

A thick cloud of dust hung upon their rear, which filled my mouth and eyes, and nearly smothered me. In the midst of this I could see nothing, and the buffalo were not distinguishable until within thirty feet. They crowded together more densely still as I came upon them, and rushed along in such a compact body, that I could not obtain an entrance—the horse almost leaping upon them. In a few moments the mass divided to the right and left, the horns clattering with a noise heard above every thing else, and my horse darted into the opening. Five or six bulls charged on us as we dashed along the line, but were left far behind, and singling out a cow, I gave her my fire, but struck too high. She gave a tremendous leap, and scoured on swifter than before. I reigned up my horse, and the band swept on like a torrent, and left the place quiet and clear.

The relief we feel with "quiet and clear" measures how fully Frémont has caught us up in the illusion of motion. The mind automatically performs intentional acts here while the body surrenders to an overwhelming kinesthesia. The pleasure of such intensity leads Frémont to abandon any hidden agenda to become distinctive and "distinguishable."

In the account of the second hunt, a band of Arapaho asks Frémont's column to halt so as to avoid raising a passing herd. "We, therefore,

unsaddled our horses, and sat down on the bank to view the scene."
Sight now reasserts its primacy over hearing. In the ensuing chiar-
oscuro, the eye is not merely indulged, but challenged:

> The buffalo started for the hills, but were intercepted and driven
> back toward the river, broken and running in every direction. The
> clouds of dust soon covered the whole scene, preventing us from
> having any but an occasional view. It had a very singular appear-
> ance to us at a distance, especially when looking with the glass.
> We were too far to hear the report of the guns, or any sound, and
> at every instant, through the clouds of dust which the sun made
> luminous, we could see for a moment two or three buffalo dash-
> ing along, and close behind them an Indian with his long spear, or
> other weapon, and instantly again they disappeared. The apparent
> silence, and the dimly seen figures flitting by with such rapidity,
> gave it a kind of dreamy effect, and seemed more like a picture
> than a scene of real life.

However these hunts actually occurred, what strikes us are the contrast-
ing modes through which Frémont has chosen to dramatize them. The
juxtaposition of these two experiences cannot be an accident; performed
cacophony gives way to a silent movie. If the tension between spectatorship and abandonment here registers a conflict between professional
and personal imperatives, it becomes one important to master in a land
where survival depends on the estimation of distance. Yet issues of
survival are not the most compelling here. Frémont's habitual concern
is with power in relation to his world, and in the means by which the
exploring self can at once abandon and assert itself within what his rival
explorer, W. H. Emory, was to call "overcoming space."

In *Plotting the Golden West,* Stephen Fender posits an analogous set of
oppositions: For him "Frémont" means a tension between two kinds of
rhetoric. "Uncertain as to what stylistic grid to impose on his material," Frémont in the first *Report* engages in a "warfare between the
pleasures of pictorial composition and the business of surveying." It is a
fruitful tension, Fender argues, one that becomes, in a sense, the text's
final subject: "There is no need even to ask which of the two descriptive modes – the picturesque or the scientific – he finally preferred, or to
which he more readily applied the adjective 'authentic'. . . . in Frémont
the rivalry becomes an issue, almost a plot, whose exciting conclusion
is felt out, and spelt out, through the hard experience of travel in, and
writing about, the West." Whether we read the first *Report* as a warfare
between kinds of rhetoric or kinds of behavior, the tensions recorded
and embodied in it produced one of the West's first answerable styles.

   If Frémont's achievement were simply a matter of stances enclosed

within a text, however, it would be difficult to distinguish it from that
of his dark twin, Lansford Hastings. Hastings published his *Emigrant's
Guide to Oregon and California* in the year of the *Reports*. He betrays the
same impulse toward self-dramatization and impersonal survey. But his
facts are wholly unreliable; he writes about what he has not seen. Eye-
witness authority is the first criterion for inclusion in the canonical texts
about the West: It is its having come to him secondhand that makes
Irving's *Bonneville,* despite its textual polish, so much less satisfying an
account of the territory than Leonard's *Adventures*. In Hastings's landscape of hearsay the Sierra becomes a range through which "loaded
wagons may now, be driven, without serious interruption." He un-
blushingly boosts California (its atmosphere is so pure that "flesh of
any kind may be hung for weeks together, in the open air . . . without
undergoing putrefaction"), and hopes to originate a state by inducing
an act of mass migration. But whereas Frémont's legacy was to help
direct a considered if passionate act of westering, Hastings's was to
bring forth a massive error. The unfortunate pioneers who in 1846
bought his guide and followed his "Cut-off" were forced, because of
delays along the ill-defined route, to winter in the Sierra in one of
Hastings's "very easy" wagon roads, a place that would one day bear
the party's name – Donner Pass.

As we follow the course of Frémont's writings and ambitions, the
ecstatic self gives ground to the theatrical self. The account of the first
expedition culminates with the assault on Frémont Peak, an event that
serves narrative rather than scientific purposes. Frémont had carried
from St. Louis an American flag that bore an eagle clutching arrows in
one claw and a peace pipe in the other. On the summit he "unfurled the
national flag to wave in the breeze where never flag waved before."
The gesture matters as much as the country revealed. (Just a few days
before, Frémont had forgotten to take any observations for longitude
and latitude of the major objective of his expedition, South Pass.) The
human figure being cut looms over the landscape. Frémont would increasingly concern himself with fulfilling an archetype. A year later he
comes upon the Great Salt Lake, and compares himself to a gazer upon
another sea:

> We reached the butte without difficulty, and, ascending to the
> summit, immediately at our feet beheld the object of our anxious
> search – the waters of the Inland Sea, stretching in still and soli-
> tary grandeur far beyond the limit of our vision. It was one of the
> great points of the exploration; and as we looked eagerly over the
> lake in the first emotions of excited pleasure, I am doubtful if the
> followers of Balboa felt more enthusiasm when, from the heights

of the Andes, they saw for the first time the great Western ocean.
It was certainly a magnificent object, and a noble *terminus* to this
part of our expedition; and to travellers so long shut up among
mountain ranges, a sudden view over the expanse of silent waters
had in it something sublime.

Self-presentations such as these won for Frémont the place of preeminent
explorer in the national imagination. Yet there is nothing original about
this moment – the lake had been seen many times before, and William
Ashley's men had sailed on it in skin canoes in 1826. Through simile
Frémont purchases the priority he could not claim in fact. In self-drama-
tizing moments like this, the story he wants to fulfill preempts the trail
he is actually furthering. These impulses would come to a head in
Frémont's fateful decisions to cross the borders of California.

Frémont portrays his first entry into California as an unplanned necessity. His second expedition struck south from The Dalles in November
1843 in search of the "great river flowing from the Rocky mountains to
the bay of San Francisco" – the mythical Buenaventura. Decades of explorers had pursued this mirage into the wastes of the northern rim of the
Great Basin. A glance at Gallatin's map of 1836 or Bonneville's of 1837
might have convinced Frémont that he went in pursuit of a legend. By
the next April, camped near the bay of San Francisco, he will confidently
declare that "No river from the interior does, or can, cross the Sierra
Nevada." That January, Frémont had in fact "abandoned all idea of its
existence." The same suspense that justified the expedition must, however, be preserved in the account of it, and Frémont approaches the
Buenaventura in the *Report* as if it were a live geographic possibility. It is
"the course of the narrative" that must be followed. Aware that he
intentionally projects a goal that will prove illusory, Frémont invokes the
imperatives of a writer rather than an explorer:

> The course of the narrative will show at what point, and for what
> reasons, we were prevented from the complete execution of this
> plan, after having made considerable progress upon it, and how
> we were forced by desert plains and mountain ranges, and deep
> snows, far to the south and near to the Pacific Ocean, and along
> the western base of the Sierra Nevada; where, indeed, a new and
> ample field of exploration opened itself before us. For the present,
> we must follow the narrative.

Fictional rather than documentary imperatives prevail here. His quest
must have its grail, even when it is only a screen for a further goal.

With the verb "forced," Frémont's pursuit of a river he knows (at the
moment of composition) to be nonexistent merges with his ambitions
to enter California, which he still needs to justify. The search for the

Buenaventura led south to the Truckee Valley of Nevada, where the party camped in January 1844. At this juncture Frémont faced two options: to follow orders and return eastward at once, or to cross the Sierra in midwinter. He was certainly not "forced" to enter California. His horses did lack shoes, and out of this inconvenience a decision to turn west seems to materialize: "It was evidently impossible that they could cross the country to the Rocky mountains. . . . I therefore determined to abandon my eastern course, and cross the Sierra Nevada into the valley of the Sacramento." But Charles Preuss, the expedition's topographer, had confided to his journal in October that "The latest plan now is to turn south from Fort Vancouver through Mexican territory. There we shall have to find the route from Monterey to Santa Fé and follow it." As Allan Nevins points out, "there was no necessity for entering California." Frémont could have let his men and horses recruit during the Nevada winter and then pushed east in the spring. But he was "forced" westward, as he will reflect when looking back from central California on the successful mountain crossing: "We here left the waters of the bay of San Francisco, and, though forced upon them contrary to my intentions, I cannot regret the necessity which occasioned the deviation." The major necessity was Frémont's ambition, skillfully masked by his narrative technique. Although apparently abandoning himself to "the course of the narrative" and the uncertainties of the trail, Frémont pursues a self-aggrandizing design. His orders had been to return from Oregon by way of the Oregon Trail. The second expedition thus culminates as had the first, in an act of extension in space that is also an act of disobedience.

No white man had ever crossed the Sierra in midwinter. The most eloquent summary of the crossing is Thomas Hart Benton's, in *Thirty Years' View:*

> It was attempted without a guide – in the dead of winter – accomplished in forty days – the men and surviving horses – a woful procession, crawling along one by one: skeleton men leading skeleton horses – and arriving at Suter's Settlement in the beautiful valley of the Sacramento; and where a genial warmth, and budding flowers, and trees in foliage, and grassy ground, and flowing streams, and comfortable food, made a fairy contrast with the famine and freezing they had encountered, and the lofty *Sierra Nevada* which they had climbed.

The poverty of ellipses gives way to the abundance of parataxis, as the unyielding Sierra opens out into the fertile Sacramento. Benton captures here the geographical irony – "the fairy contrast" – that made the crossing so painful. (Once in the valley, Frémont will observe that "It required all our philosophy and forbearance to prevent *plenty* from becoming as hurtful to us now, as *scarcity* had been before.") Like Leonard before him, Frémont was repulsed by paradise. Unlike Leonard, he knew that paradise did, in fact, await. (Carson, for one, had been in California fifteen years earlier.) He and his men often had it imaginatively and literally in view, and the foregone nature of the destination confers on Frémont the role of prophet–explorer. "I reminded them of the beautiful valley of the Sacramento" – this to his men as he tells them of his decision to cross the range. On February 20 they camp "on the summit of the PASS in the dividing ridge." The Sacramento will continue to prove a tantalizing inducement. "Having only the descent before us, and the valley under our eyes, we felt strong hope that we should force our way down. But this was a case in which the descent was *not* facile." Fires among the tulares of the bay lure them onward. "But, after our long wandering in the rugged mountains, where so frequently we had met with disappointments, and where the crossing of every ridge displayed some unknown lake or river, we were yet almost afraid to believe that we were at last to escape into the genial country of which we had heard so many glowing descriptions, and dreaded again to find some vast interior lake, whose bitter waters would bring us disappointment." Having endured the threat of mirage – "again the Buenaventura rose up in our minds" – and the biblical span of forty days, the expedition finally arrives in the promised land in March 1844.

If Frémont had been the Moses and Joshua of his second expedition, he was to portray himself as the Saul of the third. In the *Memoirs,* he plays the part of the reluctant servant of a call to arms eventually replaced by a usurping competitor. The emerging purpose of the third expedition – not to make maps but to conquer the land they diagram – surfaces in the moment where Frémont describes himself waiting, just north of the Oregon border, for the president's messenger. In this moment of acute self-consciousness, California changes for Frémont from a geographical to a political fact.

The third expedition had initially entered California in two parties in December 1845. They made a rendezvous in February near San Jose. On withdrawing toward Monterey, Frémont was ordered by a nervous José Castro to leave California. Frémont took up a defensive position in the nearby Gabilan Mountains, held it for a few days, and then consented to march slowly north and out of the territory. We now join him as he stands near the "southern limit" of his Oregon journey of 1843. He continues to maintain the stance of a simple explorer. "My plans when I started on my journey into this region were to connect my present survey of the intervening country with my camp in the Savannah, where I had met the Tlamaths in that December." Frémont spends two paragraphs summing up his hopes for the expedition – the promise of seeing old Indian friends, the chance to discover safe harbors on California's "iron bound" coast. He looks forward to exploring the Cascades: "I felt sure that these mountains were absolutely unknown. No one had penetrated their recesses to know what they contained, and no one had climbed to their summits; and there remained the great attraction of mystery in going into unknown places – the unknown lands of which I had dreamed when I began this life of frontier travel." This is a passage of farewell and summing up, one of the most effective in the *Memoirs* at creating narrative suspense. It does this through its gathering elegiac tone, as if Frémont's career as an explorer were about to end. So it is:

> How fate pursues a man! Thinking and ruminating over these things, I was standing alone by my camp-fire, enjoying its warmth, for the night air of early spring is chill under the shadows of the high mountains. Suddenly my ear caught the faint sound of horses' feet.

What he hears are Lieutenant Gillespie's outriders. We will never know what Gillespie told Frémont during their rendezvous. Frémont always claimed that the secret orders Gillespie had carried all the way from Washington commanded him to return to California and secure it for the Republic. As he continues: "The information through Gillespie had absolved me from my duty as an explorer, and I was left to my duty as an officer of the American Army with further authoritative knowledge that the Government intended to take California." And so Frémont falls out of the world of knowledge and into the world of power.

"How fate pursues a man!" It is hard to trust Frémont when he makes himself the object of an active verb. Frémont has pursued fate; there is little question that he had loitered in California and taken so long to leave it in hopes of playing his part in the inevitable rebellion. (War with Mexico had begun months earlier, and on the day Gillespie reached Frémont, the American Army in Mexico fought the battle of Resaca de la Palma.) He protests too much – "And I had my work all planned" – when he argues that he wishes simply to continue in the path of his chosen career. The expedition is openly becoming his story, not the story of "unknown lands." Aware of this, Frémont asks that our indulgence set him free: "I hope that no unfriendly eyes will travel along with me over these lines; the friends may be few and the many are the neutral minds who read without reference to the writer, solely for the interest they find." These lines were written more than forty years after the events they relate, and what they at once try to acknowledge and repress is that Frémont's appeal had always lain in getting us to read with "reference to the writer." The narrated moment by the campfire, when he looks back over the old "lines" and the old trails, proves the culmination of the entire movement of his career. It is a triumphant moment in which the emerging state of California becomes identified with the meditating figure of a single man.

This triumph of the will seems to produce a relaxation of vigilance, and Frémont, on the night he confers with Gillespie, forgets – for only the second time in his career – to post sentries. He walks among the restless horses, returns to the fire and the dispatches, resolves "to move forward on the opportunity and return forthwith to the Sacramento valley." He beds down after a conclusive one-sentence paragraph: "This decision was the first step in the conquest of California." A few moments later Carson wakes to the sound of an ax slicing through Basil Lajeunesse's skull. A bloody struggle with the Tlamaths follows in the light of the smoldering fires. In the morning, with three men dead, Frémont throws himself into one last private act of abandon. "For the moment I threw all considerations aside and determined to square accounts with these people before I left them." As he pushes south his vengeful company pursues a search-and-destroy mission that leaves twenty Indians dead and their village destroyed. These continued excitements lead the greenhorn Gillespie to expostulate, "By heaven, this is rough work."

Rougher work was to lie ahead, months and years of baffled ambition in which Frémont's reputation was to depend increasingly on the acts and texts of others. He was to assume control of the Bear Flag Revolt, only to see it collapse into comic opera. He received the capitulation of Cahuenga and so had the honor of being the man into whose hands the natives formally delivered California. But his rule as first civil governor was cut short when the appointment made by Stockton was rescinded by Kearney. He lost his army commission in the bitter court-martial that followed. A first senator from California, he served only twenty-one working days and was not reelected. The second great fire of 1851 destroyed his San Francisco home. On his fourth expedition – into the San Juan Mountains – eleven men died of starvation. For Bernard DeVoto, there was "no more shocking or more unnecessary failure in the exploration of the West." Frémont received the first Republican nomination for president and lost to Buchanan. Relieved of his first commission in the Civil War after only one hundred days, he was offered the dubious recompense of facing Stonewall Jackson in the Shenandoah. A California Eden, the Mariposas tract near Yosemite, had been mistakenly purchased for Frémont by Larkin in 1849. Consternation turned to joy when gold began pouring out of its rushing streams. Frémont and Jessie built a frame house among the huge pines and red clover of Bear Valley. There they lived for a few years with a spaciousness and style that made

2. John C. Frémont as Josiah Royce knew him

them the first family of California. Fifteen years after its purchase they
had lost the Mariposas to the very partners who had formed a company
to pay off its massive debts. A crushing financial blow came with the
collapse, in 1870, of Frémont's venture with the Memphis and El Paso
Railroad. The final blow would be struck, however, by a young professor from Harvard and a native Californian, Josiah Royce.

Royce's *California* (1886) expends nearly half its length detailing the events surrounding the Bear Flag Revolt. (He interviewed the Frémonts in the 1880s; Royce's mother, Sarah, had crossed the plains in 1849 "guided only by the light of Frémont's *Travels*.") His is a text against Frémont's texts, an act of debunking more than equal to Benton's puffery in *Thirty Years' View*. Royce structures his story around the myth of the Fall. An Eden of "humane tenderheartedness" is corrupted by this ambitious invader. California before Frémont had known only wars of "bloodless playfulness." "Civilized warfare was, in fact, introduced into California through the undertakings of our own gallant Captain Frémont. For in civilized warfare, as is well known, somebody always gets badly hurt." Frémont's actions led, in Royce's account, to "the degradation, the ruin, and the oppression of the Californian people by our own." As Kevin Starr sums up: "Frémont and the Bear Flaggers, Royce felt, committed the original sin of California history." The conquest was the key trauma in California history, and Frémont is the Satan who out of pride and ambition breaks unity with the past. The perhaps inadvertent result of such an account is to make Frémont indispensable to the unfolding myth of California. The fall of the state is embodied in the fall of the man. The disaster of his subsequent career can even be taken as reward for the rape of the garden. To no other American would it be given to think of California as quite literally his for the taking. If Royce's *California* unmasks an ambition sometimes comic in its grandiosity, it also opens onto the pathos of a man who has known what it is to "win" California, and who has had to pay the price.

Frémont's career shows the dangers of confounding an imaginative with a literal act of possession. As scientific explorer, he had balanced his desire to penetrate the ground against his ability to stand removed as spectator from it. But as ambitious invader, he turned his capacity for spectatorship upon himself rather than the landscape, and so had to elevate the will to control over the complementary experience of surrender. Where encounter with landscape has previously encouraged a complex and liberating dialectic between spectatorship and abandonment, now he imposed on it the designs of an imperial self. The figure finally overshadows the ground. This is a way of saying that Frémont fell out of an imaginative and into a political relationship with landscape. It becomes enemy territory, and, finally, property.

It is perhaps too easy to criticize Frémont for trying to possess a landscape he was commissioned to survey. To valorize landscape solely as an object of aesthetic contemplation or scientific study is to ignore the fact that it is also a commodity we are all bound to use. Frémont took upon himself the double role of seer and exploiter, and although he did develop a large tract of wilderness, his primary "use" of the land was to capitalize his history with it for political purposes. If he falls into an exploitative relationship to California space, it is a fall that makes possible the social and economic life of postlapsarian man. There is something honest in Frémont's refusal to keep his stance toward space pure. He openly accepts what so many American writers actively re-press, our necessary entanglement in the development of the material world. He stands at the beginning of the American experience in California as a man who acts out the full range of possibilities – from voluptuary participation, to scientific observation, to political and economic exploitation – for interaction with its natural space. No other Californian would experience, know, and possess so much, or fall so far.

Chapter 2

Muir and the possession of landscape

===============

> There is a property in the horizon which no man has but he whose
> eye can integrate all the parts, that is, the poet.
> – Emerson, *Nature*

John Muir's (1838–1914) landscapes do not remain solely the property
of his eye. Forty pages into *The Yosemite,* landscape description has
begun to prove tedious, and Muir decides to divert his readers with
story. The subtitle "An Unexpected Adventure" alerts us that doing is
about to supersede looking. Wishing one night "to look at the moon
through the meshes of some of the denser portions" of Yosemite Falls,
Muir ventures "to creep farther behind it while it was gently wind-
swayed, without taking sufficient thought about its swaying back to its
natural position after the wind-pressure should be removed." Muir
begins his foray from Fern Ledge, a granite shelf extending behind the
fall some four hundred feet above its base. He achieves his goal, and the
wind shifts.

> Down came a dash of spent comets, thin and harmless-looking in
> the distance, but they felt desperately solid and stony when they
> struck my shoulders, like a mixture of choking spray and gravel
> and big hailstones. Instinctively dropping on my knees, I gripped
> an angle of the rock, curled up like a young fern frond with my
> face pressed against my breast, and in this attitude submitted as
> best I could to my thundering bath.

Trapped in the shaft of California's highest waterfall, Muir begins to
weigh the chances of escape. "Would the column be swayed a few
inches away from the wall, or would it come yet closer? The fall was in
flood and not so lightly would its ponderous mass be swayed." Then,
in one of those lucky chances on which his survival so often depends,
Muir feels the crush of water "moved gently forward" by the "breath

of an 'idle wind.' " He crawls a few feet to a block of ice, wedges himself between it and the canyon wall, and waits until the "steadiness of the light" – he has been cast into utter darkness – gives encouragement to rise and get away. He slips out, builds a fire, warms himself, runs home to sleep, and wakes "sound and comfortable, better, not worse, for my hard mid-night bath."

In the classic American accounts of landscape, landscape tends to disappear. "In the woods," Emerson says, "we return to reason and faith. There I feel that nothing can befall me in life, – no disgrace, no calamity (leaving me my eyes), which nature cannot repair." Eyesight seems to be precisely the medium through which Emerson would encounter nature. But he continues: "Standing on the bare ground, – my head bathed by the blithe air and uplifted into infinite space, – all mean egotism vanishes. I become a transparent eyeball; I am nothing; I see all; the currents of the Universal Being circulate through me; I am part or parcel of God." Clearly this is no bodily seeing. The woods here prove the site of a supernatural transparency; as these sentences unfold we move step by step out of a seen place and into an invisible one. Hemingway's Nick finds himself in a wilderness so happily responsive to his rage for order – "Sharp at the edge of this extension of the forest floor commenced the sweet fern" – that it registers itself less as a place than as a wish fulfillment. A sentence like "The river was there" locates us nowhere so squarely as in Nick's repressed and haunting sense of loss. Talking about the presence of landscape becomes a way of not talking about some vacancy in the self. Williams is renowned for wanting to see clearly, and for focusing on flowers. Yet his roses and tuberoses, so rigorously portioned out through end-stopped lines, serve purposes larger than our simple seeing of them. "To engage roses/becomes a geometry." Within the descriptive space of the poem any natural object or prospect becomes an occasion for celebrating the mind's power to order the world through its own austere punctuation. Whether landscape functions as the scene of imaginative transcendence, a screen for psychological projection, or as a challenge to aesthetic contemplation, we do not often find our anthologized authors observing it for its own sake.

Muir looks at landscape as if it were there, and as if it were his subject. His writing continually validates the presence of the world. As a man who had temporarily lost his sight (he was blinded for a month after a file was flung into his right eye), Muir prefers to celebrate the apparatus of perception. He seems scarcely aware of himself as an observer who alters his world in perceiving it. He does not imagine that it may be impossible to speak of landscape without investing it with the luster of a human use. Muir's naiveté about epistemological cruxes

leaves him free to indulge a response to landscape largely unavailable to
the more self-conscious "tradition." His implicit faith in the eye allows
him to go beyond mere seeing. It frees him to penetrate the world with
his body.

Muir describes Yosemite Falls, and then he enters it. He gives himself
to "the raw, quick flesh of the mountain." Faulkner can speak of the
woods as Ike's "mistress and his wife," but even his most patient
hunter never knows an immersion in wilderness as total as Muir's.
Where in our literature does the visionary give way so readily to the
sensual as in this midnight bath? Muir enters the falls in order to enjoy a
new angle of vision; he gets instead the "sudden disenchantment" of
darkness and inundation, and is enchanted after all. He habitually vio-
lates the distance between landscape and self that makes vision chaste,
even possible. What he describes comes alive in anecdotes of which he
is the hero; the stories are nearly always of penetration. The stories no
doubt precede Muir's narration of them; yet, had they not occurred, he
would have had to invent them. Muir's two major tributes to his
adopted home – *The Mountains of California* (1894) and *The Yosemite*
(1912) – both quickly bow to the necessity to enliven a survey of the
landscape with human story. Muir intends to celebrate the natural
world that antedates and survives our wishes. Yet his books about
landscape are also profoundly self-encoding. Whenever Muir summons
a prospect into view, he can reveal the ways in which landscape serves
as a measure of the self.

Muir can be said to have brought much of the Sierra landscape into
being. He discovered the first living glacier in the mountains through
stubborn persistence in the belief that it was there. "Prior to the autumn
of 1871 the glaciers of the Sierra were unknown. In October of that
year I discovered the Black Mountain Glacier in a shadowy amphithe-
ater between Black and Red Mountains." As his most historic act of
penetration – Muir not only tracks the glacier to its lair but spelunks in
the "weird under-world of the crevasse" – it is also his most Emerso-
nian attempt to conform things to his thoughts. Muir's lifelong dispute
with Josiah Whitney and Clarence King turned on whether the Yosemite was glacial or catastrophic in origin. They were arguing less about a
theory than a metaphor. That the glaciers (those powerful carving ar-
chitects that disappear) were the prime movers behind Sierra sculpture
reaffirmed Muir's sense of a unifying hidden god. King was tempera-
mentally committed to more demonic myths of origin. The quarrel
came down to a choice between imagining origins as shaped by a
"tender" hand from above or by an unpredictable fault from below. No
wonder that Henry Adams thought King the foremost young man of
his generation, while Emerson, whom Muir entertained for a week in

Yosemite in 1871, closed out his journal list of "My Men" with the
name of "John Muir."

Muir's quest is to know the mountains, not himself. His curiosity
about the massive taluses that litter the base of Yosemite cliffs is
answered one night by a "strange thrilling motion. . . . I ran out of my
cabin, both glad and frightened, shouting, 'A noble earthquake! A
noble earthquake!' feeling sure I was going to learn something." This is
Muir's essential brand of ecstasy: He perfects the role of spectator when
plunged into a frenzy of motion. The Thoreau of "Solitude" founds his
humanity on the experience of "a certain doubleness by which I can
stand as remote from myself as from another." In such moments Thoreau asserts his essential independence of nature; he becomes a complete
society of two. Muir has this experience but misses its meaning; his
knowledge of the "spectator" and the "indweller" comes through moments of crisis rather than achieved calm. Muir narrowly avoids a fall
into self-consciousness while scaling the granite face of Mount Ritter:

> The tried dangers beneath seemed even greater than that of the
> cliff in front; therefore, after scanning its face again and again, I
> began to scale it, picking my holds with intense caution. After
> gaining a point about halfway to the top, I was suddenly brought
> to a dead stop, with arms outspread, clinging close to the face of
> the rock, unable to move hand or foot either up or down. My
> doom appeared fixed. I *must* fall. There would be a moment of
> bewilderment, and then a lifeless rumble down the one general
> precipice to the glacier below.
>
> When this final danger flashed upon me, I became nerve-shaken
> for the first time since setting foot on the mountains, and my
> mind seemed to fill with a stifling smoke. But this terrible eclipse
> lasted only a moment, when life blazed forth again with a preter-
> natural clearness. I seemed suddenly to become possessed of a new
> sense. The other self, bygone experiences, Instinct, or Guardian
> Angel, – call it what you will, – came forward and assumed con-
> trol. Then my trembling muscles became firm again, every rift
> and flaw in the rock was seen as through a microscope, and my
> limbs moved with a positiveness and precision with which I
> seemed to have nothing at all to do. Had I been borne aloft upon
> wings, my deliverance could not have been more complete.

This is the key passage in Muir, the one Gary Snyder reset as poetry
in *Myths & Texts*. Snyder omits the sentence about the "other self," the
one in which Muir equivocates about the agency of his salvation. But
the speculation is essential, given the fact that it is so rare. What Muir
here glimpses and then balks at pursuing is the Romantic sublime, that

moment in which the questing self, lost in nature, comes upon the self as a final source of power and authority. Such a moment on the Simplon Pass was to lead Wordsworth to say to his soul, "I recognize thy glory." Muir concludes that he has been saved by – "call it what you will." His conclusion measures not only his liberating naiveté but his anxiety about tension within himself and between himself and the world. The questions that arrest the English Romantics are just those over which he is prepared to glide. His dearest hope was that the self could be whole, without faults or cracks. His most moving fantasy about unity is located in Yosemite:

> No pain here, no dull empty hours, no fear of the past, no fear of the future. These blessed mountains are so compactly filled with God's beauty, no petty personal hope or experience has room to be. Drinking this champagne water is pure pleasure, so is breathing the living air, and every movement of limbs is pleasure, while the whole body seems to feel beauty when exposed to it as it feels the campfire or sunshine, entering not by the eyes alone, but equally through all one's flesh like radiant heat, making a passionate ecstatic pleasure-glow not explainable. One's body then seems homogeneous throughout, sound as a crystal.

This is Muir's original rendition of the American sublime, an ambition toward purification that runs straight from Emerson's transparent eyeball to Stevens's central man, "the transparence of the place in which/He is." In such moments all the tensions that define us as fallen historical beings are not so much resolved as ignored while the self participates in an ecstasy of resemblance.

"I never turn back": Muir prefers movement to meditation. His unremitting didacticism is the genteel complement of a much more primitive sort of curiosity. There is in him a deep desire to uncover nature's secrets at a moment of maximum turmoil. His is a meteorological imagination in which the mountains become "more plainly visible" during storm. Caught in a windstorm that rocks the Douglas spruce to the roots, Muir decides "it would be a fine thing to climb one of the trees to obtain a wider outlook." He quickly scales a tree a hundred feet high. "Never before did I enjoy so noble an exhilaration of motion. The slender tops fairly flapped and swished in the passionate torrent, bending and swirling backward and forward, round and round, tracing indescribable combinations of vertical and horizontal curves, while I clung with muscles firm braced, like a bobolink on a reed." In flood Muir thrusts himself into "the heart of the storm," stands on a "slim boot-bridge . . . scarcely above the current" of Dry Creek, and listens to "the smothered bumping and rumbling of boulders on the bottom as they were shoving and rolling forward against one another in a wild rush." In periods of calm, he seeks out avalanches. After a heavy snowfall his "trampling near the cañon head" triggers a cascade.

> When the avalanche started I threw myself on my back and spread my arms to try to keep from sinking. . . . I was only moderately imbedded on the surface or at times a little below it, and covered with a veil of black-streaming dust particles; and as the whole mass beneath me and about me joined in the flight there was no friction, though I was tossed here and there and lurched from side to side. When the avalanche swedged and came to rest I found myself on top of the crumpled pine without a bruise or scar. This was a fine experience. . . . This flight in what might be called a milky way of snow-stars was the most spiritual and exhilarating of all the modes of motion I have ever experienced.

Muir's imaginative flights depend for their stimulus on such displays of physical pluck.

Muir's favorite animal lives, naturally, in perpetual storm. Every Sierra waterfall houses its little water ouzel, the bluish-gray thrush who feeds among the torrents. In winter dawns the ouzel busily gleans a breakfast from the brook while robins shiver and mutter in the trees. So his human counterpart insists on being up and about, braving perhaps this morning the white water of the Upper Fall to explore the "huge course mouth" of the ice cone piling up at its base. Bird and admirer think nothing of obstacles; both move in "one homogeneous buzz." Through the ouzel, Muir develops his most discreet self-portrait. The bird proves "ever vigorous and enthusiastic, yet self-contained, and neither seeking nor shunning your company." Above all, the ouzel never slows his pace. "He *must* sing though the heavens fall." As a guide in Yosemite Valley, Muir loathed the boarding school girls with their "cheap adjectives," yet his own work was never to escape the gush of superlatives that even a friendly critic labels "grandiloquent." We can catch in Muir's praise of a voice that knows "no wavering notes between sorrow and joy" a spirited defense of his own "unmodulated" style.

Muir's pleasure in storm flows from the "multitude of separate and apparently antagonistic impressions" it stirs up. During storm the human observer must "ascend" toward whatever vantage point renders its effects "united and harmonious." The successful struggle to unite oneself with this teeming variety proves that one can, like the ouzel, make any place a home. In calm weather, landscape affords antithetical pleasures, achieved triumphs of proportion. Muir's most succinct description of Yosemite Valley, the landscape with which he was to become identified, offers perhaps too seamless a prospect:

It is easier to feel than to realize, or in any way explain, Yosemite grandeur. The magnitudes of the rocks and trees and streams are so delicately harmonized they are mostly hidden. Sheer precipices three thousand feet high are fringed with tall trees growing close like grass on the brow of a lowland hill, and extending along the feet of these precipices a ribbon of meadow a mile wide and seven or eight long, that seems like a strip a farmer might mow in less than a day. Waterfalls, five hundred to one or two thousand feet high, are so subordinated to the mighty cliffs over which they pour that they seem like wisps of smoke, gentle as floating clouds, though their voices fill the valley and make the rocks tremble. The mountains, too, along the eastern sky, and the domes in front of them, and the succession of smooth rounded waves between, swelling higher, higher, with dark woods in their hollows, serene in massive exuberant bulk and beauty, tend yet more to hide the grandeur of the Yosemite temple and make it appear as a subdued subordinate feature of the vast harmonious landscape. Thus every attempt to appreciate any one feature is beaten down by the overwhelming influence of all the others.

The gathering cry of protest here nearly undoes the intent to praise. "Beaten down" sounds like anathema from a witness so fond of salience. Yet Muir means to praise; "similitude in dissimilitude" is his consciously adopted refrain. His first sight of the Sierra – the Pisgah Vision from Pacheco Pass – reveals even the "summit-peaks" of his promised land as "comparatively smooth and featureless." The mountains swell up in "one vast wave of stone." The Sierra is, in fact, a single rock whose felt wholeness may justify Muir's conclusion that "when we try to pick out anything by itself, we find it hitched to everything else in the universe."

Muir's vision of the Sierra as one vast simile may have hastened the loss of one of its most favored gardens. Yosemite National Park had been created in 1890, and Yosemite Valley, run by California as a separate concession, was receded to federal control in 1906. The entire Merced and Tuolumne watershed was now secure. But in that year earthquake struck San Francisco. Since the establishment of the park the city had pressed the Department of the Interior for a reservoir in the Sierra, and in the wake of the fires that ravaged the city unchecked the cry went up to "Dam Hetch Hetchy!"

Located sixteen miles north of Yosemite Valley, Hetch Hetchy has entered the American imagination more as a cause than a place. It is a place now seldom seen; the dam that secures its waters leaves an ugly, fluctuating margin of mud and stumps around the lake's shore. Those who saw the valley before the dam marveled with Josiah Whitney at "how curiously nature has repeated herself," though some preferred the smaller defile as a welcome luminist rendition of Yosemite's operatic sublime. Muir fell also into the habit of describing Hetch Hetchy as the double of Yosemite. In "Rambles of a Botanist" he wrote that the valley "is bent northward in the middle like Yosemite." It contains a "vast perpendicular rock" that "resembles El Capitan." "The first conspicuous rocks on the right are a group like the Cathedral Rocks of Yosemite." Hetch Hetchy Fall occupies "a position relative to the valley like that of Yosemite Fall." And the benches along its margin "correspond with astonishing minuteness to the benches of the same relative position of the Yosemite wall." In Muir's writing about the two valleys, Yosemite emerges as the transcendental referent of which Hetch Hetchy is the best available copy. This is high praise indeed for any valley, but such thinking had the unfortunate effect of suggesting to an aroused public that Hetch Hetchy was, in fact, expendable. When Muir took up the fight for Hetch Hetchy in 1905, he had then to combat not only the impending earthquake (catastrophe would literally reshape *this* valley), but the logic of his own running comparison. The habit of perceiving connection and likeness turned against him; the fight was lost in 1913, and Muir died the next year.

What had been at stake, Muir seemed to feel, was his very life. "Anyhow I'll be relieved when it's settled, for it's killing me." He consoled himself for the double loss by assimilating defeat to an Edenic paradigm: "The first forest reservation, including only one tree, was likewise despoiled." The ultimate discrimination of likeness had been achieved, and Muir could die while emulating his first parents, by paying for the gift of the garden through the appropriate experience of fall. What he could not have known was that the earthquake had done more than destroy Hetch Hetchy. The fight it unloosed was, as William Everson says, "one of the turning points in the spiritual life of the nation," and the anger over the valley's loss secured the future of the conservation movement in America.

Although Muir habitually argues for the underlying continuity of natural impressions, it is incongruity that ignites his eye. The botanical amplitude of the Sierra belies its unvarying geology. "California forests are made up of a greater number of distinct species than any other in the world." Distinguished by "inviting openness" rather than "monotonous uniformity," these forests grow in "long, curving bands" punctuated by the absence of soil-bearing moraines. Muir's masters of extravagance, the sugar pines, are "never so interblended as to lose their individuality." Their very pattern of growth is a pattern of hope:

3. The Hetch Hetchy Valley before the flood

The sugar pine is a remarkably proper tree in youth—a strict follower of coniferous fashions—slim, erect, with leafy branches kept exactly in place, each tapering in outline and terminating in a spiry point. The successive forms between the cautious neatness of youth and the bold freedom of maturity offer a delightful study. At the age of fifty or sixty years, the shy, fashionable form begins to be broken up. Specialized branches push out and bend with the great cones, giving individual character, that becomes more marked from year to year.

In praising his favorite tree, Muir elaborates an apology for his own late-blooming independence.

If we return now to the quotation about Yosemite Valley, we can better understand why Muir seems half oppressed by its vast harmonies. It cannot be seen at all without sacrificing the proximity that discloses difference. The protest lodged by the two artists Muir guides to Tuolumne Meadows—" 'here are fore-grounds, middle-grounds, backgrounds, all alike' "—finds echo in Muir's frustrated attempt to appreciate any one feature of this landscape. The scene simply provides no point of entry. So, like Wordsworth projecting the hermit into the vacancy of the Wye Valley, Muir begins to insinuate the presence of the human. The image of the farmer mowing his Yosemite field, surrounded by "wisps of smoke" from so many imaginary chimneys, adjusts the scene to human scale. Inviolate landscape becomes working homestead. In a few months after sketching this passage Muir was to build a cabin, with floor slabs spaced to permit the unfolding of ferns, in the midst of this very scene. At a total outlay of four dollars, Muir's cabin was one-seventh the cost of Thoreau's.

This is the final significance of the Sierra landscape for Muir: It was the garden that had originally been set apart for him. In *My First Summer in the Sierra* (written in 1869; revised and published in 1911), Muir begins to redefine the nature of home. Years later he will sum up the perpetual sense of *déjà vu* inspired by that first visit: "Going to the mountains is like going home. We always find that the strangest objects in these fountain wilds are in some degree familiar, and we look upon them with a vague sense of having seen them before." In his first journal about the mountains, Muir is not so aware of their uncanny effect. He repeatedly likens the Sierra to a domesticated human space. At one moment he feels himself in a "majestic domed pavilion"; at another his "mountain hollow is home, sweet home." He seeks out enclosures in which he can feel the "influences" of nature "acting at short range as if in a quiet room." The totem animal here is not the ouzel, domesticator of the inhospitable, but the common housefly, the thing always at home. Though "fond of domestic ease," the housefly "seems to be everywhere. I wonder if any island in mid-ocean is flyless. The bluebottle is abundant in these Yosemite woods, ever ready with his marvelous store of eggs to make all dead flesh fly." As ubiquitous as the imagination (and as strangely powerful an antidote to death), the housefly is for Muir the thing that cannot suffer exile. Through the image of the fly Muir explores the possibility that an errant flight into wilderness has all the logic of a perpetual return.

When Muir had left home, his father had refused even to say good-bye. The "one well-defined marvel of my life of the kind called super-natural" shows him as haunted by the lack of a blessing. Standing one day on the wall above the valley, Muir has the premonition that a favorite professor from Wisconsin is at that moment somewhere below. "He seemed to be wafted bodily almost against my face." The next day Muir finds Professor Butler "lost in the brush" on the brow of Vernal Falls. So the sponsor figure appears to sanction the "homecoming" of the prodigal son.

Muir was in flight from a "half-happy" childhood. "Father was proud of his garden and seemed always trying to make it as much like Eden as possible." " 'Play as much as you like in the back yard and garden,' " this Scots Jehovah would warn, " 'and mind what you'll get when you forget and disobey.' " What John got was perpetual thrash-ing. So in *The Story of My Boyhood and Youth* (1913) a parody of the ancient script is acted out. Muir was to know firsthand the connection between human freedom and escape from the strictures of a garden. The family's emigration to America in 1849 only added toil to prohibi-tion. When Muir was a young man in Wisconsin, his life was one of sixteen-hour days in the fields. He was allowed two holidays a year. Knowledge was a fruit more forbidden than leisure. John kept his books – the Bible was the only text a man needed – "carefully hidden from father's eye." He rose at one in the morning to steal time for his inventions. A tinkerer in hickory, John was forced by his overseer into Promethean attitudes:

> "John," he inquired, "what is that thing you are making upstairs?"
> I replied in desperation that I didn't know what to call it.
> "What! You mean to say you don't know what you are trying to do?"
> "Oh, yes," I said, "I know very well what I am doing."

He was inventing his way off the farm.

Muir's childhood reverses the traditional myth of human beginnings. He grows up to gain rather than lose the garden. Muir fell into landscape in 1864. "Eden" had lain always about him, but not until quitting the University of Wisconsin for Canada did he truly enter into it. "I really do not know where I shall halt. I feel like Milton's Adam and Eve – 'The world was all before them where to choose their place of rest.' " Like Wordsworth at the beginning of *The Prelude,* Muir begins his story at twenty-five by going out into the world *as if* it were the Garden. His autobiography ends with this moment, but his life begins with it. How does he get from the false to the true Eden? He simply walks away. Adam and Eve lose paradise through an act of choice; Muir regains it through an act of abandon. At Wisconsin, he concludes, "I was far from satisfied with what I had learned, and should have stayed longer. Anyhow I wandered away on a glorious botanical and geological excursion, which has lasted nearly fifty years and is not yet completed." The abrupt "Anyhow" expresses Muir's sense that we are redeemed less by the will than by the "constant and cumulative" obedience to "impulse." With its endlessly surprising prospects, landscape offered such a sensibility the largest possible sense of *invitation.* It would always beckon, in Frost's words, with "the wonder of unexpected supply."

The world of disciplined labor was one Muir could never entirely leave behind. He wavered in his resolve to enroll in "the University of the Wilderness"; four years of dallying in machine shops would intervene between his first plunge into Canada and his final departure for California. In the interim Muir would become one of America's first efficiency experts. His assignment to study conditions in a carriage factory culminated in his attack on the ten-hour day and the self-defeating competitiveness of "the gobble gobble school of economics." As an adolescent Edison, Muir had devoted every spare minute to inventions of dubious ingenuity. First there was the procession of intricate clocks, then the thermometer and barometers by which favorable laboring conditions could be judged. His "early-rising machine" – a trick bed that violently ejected its occupant at a forty-five degree angle – was nicely complemented by his "Loafer's Chair," primed to fire a blank cartridge under anyone prone to linger in it. His triumph was a study desk that used cogwheels to rotate books before his eyes at fifteen-minute intervals as soon as he had been catapulted from bed. These "labor-saving" devices might seem at first to rebuke his father's vision of a world of toil. In fact they simply perpetuate a more subtle enslavement. An internalization this complete could only be undone by a reaction as profound. In Frost, work and play remain mutually interpenetrating activities because he locates himself in semicultivated nature: Muir's opting for wilderness ensured that labor and leisure would be consigned to separate realms. During the 1880s, Muir married and strictly curtailed his trips to the wilderness. He became renowned instead for his Tokay grapes, Bartlett

4. John Muir among the vineyards he planted on his Martinez Ranch

pears, and the stringency with which he drove a bargain. But his health would waste away while he labored at "home"; the weight he lost on his Martinez ranch had to be gained back climbing mountains. By 1889 his finances were secure and he again began to travel and to write.

Equipment became something Muir carried only with reluctance into the wilderness; he almost froze on Mount Whitney for lack of a coat and blanket. His one inevitable supply was a crust of bread, though the humble staff of life had a way of mocking his independence. It is early July in his first summer in the Sierra, and supplies are running low. All that remains is mutton, sugar, tea. "Rather weak and sickish this morning, and all about a piece of bread. Can scarce command attention to my best studies, as if one couldn't take a few days' saunter in the Godful woods without maintaining a base on a wheat-field and grist-mill." A strange languor overtakes the camp. "The stomach begins to assert itself as an independent creature with a will of its own." Muir's will to meditate does not withstand his hunger for bread, though he is not quite willing to conclude that freedom in the mountains depends on cultivation in the valleys. "Bread without flesh is a good diet, as on many botanical excursions I have proved. Tea also may easily be ignored. Just bread and water and delightful toil is all I need, – not unreasonably much, yet one ought to be trained and tempered to enjoy life in these brave wilds in full independence of any particular kind of nourishment." Bread in Muir becomes the unconsciously mediating metaphor, the substance that *could* unite the worlds of work and play. Could we but solve "the bread problem, so troublesome to wanderers," we might reconcile the opposing claims of our inspiring (elevated) and our nourishing (lowland) homes.

The extreme tensions in Muir's recorded experience of landscape – between spectatorship and participation, harmony and salience, discipline and freedom – urge him into stances in which one side of the tension is consciously repressed, while being unconsciously maintained. He does not imagine, as have so many of our writers, that his final subject might become a meditation on these conflicts themselves. Muir is the least double-minded of our great naturalists. His style moves toward unmeasured exclamation; his stances toward unqualified assertion. His is a language aimed at something beyond the interrogation of its own procedures; it is aimed at changing the world. It magnificently passes this political test. Emerson and his heirs build their own worlds at the price of powerlessness in any immediate historical arena; Muir sacrifices an answerable style in order to locate a place in the popular mind. Muir finds salvation in surrender to landscape, and his attempts to know it from within can preclude a more visionary possession. He had almost persuaded Emerson to camp one night with him among the sequoias when at the last minute his guest was whisked into the hotel by his literary friends. So visionary power maintains itself by forsaking the lure of concrete knowledge. Each author has his appropriate legacy, bequests that in their generosity may suspend the temptation to valorize style. Emerson fathers Thoreau and Frost, but Muir saves Yosemite.

Chapter 3

King and catastrophe

―――――――――――

Lunching on the abyss was Clarence King's (1842–1901) idea of a good time. King and his fellow surveyor have been toiling over the ice fields on Shasta's flanks. Lost among "impassable gulfs," King decides to break for lunch:

> a lately quieted stomach is the best defence for nerves. So when we got into a pleasant, open spot where the glacier became for a little way smooth and level, we sat down, leisurely enjoying our repast. We saw a possible way out of our difficulty, and sat some time chatting pleasantly. When there was no more lunch we started again, and only three steps away came upon a narrow crack edged by sharp ice-jaws. There was something noticeable in the hollow, bottomless darkness seen through it which arrested us, and when we had jumped across to the other side, both knelt and looked into its depths. We saw a large domed grotto walled in with shattered ice and arched over by a roof of frozen snow so thin that the light came through quite easily. The middle of this dome overhung a terrible abyss. A block of ice thrown in fell from ledge to ledge, echoing back its stroke fainter and fainter. We had unconsciously sat for twenty minutes lunching and laughing on the thin roof, with only a few inches of frozen snow to hold us up over that still, deep grave.

Courtship of disaster recurs in King's story as a curiously obsessive pattern. What will to risk himself was it that he tested by chasing an aroused grizzly, headfirst, into a smoky cave? (He sailed out safely with the bear shot through the brain.) Was it a scientist's duty that sent him up under the thunderheads of Job's Peak to be struck by the inevitable lightning bolt? (For a week his "right side turned the color of coffee.")

And whence came the bravado that inspired him to deter the Walapais of Arizona from kindling a fire on his chest by brandishing his barometer like a gun? (The cavalry arrived in the nick of time.) King loved to coolly seat himself in the door of death. Such near misses were for him bracing metaphors for the human condition. He sought to celebrate with defiance the liability of life to sudden fall. For all that, the career of Clarence King became one of the great American stories of unsuccess. The closest he came to avoiding the catastrophe that was to become his life was while risking it, with his inimitable good humor, in the mountains of California.

If King loved the emotion of descent – "I always feel a strange renewal of life when I come down from one of these climbs" – he was bound to find it an oppressive refrain in the unfolding story of his life. In 1848, James King died of fever in the China Sea. Six-year-old Clarence was left the son and heir of a Newport trading family of declining fortunes. His mother, Florence, would remarry and outlive her son to claim that "I have never known a more perfect human tie than that which bound my son and myself." King discovered his first fossil (a fern) at seven and entered the new Yale Scientific School at eighteen. He pitched for the varsity and captained the Yale crew. Resolved to become a geologist, King traveled on horseback across the plains with his friends Gardiner and Hyde in the spring of 1863. On a riverboat in the Sacramento delta King spied a bearded, roughly dressed stranger and guessed his name. It was William Brewer, field general of Josiah Whitney's Survey of California. King and Gardiner introduced themselves and were promptly enlisted in the assault on the Range of Light. *Mountaineering in the Sierra Nevada* (1872), King's masterpiece, would refigure the experiences of the next three years. King would go on to head the Survey of the 40th Parallel (it covered a belt one hundred miles wide from Reno to Cheyenne), and in 1876 would become the youngest member of the National Academy of Sciences. He reached the summit of his public career with his appointment in 1879 as the first Director of the U.S. Geological Survey.

In the meantime King had found and renounced the love of a Virginia City schoolteacher (family "duty" called) and befriended Henry Adams. In after years Adams would eulogize King as "the most remarkable man of our time"; they became so linked in the public mind that King became the stalking horse for those offended characters in search of an author for Adams's anonymously published novel, *Democracy*. King was the beloved center of the "Five of Hearts," a club composed of Clara and John Hay and Clover and Henry Adams. (King, Hay, and Adams were all within two inches of five feet.) His conversation was of a legendary wittiness never quite recapturable in stories such as the one in which he replies to Ruskin's offer of a choice between two Turners: "One good Turner deserves another." Friends called King "Scheherazade."

King served just two years as Director of the Survey; the last twenty of his life were spent as a "geological Micawber." He had published the authoritative *Systematic Geology* in 1878, but his own ventures into mining were to prove catastrophic. King wanted money, and after a stint as a cattle baron he turned to the buried treasures of the Sierra Madre. For a few years King ran three of Mexico's richest mines. With his early fortune he spent two years in Europe. Then his luck changed. When a mine's upper ores weren't giving way to country rock or the Yacqui weren't on the warpath, King found himself unable to drive his labor gangs with the mercilessness he associated with capitalist success. His European backers pulled out. Forced to resign from one directorship after another, King was finally broken in the Panic of 1893, when the director of his El Paso bank was indicted for "willful misapplication" of funds. On Halloween of that year King was committed to Bloomingdale after an arrest and fine of ten dollars for disorderly conduct in Central Park. Bouts with malaria, rheumatism, and inflammation of the spine finally converged to rationalize his doctor's diagnosis of mental disturbance. After one last lark with Adams in Cuba, King simply "evaded into space." He blew like a tumbleweed through the mining towns of the West, barely meeting expenses. He had pneumonia by the time his testimony, in 1900, cinched victory for Anaconda in the War of the Copper Kings. A few months later a tubercular patch surfaced on King's lung while he was appraising lead deposits on the Flat River. He died punning on the day before Christmas, 1901, in Phoenix, Arizona.

If King's biography evokes a paradigm of eminence and fall, it was with such themes that he was directly associated in the intellectual life of his time. In 1877 he addressed his alma mater on the subject of "Catastrophism and the Evolution of Environment." In this intellectual credo King attempted to frame the debate between two views of geologic change. It became as well his defense of poetry, a treatise on the origins of creativity in human as well as telluric life.

The face of the earth enjoyed two rivals for its biography in the later nineteenth century. The Uniformitarians and the Catastrophists quarreled over the character and rate of geologic change. The conservative and established view was that "the present is the key to the past." Uniformitarians saw the current configuration of the earth as the product of a steady evolution under the operation of uniform physical laws. Continuity and harmony were key; creation had proceeded from its inception in an unbroken and moderately paced series of steps. Opponents of such a view were likely to prefer the drama of volcanoes to the stateliness of rivers. Catastrophists saw geologic processes as discontinuous and given to varying rates of change. Although the current rate of geologic change might seem negligible, the past was characterized by sudden turns and great upheavals. The present was not so much the key to the past as its unpredictable outcome. In short, one school saw its own moment as more or less determined; the other, as all too frighteningly free.

As a "modified" catastrophist, King could not agree with the extreme advocates of the theory that catastrophe had "extirpated all life at oft-repeated intervals from the time of its earliest introduction." God's *Put out the light* had never been that terribly spoken. It was the geology of "the west" that "was distinctly catastrophic in the wildest dynamic sense," and King never had more trouble stationing himself between theoretical extremes than in his quarrel with John Muir over the origin of Yosemite Valley. Muir claimed that the slow work of glaciers had formed the granite defile. King could not openly contradict the insistence of Josiah Whitney that only a massive subsidence of the valley floor could account for its present shape. The one index reference to Muir in *Systematic Geology* consists of a short editorial: "Muir, John, his glacial blunders." In fact in *Mountaineering* and elsewhere King was willing to admit that "those terrible ice-engines" performed their work along with a catastrophic "rending asunder." Only such a modified view, of a world in which catastrophe can be survived, left the responsive human any role to play in the scheme of creation. Plasticity was what King cherished, and "*plasticity* became the sole principle of salvation" in a world given to "terrible and destructive exhibitions of sudden, unusual telluric energy." It was his own imperative drive to be and remain creative that King's insistence on a world of past and "impending crises" was meant to guarantee.

How else but through catastrophe would power reveal itself in a world once so suddenly created? King's work forges everywhere a link between creation and catastrophe. The Creation *is* a catastrophe; not, as Blake meant, a falling off from a world of undivided light, but rather a happy display of "novelty" at/as the source. Creation and catastrophe presume a breach, a sudden intrusion of pattern previously unknown. After the original "abruption" (as Frost would call it) of spirit into matter, matter was unlikely to settle, down the long perspective of the years, for no further "intake of fire":

> He who brought to bear that mysterious energy we call life upon
> primeval matter, bestowed at the same time a power of develop-
> ment by change, arranging that the interaction of energy and
> matter which make up environment should, from time to time,

burst in upon the current of life and sweep it onward and upward to ever higher and better manifestations. Moments of great catastrophe, thus translated into the language of life, become moments of creation, when out of plastic organisms something newer and nobler is called into being.

King's theory of change thus allows him to think of histories – be they biographical, regional, literary, or geologic – as composed of a series of fresh starts. The debate over models of continuity is as old as the ancients and the moderns and as new as the romantics and the self-scatterers. Whether one reviewed a personal or a planetary past, the pattern thrown up was riddled, in King's view, by instability.

Surface landscape was bound to present King with a suspiciously stable prospect. As a geologist rather than a geographer, King was destined by professional training as well as conceptual bias to concern himself with origin rather than function. As a scientist, he found the morphology of landscape less pertinent than its unapparent past. He saw the world less as relief than as process. If "mirage" is the key image in the opening of *Mountaineering,* it is because King looks *through* rather than *at* "The Range." "Geology itself," King told his mother, "is chiefly a matter of imagination. One man can actually see into the ground no farther than another. Geology is the best training conceivable in constructive imagination." The patterns geology reckons with are invisible; its succession of upheavals, folds, and collapses render the earth up as that which is crumpled. "Orography" (the study of mountain building) dissolves in its fluid perspectives the planet's most massive solids. The most disturbing discovery of nineteenth-century geology may have been not that history had no beginning but rather that landscape, the place in which human history has been acted out, will fold back eventually into the surface of the earth. Such prospects undermine interest in place as that which meets the eye.

THE REGIONAL SUBLIME

King was diverted from a career in the mirage of geology or the fictions of literature by his fascination with triumph in the visible world. His major metaphor for success became the scaling of a mountain. His climb of Mount Shasta becomes, in *Mountaineering,* the dark emblem of his drive toward measurable achievement. Of the three great climbs in the book, it is the one consciously dominated by a sense of manifest rather than spiritual destiny.

Manifest Destiny is in fact the theme of the climb. King's was an inadvertent epic of the Gilded Age: Few had reason to be more sensitive to the momentum that led it west. On Shasta conquest comes too easily: "Indeed, I have never reached a corresponding altitude with so little labor and difficulty." Two young girls had beaten King to the top. He finds himself standing "upon a great shield which rose gently in all directions to the sky." As he lingers through sunset, the natural eminence achieved by the self becomes the token of a regional destiny:

> Afar in the north, bars of blue shadow streamed out from the peaks, tracing themselves upon rosy air. All the eastern slope of Shasta was of course in dark shade, the gray glacier forms, broken ridges of stone, and forest all dim and fading. A long cone of cobalt-blue, the shadow of Shasta fell strongly defined over the bright plain, its apex darkening the earth a hundred miles away. As the sun sank, this gigantic spectral volcano rose on the warm sky till its darker form stood huge and terrible over the whole east. It was intensely distinct at the summit, just as far-away peaks seen against the east in evening always are, and faded at base as it entered the stratum of earth mist.
>
> Grand and impressive we had thought Shasta when studying it in similar light from the plain. Infinitely more impressive was this phantom volcano as it stood overshadowing the land and slowly fading into night.
>
> Before quitting the ridge, Fred Clark and I climbed together out upon the highest pinnacle, a trachyte needle rising a few feet above the rest, and so small we could barely balance there together, but we stood a moment and waved the American flag, looking down over our shoulders eleven thousand feet.

King might have better waved the Bear Flag: This is a vision of Manifest Destiny in reverse. West rises "huge and terrible over the whole east" here in what we might call a "regional sublime." King had little doubt that California would overcome the turbulence of her early beginnings ("We must admit the facts. California people are not living in a tranquil, healthy, social *régime*") to cast a shadow over the land that lay behind her. In his imperial moment on Shasta, King becomes a type of all that he believed the state would call forth: "Out of the race of men whom they have in the same shallow way called common, I believe Time shall separate a noble race."

A "Shasta complex" seemed to pervade the state survey. King's epiphany was finally amateurish compared to the dogged insistence of William Brewer on the mountain's preeminence. Of all California onlookers, Brewer tried to see California clearly and to see it whole. He is not a patron of a region within the region. Brewer's is the only account of the state from which one could construct a map; he covered more than fifteen thousand miles in four years. There is nevertheless in the pattern of his movement (an arc up the Coast Range and down the Sierra Nevada – *Up and Down California*) a logic that throws one pattern into relief: Shasta. Brewer judged Shasta the highest mountain in the state. He saw it as "the grand goal of this trip." He was to refer estimates of Sierra evaluations to Shasta. His expectations and memories of the solitary volcano suggest that he saw it as California's distinctive topographical feature *because* it marked the climax of his trip. Brewer's pleasure in coming upon the mountain shows to what various uses a natural fact can be put; whereas King identified Shasta with imperial selfhood, Brewer prized it as completing the text of a relentlessly logical grammar – as the region's exclamation point.

Mountaineering contains three great climbs: Tyndall, Shasta, Whitney. The original set of chapters published in *The Atlantic Monthly* in 1871 ended with Shasta. King added five chapters to the first edition and ended with Whitney. In this edition Shasta proves a false climax, an elevation too easily won. Whitney replaces it only as a formal climax; the climb is actually a failure so profound that it had to be made good in a second edition. Tyndall remains the triumphant climb, the one in which King enjoys the naive success of a firstcomer and the certain knowledge of catastrophe overcome. Before comparing King's experience of these two summits, I would like to digress, however, into a story of emotional rather than physical conquest.

FRIENDSHIP AND ORDEAL

"I looked at it as one contemplating the purpose of his life": This is King in 1864 facing the most gigantic mountain wall in America. His purpose was to reconnoiter the Kings–Kern divide and to stand on its highest peak, the yet unnamed Mount Tyndall. Brewer pronounced impossible King's "campaign for the top of California"; King had proven hapless enough in the months previous by "getting his ears frostbitten" and allowing to be stolen Indian bows the expedition had carried for seven hundred miles. But he had "the greatest muscular endurance" Brewer had ever seen as well as his Chingachgook, "the one comrade I would choose to face death with," his man Cotter. The story of King and Cotter on Tyndall is one of the classic American accounts of friendship and ordeal.

King no doubt thought of the conquest of the peak as the climax of the five-day trip. Its emotional center lies rather in two linked moments

5. James Gardiner, Richard Cotter, William Brewer, and Clarence King, the 1864 field party of the California Geological Survey

of risk-taking and love. Dick Cotter is a nearly anonymous figure in King's narrative, a drover whom King had borrowed from Brewer's service. They were fated to share an ecstatic intimacy that appropriated a mythic dimension for the simple word "friend."

The most arresting moment of the ascent comes on the first night out. King beds down on "a sort of shelf just large enough for Cotter and me." As the temperature drops the sudden leverage of the frost sends immense blocks whizzing past the the lee of their cliff:

> A single thickness of blanket is a better mattress than none, but the larger crystals of orthoclase, protruding plentifully, punched my back and caused me to revolve on a horizontal axis with precision and frequency. How I loved Cotter! how I hugged him and got warm, while our backs gradually petrified, till we whirled over and thawed them out together! The slant of that bed was diagonal and excessive; down it we slid till the ice chilled us awake, and we crawled back and chocked ourselves up with bits of granite inserted under my ribs and shoulders. In this pleasant position we got dozing again, and there stole over me a most comfortable ease. The granite softened perceptibly.

The one domestic scene in *Mountaineering* that the hero does not shun, he shares with a man.

King's unblushing interdependency with Cotter passes a less perilous test on the descent from Tyndall. King and Cotter are scaling "forty feet of smooth granite" above a frozen lake. Cotter makes a bold spring for a crack beyond King's reach, clambers to a ledge, and calls down cheerfully,

> "Don't be afraid to bear your weight." I made up my mind, however, to make that climb without his aid, and husbanded my strength as I climbed from crack to crack. I got up without difficulty to my former point, rested there a moment, hanging solely by my hands, gathered every pound of strength and atom of will for the reach, then jerked myself upward with a swing, just getting the tips of my fingers into the crack. In an instant I had grasped it with my right hand also. I felt the sinews of my fingers relax a little, but the picture of the slope of ice and the blue lake affected me so strongly that I redoubled my grip, and climbed slowly along the crack until I reached the angle and got one arm over the edge as Cotter had done. As I rested my body upon the edge and looked up at Cotter, I saw that, instead of a level top, he was sitting upon a smooth roof-like slope, where the least pull would have dragged him over the brink. He had no brace for his feet, nor hold for his hands, but had seated himself calmly, with the rope tied round his breast, knowing that my only safety lay in being able to make the climb entirely unaided; certain that the least waver in his tone would have disheartened me, and perhaps

made it impossible. The shock I received on seeing this affected me for a moment, but not enough to throw me off my guard, and I climbed quickly over the edge. When we had walked back out of danger we sat down upon the granite for a rest.

In all my experience of mountaineering I have never known an act of such real, profound courage as this of Cotter's. It is one thing, in a moment of excitement, to make a gallant leap, or hold one's nerves in the iron grasp of will, but to coolly seat one's self in the door of death, and silently listen for the fatal summons, and this all for a friend, – for he might easily have cast loose the lasso and saved himself, – requires as sublime a type of courage as I know.

The manuscript version of the descent is curiously diffident. The entire five days on Tyndall receive only twenty-nine lines in a small notebook King carried into the mountains, and "The Descent of Tyndall" is compressed into this:

> I will not fatigue you by a detailed account of the climb homeward it was very difficult twice Dick came within a hair's breadth of losing his life in different places I too thought myself gone

The notes of the ascent claim even less – "We reached the summit without accident." Gone here is the saving slide to the gooseberry bush, King's sweet vertigo on the rope, or the final creep up the gigantic icicle. The lines alluding to Cotter's "real" act of courage are fragmentary and crossed out. "Dick climbed up one face of granite which was 40 feet and a little overhanging clinging w̄ almost nothing." From the evidence of the notes, it appears that King as author elaborated catastrophes that would give him the chance to measure a man's aptitude for sacrifice and love.

As the later encounters with women in *Mountaineering* make clear, King chose to project a persona of a man in flight from the lure of the hearth. He turns instead to Cotter. In giving these perhaps apocryphal catastrophes on Tyndall such full play in the published text, King was setting out again on a national errand into the wilderness. The jaunty make-believe may hail from Leslie Stephen's "A Bad Five Minutes in the Alps," but King's claim to "the territory" of passionate male friendship is pure Cooper, Melville, and Twain.

ON TYNDALL AND WHITNEY

As King stood on Mount Tyndall he saw a peak even higher. "Whitney" was the name he gave to this "cleanly cut helmet of granite." On

Whitney seven years later the "rocky tower of Mount Tyndall" would beckon to King through the mist. On each mountain King is acutely aware of the other. If they provided the peak experiences in King's narrative, they could scarcely have presented more startling contrasts to the eye.

King can seem a man beset by light. Nature's reflecting surfaces could offer after all only a frozen mirage of a fundamentally fluid world. "Distinctness" can be, for King, literally "terrible." Doré's Dante tries to "shut in our imagination" with its overbalancing love of unmodulated light. "There is in all his Inferno landscape a certain sharp boundary between the real and unreal, and never the infinite suggestiveness of great regions of half-light, in which everything may be seen, nothing recognized." On Tyndall the light creates, by usurping the suggesting power of the eye, a "desert of death." The "tumult of form" only amplifies a "silence . . . like the waveless calm of space." The world can be seen but not realized:

> The serene sky is grave with nocturnal darkness. The earth blinds you with its light. That fair contrast we love in lower lands between bright heavens and dark cool earth here reverses itself with terrible energy. You look up into an infinite vault, unveiled by clouds, empty and dark, from which no brightness seems to ray, an expanse with no graded perspective, no tremble, no vapory mobility, only the vast yawning of hollow space.

No tremble: What is this but a vision of a heaven – and an earth – in which all processes have stopped? Light and sound here insist on a world separate from man in space and time. "I have never seen Nature when she seemed so little 'mother Nature' as in this place of rocks and snow, echoes and emptiness. It impresses me as the ruins of some bygone geological period, and no part of the present order." On Tyndall, King confronts that thing most terrible, a finished creation.

On Whitney, weather offered King the chance to participate in the construction of the landscape, but it was a chance not taken. Anticipation threw up a barrier to experience. King had tried to climb Whitney twice before; now the assault was a thing to be done. Reaching the top proves at once foreshortened and anticlimactic: "Above us but thirty feet rose a crest, beyond which we saw nothing. I dared not think it the summit till we stood there, and Mount Whitney was under our feet." Catastrophe becomes afterthought on Whitney; both King and his companion, Pinson (they scarcely seem to have spoken), enjoy the obligatory but unelaborated fall through the ice. On the summit the range is obscured by cloud. Instead of projecting himself into the half-light, however, King assimilates the mountains he does see into a catalogue of

past climbs. "I saw the peaks and passes and amphitheatres, dear old
Cotter and I had climbed." He sees little else. Dense clouds soon close
in, and, "feeling quite assured of our direction," King promptly gets
lost. After sitting down "to carefully recall every detail of topography,"
he makes his tired way home.

King had been more lost than he thought; it was the wrong mountain. Two years after King's 1871 climb, W. A. Goodyear read a paper
before the California Academy of Sciences that made a conclusive re-
joinder to King's claim: *"This peak is not Mount Whitney."* King
promptly headed west and climbed – it was his fourth attempt – the true
Whitney. "All honor," King remarked, "to those who came before
me." King had actually been on a peak he himself had named Sheep
Rock, the present Mount Langley. The "rocky tower" King had seen
through the fog was not Tyndall but the true Whitney. Whitney and
Tyndall are thus linked not only by a reciprocal glance – on each peak
King "sees" the other – but by an act of unconscious substitution. When
King sees Whitney and thinks it Tyndall, he confounds the site of
priority and triumph with that of belatedness and loss. The confusion
between the experiences on Tyndall and the false Whitney eventually
found resolution in a wisdom beyond gain or loss. In the 1874 edition
of *Mountaineering,* King added seventeen pages on the climb of the true
Whitney. The revised chapter becomes a meditation on and farewell to
the pursuit of desire in the natural world.

Wordsworth had had his Goodyear – the chastening peasant who told
him that he had also missed his mountain, *"that we had crossed the Alps."*
The disappointment ensuing from such loss led to a literal "break
through," a discovery that our destiny lies less in outer nature than in
the far reaches of human nature. "Our being's heart and home" is in the
"invisible world." It is the shape and strength of his own desire that he
comes upon in the Simplon Pass when, after nature has failed to guide
and satisfy him, Wordsworth loses his way. Actually being lost is for
him a state preparatory to some discovery about mental power. Wordsworth enjoys these sudden encounters with the dimensions of his own
need and power – with the sublime – after he has abandoned himself in
natural space.

King's moments of sudden grace do not come unsought, and so they
scarcely come at all. He refuses to get lost. If the promise of catastrophe
is the free response to the unexpected, King arms himself against the
promise. (He was, after all, nearly always making a map.) By so aggressively asserting his will to achieve the eminence from which everything could be seen, King tends to impose rather than to discover.
Wordsworth knew that geographical and psychological dispositions
converge; his theory of attention holds that the mind in creation must

absent itself from the will in the way that a hiker does from a map. De Quincey likens a Wordsworth waiting for the mail to the responsive Boy of Winander:

> At intervals, Wordsworth had stretched himself at length on the high road, applying his ear to the ground, so as to catch any sound of wheels that might be groaning along at a distance. Once, when he was slowly rising from this effort, his eye caught a bright star that was glittering between the brow of Seat Sandal, and of the mighty Helvellyn. He gazed upon it for a minute or so; and then, upon turning away to descend into Grasmere, he made the following explanation: – "I have remarked, from my earliest days, that if, under any circumstances, the attention is energetically braced up to an act of steady observation, or of steady expectation, then, if this intense condition of vigilance should suddenly relax, at that moment any beautiful, any impressive visual object, or collection of objects, falling upon the eye, is carried to the heart with a power not known under other circumstances. Just now . . . at the very instant when the organs of attention were all at once relaxing from their tension, the bright star hanging in the air above those outlines of massy blackness, fell suddenly upon my eye, and penetrated my capacity of apprehension with a pathos and a sense of the Infinite, that would not have arrested me under other circumstances.

Creation for Wordsworth, as for King, issues from a moment of sudden fall. The world is always "falling upon the eye." (Wordsworth's theory of attention nearly guarantees the existence of the imagination we call Romantic: His "sense of the Infinite" may have its source in a subliminal awareness of his own steady willingness to receive.) But while these falls are for Wordsworth (and his Boy of Winander) "a gentle shock of mild surprise," in King they are catastrophes. King's violent taste in surprise demands a vigilance that nearly rules out anything more than muscular responsiveness to the surprises that come. Braving catastrophe discourages the free exercise of the very power – plastic imagination – it is meant to stimulate. Perhaps the central and somber lesson of King's work is that landscape can never lead beyond landscape – into a knowledge of how we inspirit it – until we have relinquished enough to allow it to inspire us.

This is what gives the final assault on Whitney such pathos, for the very pages in which King inaugurates a consciously imaginative career also complete his first and last major fiction. As the preface to the 1874 edition bids farewell to youth and to literature, so the revision of Whitney acknowledges and bids farewell to a higher self-consciousness. The bravado on Tyndall gives way here to a meditative mood. At his camp at twelve thousand feet King is relieved to give up control. "One's own wearying identity shrinks from the broad, open foreground of the vision, and a calmness born of reverent reflections encompasses the soul." Tyndall's "vacant solitudes" are replaced by a "sheltering nearness." Where the false Whitney parodied the triumph on Tyndall, the true Whitney proves its true contrary:

> That fearful sense of wreck and desolation, of a world crushed into fragments, of the ice chisel which, unseen, has wrought this strange mountain sculpture, all the sensations of power and tragedy I had invariably felt before on high peaks, were totally forgotten. It was the absolute reverse of the effect on Mount Tyndall, where an unrelenting clearness discovered every object in all its power and reality. Then we saw only unburied wreck of geologic struggles, black with sudden shadow or white under searching focus, as if the sun were a great burning-glass, gathering light from all space, and hurling its fierce shafts upon spire and wall.

The failure of past ambition here finds emblem in a humbled landscape in which all eminence is muted in "a strange harmonizing of earth and air." What could have been King's Simplon becomes his Snowdon; the mood is one in which nature can be read as a harmonious text. Imagination withdraws from self-assertion in the name of a higher order. The mind is drawn to resemblance rather than difference. The "highest bliss" is not to overreach, fall, and discover the imagination's "awful Power," but simply to enjoy, as Wordsworth did on Snowdon, "the consciousness/Of Whom" one is.

Once safely back on the valley floor King looks back at Whitney and feels himself "on the edge of myth-making." He can now play with imaginative projection – "It is hard not to invest these great dominating peaks with consciousness" – because he has withdrawn any hope of lending, through the embodiment of irrepressible force, a myth to nature. As King tries to realize again "the hard, materialistic reality of Mount Whitney," an old Indian crouches beside him and sights an arrow toward the peak. For a last moment he entertains a notion of the peak as the old earthshaker of the valley. He concludes by letting be be finale of seem: "I saw the great peak only as it really is, a splendid mass of granite, 14,887 feet high, ice-chiselled and storm-tinted, a great monolith left standing amid the ruins of a bygone geological empire." King entertains and rejects the notion of nature as symbol in the same short interval. In this abbreviated romance with resonance he could have found no more fitting monument than Whitney for his own sadly truncated career.

The revised experience on Whitney throws light back on the vision

6. "Winter Sunrise, the Sierra Nevada from Lone Pine, California, 1944"

from the top of Tyndall. The 1874 text revises the experience on Tyndall and allows us to complete the following chart:

Summit experiences

Tyndall (1872):	"eye" usurped by landscape
False Whitney (1872):	"I" lost in landscape
True Whitney (1874):	"eye" withdrawn from landscape
Tyndall (as revalued in 1874):	"I" as measure of landscape

In the 1872 text King had refused to project himself into Tyndall's "inanimate forms out of which something living has gone forever." This had seemed like a principled refusal of the Romantic sublime. But in the 1874 text it becomes apparent – the strongest writing here is reserved for the *contrast* with Tyndall – that on that lower peak King had been celebrating, over and above "the eloquence of death," the appropriating power of language itself. The description at the summit had testified to the toughness of a mind in its unblinking focus on man's unique gift of mortality. The "unrelenting clearness" of the sun can be seen as an emblem of King's unique powers of "searching focus." For this one moment he is perhaps less beset by light than identified with it, gazing calmly down on a universe of death like the sun's "great burning-glass." King does not promote such an identification; it is precisely any resonance between nature and human nature that the vision on Tyndall had been meant to deny. But the resonance is there, and it is this habit of inscribing himself in the rhythms and forms of landscape that gives his work its naive power. He purchases knowledge of such practice with a loss of power; on the true Whitney, King's admission of "myth-making" and his renunciation of further myths are, in fact, one.

NADIR AND ZENITH

If we stand back from the sequence of chapters in *Mountaineering,* its introduction, conclusion, digressions, and climaxes form a double parabola, a valley with two peaks (see opposite). The two episodes of "zenith" are structurally bound together by their antithetical relation to the book's "nadir," King's discovery of the fossil in "Merced Ramblings." In this model the book begins and ends with a long perspective, alternates between chapters of quest and flight, and takes for its middle a comic anticlimax. The quest is toward triumph over catastrophe risked; the flight is from emblems of domestic entanglement. The counterpoint provided by the chapters of flight shows how careful King was to arrange his chapters in a dialectical sequence.

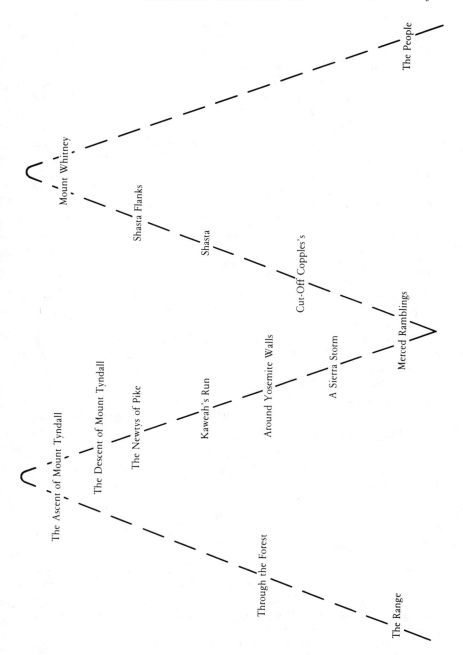

The People

Mount Whitney

Shasta Flanks

Shasta

Cut-Off Copples's

Merced Ramblings

A Sierra Storm

Around Yosemite Walls

Kaweah's Run

The Newtys of Pike

The Descent of Mount Tyndall

The Ascent of Mount Tyndall

Through the Forest

The Range

In "The Newtys of Pike" and "Cut-Off Copples's," King runs
smack into the seductive world of the hearth. King comes upon Susan
Newty "flat upon her back" beside the fire, "her mind absorbed in the
simple amusement of waving one foot (a cowhide eleven) slowly across
the fire." (She and her folks are surrounded by "acres of tranquil
pork.") Mother Pike snaps at Susan not to "spread so," and the tone of
the episode is set. No matter how much King comes to admire her
"riding, her firm, immovable seat," no matter how "determined" he
becomes "to probe Susan," he cannot get around the impending chance
of entrapment. When Pa Pike finally proposes for her ("Thet – thet –
thet man what gits Susan *has half the hogs!*"), the threat to mobility fully
surfaces and King is soon gone. (Susan was six feet and a breaker of
horses.) So it is with "*Venus de* Copples"; King cannot rid himself of "a
fear that her buttons might sooner or later burst off and go singing by
my ear." King may be a match for his mountains, but not for the erotic
frankness of such "vast potatoes or massive pears." There are women,
like "mules," who can "place men under their spell." These chapters
become climax rather than digression if one reads the book as a parable
of displaced eros. *Mountaineering* proves so abundant with antithetical
themes that any map of its peaks and valleys depends on which thematic function one has chosen to graph.

There can be little doubt, however, that King sees his discovery of
the fossil in "Merced Ramblings" as the "nadir" of the book. He has
been chipping with his hammer in "a canõn whose profound uninter-
estingness is quite beyond portrayal." He wishes he were on a mountain – "it seemed to me the place of places for a fossil. Here was nadir,
the snow-capped zenith of my heart banished even from sight." While
turning homeward he notices

> in the rock an object about the size and shape of a small cigar. It
> was the fossil, the object for which science had searched and
> yearned and despaired! There he reclined comfortably upon his
> side, half bedded in luxuriously fine-grained argillaceous ma-
> terial, – a plump pampered cephalopoda (if it is cephalopoda),
> whom the terrible ordeal of metamorphism had spared. . . . The
> age of the gold-belt was discovered.

King would later take great pride in Whitney's assertion that this find
conclusively established the age of the Mother Lode. It was the climax
of King's work in the field. But in the text professional success is
redefined as a kind of failure and located in a valley. King experiences
the discovery as pure bathos: "All this came and went without the
longed-for elation. There was no doubt that I was not so happy as I
thought I should be." Why was King so ambivalent about success?

FOSSILS AND TEXTS

King spent a lifetime torn between the claims of invention and discovery. When he found a fossil, he discovered literal evidence of a world man did not create; when he invented a text, he produced evidence of a world only man possesses. Discovery of fossils and minerals would ensure his professional and financial success; invention of a fictive world would make his literary career. King was gifted at both modes of bringing something new into being. He had hoped to achieve eminence in both orders of time, but his literary ambitions demanded that he take an ironic stance toward success in the immediate temporal world. The demands of that world he would however find too urgent to ignore, and the incipient knowledge of this compromise underlies his long look here "Down the perspective of the years":

> I could see before me spectacled wise men of some scientific society, and one who pronounced my obituary, ending thus: "In summing up the character and labors of this fallen follower of science, let it never be forgotten that he discovered the cephalopoda"; and perhaps, I mused, they will put over me a slab of fossil rain-drops, those eternally embalmed tears of nature.

This is King's prefiguring of his eventually frozen creativity, a monument to power blocked at the source. He would go on digging in the earth for the rest of his life. With his usual easy irony he sensed that the immortality parodied here could be guaranteed not by the discovery of a thing but by the invention of a text.

His friend Henry Adams would after all make a text of *his* "failure." When King and Adams met in Estes Park in 1871, the historian saw each as "at that moment passing the critical point of his career." King was in the midst of writing *Mountaineering*. The irony of the meeting was that Adams, whose career was to display an underlying integrity of purpose, judged himself to be, in the conduct of life, a Catastrophist next to King's assured Uniformitarian style. "He had given himself education all of a piece, yet broad. Standing in the middle of his career, where their paths at last came together, he could look back and look forward on a straight line, with scientific knowledge for its base. Adams's life, past or future, was a succession of violent breaks or waves, with no base at all." The most violent break in *The Education* occurs just at this point – on meeting King the narrative of youth breaks off to resume from the perspective of "Twenty Years After." King's early success and later failure parenthesizes Adams's unchronicled middle years: "Much that had made life pleasant between 1870 and 1890 perished in the ruin, and among the earliest wreckage had been the

fortunes of Clarence King." In 1871, Adams had thought "King's education ideal, and his personal fitness unrivalled." Now he is forced to
concur with King's "California instincts" in a way he had never expected: "catastrophe," proclaimed King's life, "was the law of change."
(The "instincts" were more native to California than Adams probably
knew. In *California: An Intimate History,* Gertrude Atherton was to
deploy an analogy between the state's rebounding from earthquake and
the power of its representative men – Broderick, Ralston, King of William – to triumph over "grave faults" in their careers. *Mountaineering*
was the one book she read every year.) If *The Education* does King the
favor of writing his most memorable "obituary," King serves Adams
as the "self-character" through which he can explore his fascination
with energy unconstrained by form.

King and Adams might not have changed places had the mountaineer
found an adequate vehicle for musing on his own history of waste. In
the years during which catastrophe became King's governing script
rather than his chosen metaphor, he essayed only one brief fiction,
"The Helmet of Mambrino." This detour into the landscape of Don
Quixote finds King in pursuit of a fossil (a barber's basin) by which he
could authenticate the existence of a wholly fictive career. Too many
basins turn up, and the choice of the battered old over the shiny new
proves a comically arbitrary one. These are not the "literary remains"
through which Cervantes lives on. "The Helmet of Mambrino" is a
charming and rueful parable on the form in which the self ensures its
survival: by re-creating rather than prospecting in the world.

King's career raises important questions about the integrity of any
career. Integrity itself is the issue – his geological theory and psychological dispositions converge on the question of continuous and unbroken development. Time itself was defined by King's geology as a
series of fresh starts. And if one glances at the life, it looks like a
radical self-scattering. But to study the career is to discover that it
returned again and again to its central theme and so transformed catastrophe into a kind of fate. With every opportunity to stray from his
abiding principle of being, King did not stray. Even his failures took
their place in a gathering refrain. The integrity was not in the recurrence of catastrophe but in the will to encounter and survive it. What
had begun as a desideratum became, of course, an oppressive script. If
integrity was finally a condition that befell King, it was integrity
nevertheless. Although the self here may appear to be only a "mobile
desiring fantasy," it is just as deeply centered in a lifetime of half-
conscious fidelity to an image of possibility. King could have given
his story no greater permanence than by appropriating the catastrophic
history of the Sierra as the self's most accurate lithograph.

Chapter 4

Mary Austin: nature and nurturance

===============

THE EAGLE AND THE TROUT

Austin's (1868–1934) landscapes are charged with the drama of care. It is summer in Inyo, and a cloudburst has just blown through the canyon:

> Mary went out with the baby on one arm and a hoe on the other to look for what it had left, a very large and lively lake trout thrashing indignantly in a transient pool. Mary laid the baby under a sagebush while she dammed the shallow trickle below it before undertaking to flip the trout out with the hoe. At that instant an eagle hovering, who must have already marked it for his own, swooped and snatched. Mary struck him with the hoe, so that he dropped the trout, which Mary fell upon; the eagle sharply with a resentful scream darted for the sleeping child. Mary sweats still to think what might have happened if she had not laid it so close up under the covering sage. Once more the hoe came into play and the eagle swooped, this time raking the raised arms with a long claw before, screaming, he made off into invisible blueness. I do not even yet recall how Mary got back to the house – with the trout; but it was days before she would so much as take the child outdoors without a preliminary survey of the wide haunt of eagles, and she left out that part when she accounted to Wallace that night for the trout at supper.

In this episode from her autobiography, *Earth Horizon* (1932), Austin rises to an occasion that life did not generously offer her: the chance to choose decisively for her child. Negligence mingles with nurturance; by putting her baby, Ruth, in harm's way, Mary initiates a passionate test of her love. If her carelessness is redeemed by her courage in the act, it is Austin's ambivalence that survives. The episode seems a battle between two over a cherished third. But it also images a conflict in which

Austin will identify with the aggression and freedom of the bird. She fishes in the waters of nurturance to feed her child, but her life choice will be for the transcendence of the sky.

The capacity of Austin's experience to arrange itself in significant "pattern" was not lost upon her. Ruth was, in fact, one of those "hostages of faith and affection" by which Austin felt herself "engaged against the pattern and so delayed of fulfillment." It was in moments like this, where the claims of motherhood and the land are starkly opposed, that the pattern leapt out at Mary in all its fierce simplicity. With her inhuman surroundings she was to identify her ambitions as an artist. Her human bonds led her naturally back to her identity as a woman. The story of Austin's career is of a painful weaning of herself, through the stimulus of arid land, from the conventional acts of care that she had been raised to believe a woman's part.

The husband here is the thing left out; he neither hears nor helps. He gets to eat the fish. In later years Austin was to write "that the true ground of intimacy between men and women is their common fixation on an undescribed Third – a Way of Life, a child, a common attack upon the Wilderness." Wallace will remain the more than absent partner, the man who was never there at all. Austin's nostalgia here imagines a world of reproduction and bonds, in which one plus one makes three. Hers was instead a lonely and a complex fate; she was destined to substitute the oppositions of the dyad (self/landscape) for the rich tensions of the triangle. Austin bypassed the figure of love because she insisted on standing at the center of a diagram of her own devising. Her career redefined a woman's "middle" as the creative mind rather than the hearth. She imagined this place as the center of a circle, Earth Horizon, "the Sacred Middle from which all horizons are equidistant." At the circle's four cardinal points, as Rae Ballard has shown, stood Austin's four chosen roles: mystic, folklorist, naturist, writer. Unlike life in a triangle, life at the center promised order and completion, experience purged of instability and desire. But the figure traced its darker dimensions, and as her story unfolds Austin's soul is not always able to swing "freely to its proper arc." Austin stood also at the center of an emotional mandala in which she found herself quartered by the conflicting claims of the four women who drew her back into the traditional roles from which writing about the West had promised to deliver her.

FOUR AND ONE

The second daughter of George and Susannah Hunter was born into a green and malarial Illinois. Fever took away both father and sister when

Mary was ten. But by then (1878) she had learned to depend on solitary intimations of immortality from the natural world: "God happened to Mary under the walnut tree" when she was five. Coppery brown hair still fell below her knees when the Class Poet took her degree from Blackburn College in 1888. In that year Mary's family moved to California. They homesteaded first at the tip of the lower San Joaquin, at a place called Tejon. Edward Beale – he who had saved Kearney at San Pasqual and carried the secret news of gold to Washington – ushered Mary into Indian villages and shared with her old reports of military expeditions and geological surveys. Mary began to write about the land. Three years after coming to California she married Stafford Wallace Austin, son of declining gentry from Hawaii. They moved east of the Sierra, to the Owens Valley. The Austins lived and taught in Bishop, Independence, Lone Pine. As she lay on her childbed in 1892, Mary's first story was accepted by the *Overland Monthly*. Wallace's business failed. And it soon became clear, in Austin's words, that something "was the matter with the child."

In 1900, Mary built "the brown house" in Lone Pine and placed her daughter in a foster home. (Ruth would die in an institution in 1918.) She finished writing her first and most famous book, *The Land of Little Rain*. Already a member of the Lummis Salon in Pasadena, Austin would soon help to found the artists' colony at Carmel. As her career flourished, her marriage foundered. Ten years of estrangement ended in divorce in 1914. By 1906, Austin was done with California; although she lived through the San Francisco earthquake, it was the destruction of the Owens Valley by the Los Angeles Water Department that exiled her spiritually from the Lands of the Sun.

Austin would seek out a cancer cure in Italy and sojourn in New York before settling permanently, in 1924, in New Mexico. Over the years she produced plays (*The Arrow Maker*), feminist novels (*A Woman of Genius*), collections of folklore (*One Smoke Stories*), studies in mysticism (*The Man Jesus*), and works on prosody (*The American Rhythm*). It was a public life. She toured England with the Herbert Hoovers. H. G. Wells huddled with her over his marital difficulties. (He called her "the most intelligent woman in America.") Conrad handed her a rose, still pressed in the Huntington Library, on her departure from England. Austin claimed that Willa Cather wrote *Death Comes for the Archbishop* in her Santa Fe adobe. The high priestess of the Southwest, she wept over the murals of Diego Rivera and served as a delegate to the Seven States Conference on the fate of the Colorado. In 1937 her ashes were buried on Mount Picacho, three years after her death in Santa Fe.

There is a pattern here, one laid down by places: Illinois, California, Europe, New York, New Mexico. Austin wrote about the land, but what gave her works power were the people left out. The galvanizing pattern is not accessible through the public record of movement from place to place. It begins in a scandal before Mary was born, and ends in an expiating interview in San Diego. Its major themes are betrayal, adoption, nurturance, and its entire cast is female.

In her autobiography Austin traces her legacy through the line of "mother-wit." She names the first section for her maternal great-grand-mother – "The Saga of Polly McAdams." (Polly was the ancestor who discovered that a woman ought to be judged by a "result achieved" rather than an "effect produced.") Life stories are here sagas of a chain of women. The chain culminates in a ring of which Austin forms the center:

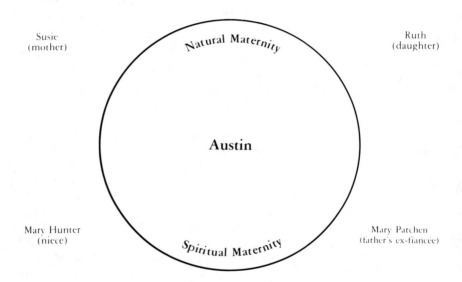

Susie
(mother)

Ruth
(daughter)

Mary Hunter
(niece)

Mary Patchen
(father's ex-fiancée)

The cardinal points in Austin's emotional compass are held by two functionally linked pairs. We can begin by saying that as Austin grew older, she swung away from the arc of natural and toward the arc of spiritual maternity. And we can't really appreciate Austin's landscapes until we understand how her displaced love for these figures found expression through California's barren ground.

Austin's autobiography can be read as a mystery, a search for the true mother. Along the way she must give up her child. The story begins before Mary was born, with her father's courtship of a woman not her mother. George Hunter met and began to court Mary Patchen "a year

or two previous to his marriage." She is the one woman in the autobiography to whom Mary uncritically allows the attribution of beauty:
"Mary Patchen was beautiful, with a beauty of the essential inner structure of the mind which, when Mary first knew her nearly forty years
afterwards, was still evident. She had a figure called in her day 'statu-
esque,' and that clear, white, and rosy skin which goes with the bluest
of blue eyes and pale gold hair." Shortly after the engagement by the
local Lyceum of a lecturer named Hutchinson, George received a "note
from Miss Patchen notifying him that their friendship was at an end."
It seems that Hutchinson had overheard the young Hunter speaking
lightly of the lady. Sometime later, Miss Patchen became Mrs. Hutchinson. A warrant for Hutchinson's arrest as a bigamist reached Carlinville before the couple had returned from their honeymoon.

Ten years later–in the summer of Mary's birth–Mary Patchen
Snyder (she had married a second time) retracted all blame through the
compliment of a visit. The scandal seemed dead and buried. "It remained for Mary Patchen herself, many years after, to take up the
experience and hang it about young Mary's neck, as an amulet against
loneliness of heart." A dropped stitch in the fabric of Austin's narrative,
this comment is not picked up again for nearly three hundred pages.
Mary Patchen makes her one and only encore in a hotel in San Diego,
where she gives Mary Austin this gift:

> "I didn't know your mother," she said, "but I know she didn't
> want you." She told me how she had called on the Hunters in the
> summer before Mary was born, and seeing my mother's condi-
> tion, it came over her that the child was not welcome. She was
> grieved, because she wanted nothing so much as a child herself;
> and George Hunter's child; she felt a warm flooding of emotion
> going out toward him and his unwanted child. It came over her as
> though he had said, "This should be your child, Mary," and she
> felt the stir of the child in her body; "if it could be," she said, "if
> it could be." She felt the stir in him, the comfort of acknowledge-
> ment. She sat there and experienced communication with my
> father about the child.

They talk of George Hunter's books, of Mary Austin's writings. "We
talked long and lovingly of these things." Mary Patchen shows her
adopted daughter the spray of grass and flowers she had gathered from
the father's grave. "It was the most real and moving contact I have ever
known." The autobiography comes to a climax in a scene in which
Mary Patchen's eagerness to establish her spiritual maternity is matched
by Mary Austin's eagerness to acknowledge it.

How could this have happened? Perhaps because what Mary Patchen
said was true. In one of her notebooks, Austin was to admit that while

"never homesick out of doors . . . I used to be homesick in our own house." It was a house rife with rejections. From her earliest years, Susie's daughter (Austin's sisterly nickname for her mother is one index to the obliquity of the bond) had felt herself an unwanted child. In a major deletion from *Earth Horizon,* Austin suppressed from the record a comment overheard after her sister Jennie's death: "I can't help wishing that Mary had been the one to be taken." Mary's diphtheria had fatally infected the beloved Jennie, and mother and daughter now stand over the fresh grave:

> I remember in the bleak little burying-ground looking up at my mother in her weeds and making toward her for the last time in my life the child's instinctive gesture for comfort, and being thrust off in so wild a renewal of Susie's own sense of loss, her rejection of what life had left for her, as leaves me still with no other comparison for the appalling shock and severance of widowhood.

In *A Woman of Genius* (1912), Olivia Lattimore was to turn such rejections into the desideratum of genius. There is a terrible pride in an imagination that, having conceived a character so desperately in "need of mothering," subjects her to this scene:

> It came back . . . the need of mothering. There was a time when I had lain abed some days with the measles or whatever. I was small enough, I remember, to lie in the crib bed that was kept downstairs for the prevalent baby . . . and my mouth was dry with fever. I recall my mother standing over me and my being taken dreadfully with the need of that sustaining bosom, and her stooping to my stretched arms divinely . . . and then . . . I asked her to put me down again. I have had drops and sinkings, but nothing to compare with this, for there was nothing there you understand . . . the release, the comforting . . . it wasn't there . . . *it was never there at all!*

Such denials sought to anticipate childhood's insistent refrain: "my mother thrusting me away."

Selfhood comes early to be associated for Mary with the withdrawal of nurturance. It is storytime, and Susie rocks the baby while brother Jim leans against his mother's shoulder. "You forgot and leaned against her knee until you felt it subtly withdrawing . . . 'hadn't you better get your stool, Mary?'. . . So Mary sat on her little stool, Jim leaned against Mother's shoulder, and Jennie sat in her lap. But I-Mary suffered no need of being taken up and comforted; to be I-Mary was more solid and satisfying than to be Mary-by-herself." "I-Mary" was to

become the primary relationship in the life. It was a unique version of
doubleness, one founded on a history of failed nurturance as much as in
a revenge against time. Creativity arose in response to the tensions of a
profoundly feminine duality. Whereas Thoreau achieves a kind of immortality by asserting the timelessness of the spectator, Austin sees
self-consciousness as a romance between the forlorn and the comforter.
What Austin lacked was something a woman could only get from a
woman, perhaps it was something only a woman needs. She was to
compensate for her past through devotion to an act of self-cherishing.
She never found another to perform the service for her; as she admits
near the end of *Earth Horizon*, "I have never been taken care of."

Mary, too, would have trouble taking care. Susie's dying words were
" 'Take care of Mary,' " but by then it was too late to generate a
tradition of tenderness. Pregnancy momentarily brought them close;
the "one voluntary caress she had to remember" was Susie's coming to
her bed and kissing her as they waited for Ruth to be born. Ruth was to
bring them no closer. "During all the years I lived in Inyo, I went every
summer to visit my mother, being in great need of her, and yet somehow always failing to make a vital connection." Something "had happened to my child," as Mary put it, something that raised the ordeal of
motherhood beyond the range of the usual tragedy.

In writing her autobiography, Austin was to interpret Susie's habitual
reserve as the universal doom of a generation of women with large
families and meager resources. Mary's sufferings as a child are thus
sublimated to one of her major themes. They constitute evidence for
the necessity of domestic reform – above all, for birth control, breaking
the chain. (Olivia Lattimore's mother can't even pass on the facts of life:
" 'I can't help you. I don't know . . . I never knew myself.' ") There
was no such context in which to rationalize Mary's history with Ruth.
It is a story repressed by the very words called upon to express it:

> I know now that he must have known from the beginning what
> was the matter with the child. . . . There was also the distress
> growing out of my increasing knowledge of what had happened to
> my child. . . . There was the trouble about the child. . . . There
> was a reason that had come into her life; a strange compelling
> reason that hung like a weight about her knees. She knew now
> what ailed her child. . . . Too late; too late; a tainted inheritance –
> recessive traits on both sides of the house. Mary had it out with her
> husband, with reluctance. . . . It was not long after that she put
> Ruth in a private institution at Santa Clara where the difference
> between herself and other children, which was beginning to trouble
> her, would not be felt, where it would not be known.

The child passes into and out of her mother's story in a haze of impersonal pronouns. It is Austin's pain that we are asked to feel; it is Austin's "blame" that we are asked to forgive. After Charles Lummis lost his son, Austin wrote to him about her Ruth, four years dead:

> There were so few people who ever had the courage to know about my Ruth, even my own family found it easier to speak of her as lost. But you like me, have eaten the bread of sorrow on which the Gods feed those they specially endow. You never knew perhaps, because I did not know it myself until it was too late, that the trouble was hereditary on her father's side, and the facts were suppressed out of that strange vanity called Family Pride.

If "the courage to know" is the standard by which Austin judges her intimates, it is a courage denied her reader by her own incapacity to tell.

Ruth's "vacuity of mind in a lovely vessel" was at times something for which her mother was willing to take all the blame. A neighbor in Tejon recalls Austin's self-doubts:

> I never expected to have a child. When I realized that I was pregnant, I promised myself that I would give birth to the smartest child that was ever born. I doubled my working hours. I hardly ate nor I hardly slept during that pregnancy. I figure that I took away from my child's brain. I did not give enough to my child.

This was inverted nurturance, a punishment disguised as a sacrifice. Things had worked against Austin from the start; during Ruth's birth the doctor had been "called away in the midst of things" to amputate a leg. Austin's maternal fantasies, as expressed in the unpublished essay "If I Had a Gifted Daughter," were inversely proportional to her successes. She argued that a "well organized home, which the ambitious young woman was expected to take part in making, is a better background for the normal development of emerging talent than any of the schools." But Ruth and her mother were unable to make a home together:

> Neighbors told how they would hear the child crying until they could endure it no longer and would go to the house to find out what was the trouble. There they would find the child strapped in a chair, screaming, and Mary, pacing the floor, her hair down her back, trying to capture some idea that eluded her for the writing she was always working at. They did not remind themselves that it was impossible to control Ruth or teach her anything and that no one was willing to keep her for long because it was too nerve-wracking.

Helen Doyle gets at the pathos of Austin's dilemma. The choice between mothering and creating was one she finally resolved by placing
Ruth in nearby homes and finally in the institution at Santa Clara. In
Earth Horizon there is a clear connection between giving up the child
and fully assuming the career. (Olivia Lattimore noticed that the "opening movement of my artistic career" followed "closely on the loss of
my baby.") The paragraph in which the mother says good-bye to the
years of "needless blight and pain" is followed by this one:

> The first thing that Mary did after settling back into Inyo was to
> build a house there, the brown house under the willow tree by the
> creek that came down from Kearsarge.

This is where she wrote her first book, *The Land of Little Rain*.

Ruth died in October 1918 of acute spasmodic asthma. Her remains
were held in San Mateo until August 1922, when Austin deposited the
ashes at the First National Bank of Monterey. Seven years later the bank
wrote Austin asking for a storage fee of $20.50; they had been trying "to
get in touch with Mrs. Austin for the past few years." These were the
years in which the now successful author had turned toward her niece,
Mary Hunter. The daughter of Austin's brother Jim, she had lost her
mother at birth. Mary Hunter's childhood letters to her aunt show her
graciously accepting gifts of hatbands and quirts while fending off an
overweening solicitude. ("You have gotten entirely the wrong idea. I am
not 'studying art' with Mr. Shrader.") The aunt tried unsuccessfully to
formalize the tie upon Jim's death in 1917. "I am ready and anxious to
adopt Mary for my daughter and give her my entire interest and care."
The struggle for custody became a violent one. Austin seems to have
kidnapped her niece in 1918 – "Finding that the child needed me, I went
home and carried her off, willy-nilly, to Carmel." What appeared to be a
simple case of compensation became complicated by the fact that, in the
ensuing years, Mary Hunter did not after all prove a "gifted" daughter.
This potential spiritual heir had from the first "shown marked artistic
and creative ability." But while Austin raged at her brother George for
his "stupid and base" guardianship, she found herself "being forced to
agree with Dr. Foster, that Mary will never be entirely normal." A
"disfiguring skin disease" had led the niece to drop out of Wellesley and
she and her aunt were periodically estranged during her college years.
On accomplishing a rendezvous in Santa Fe, they both fell sick. Although letters and visits were exchanged over the years, the relation was
one Austin proved unable to perfect, a reprise in a minor key of the loss
of her natural child.

The names matter less here than the pattern: the rejecting mother and
the abandoned daughter, the adopted mother and the saving niece.

Austin could not escape from the natural into the imagined triangle; this Family Romance of the three Marys never quite made good on the loss of Susie and Ruth. The autobiography refrains from taking the measure of this loss; it serves Austin instead as a brilliant self-defense in which the fulfilled pattern of a fourfold career superimposes itself on the story of the four and the one. Only in her books about the inhuman world did Austin reckon the costs of her lost human bonds. Beneath all she ever wrote about place ran the undersong of an unrequited human love. It was the broken circle of caring that Austin tried to perfect when she directed her gaze out onto the poverty and permanence of the landscape of California.

THE WALKING WOMAN

Austin's career explores the connection between a woman's experience of maternity and her orientation toward place. The first mention of the connection is found in the unpublished "Tejon Notebook," and is made by her mother. It is the spring of 1889 at San Emigdio Ranch in the lower San Joaquin. Susie and Mary are watching the figure who was to become Austin's "self-character," the Walking Woman:

> Over on the Temblor we met the Walking Woman. I had heard of her. The cow-boys call her Mrs. Walker but nobody knows her name. She told one of the women at Temblor that her first name is Jenny, but she answers to Mrs. Walker. She is not very tall, but her hair is thick and greyish and it is impossible to tell how old she is. She has a black bag which she carries over her shoulder on a stick. The men say she does not allow any liberties. They say she has just as good sense as any body, except that she is a little bit crazy. Mother says she looks like a woman who has had a child.

Here we can begin to see the figure fade into the ground. "Mrs. Walker" is married to her habitual behavior – it is her way of moving through space that gives her a name. But what arrests us here is Susie's clairvoyant surmise: "Mother says she looks like a woman who has had a child." It somehow seems to explain the rest – "Ah, yes," we say, "such a loss could make a woman act in such a way." For we do read "had" as "lost," not only because of the abrupt finality with which Mary conveys the surmise, but because the Walking Woman seems dispossessed of all things human – she is ageless, nameless, mindless, loveless too. The Walking Woman's wanderlust is read by no less an authority than Austin's mother as a function of her experience in the maternal role. Care has been displaced into landscape, down the road.

7. The San Emigdio Ranch in the lower San Joaquin Valley, where Mary Austin met the Walking Woman

As Austin eventually tells the story, the Walking Woman will have had a child. The last story in the collection *Lost Borders,* "The Walking Woman" creates a myth out of Susie's surmise. The story unfolds through the activities of seeking, meeting, and talking. Austin's "wish for a personal encounter" with the Walking Woman sends her out (she is the narrator) after a figure of hearsay. Bits of local lore drift back – she had been seen at the Maverick at the time of the Big Snow, and at Tres Piños when they brought home the body of Morena, and at Tunawai at the time of the cloudburst. "She came and went, oftenest in a kind of muse of travel which the untrammelled space begets, or at rare intervals flooding wondrously with talk." It is talk Austin is after, and as the story proceeds the Walking Woman's "own account" gradually begins to crowd out the rumors. The figure that has been built up out of "the contradiction of reports of her" stops to talk with Mary in her own voice. And the surmise is confirmed. "The best of our talk that day began in some dropped word of hers from which I inferred that she had had a child."

Out of all the stories surrounding the Walking Woman, there is one worth her telling – about the "three things which if you had known you could cut out all the rest." In a sandstorm on the south slope of Tehachapi she had come upon the camp of the shepherd Filon Geraud. They run together with the wind:

> "The flock travelled down the wind, the sand bit our faces; we called, and after a time heard the words broken and beaten small by the wind. . . . Such was the force of the wind that when we came together we held one another and talked a little between pantings. . . . we slept by turns; at least Filon slept. . . . I lay on the ground when my turn was and beat with the storm. I was no more tired than the earth was. . . . we kept the flock together."

After the wind drops and they cook their first meal, Filon comes over from his side of the fire:

> "I stayed with Filon until the fall. . . . All that summer in the Sierras, until it was time to turn south on the trail. It was a good time, and longer than he could be expected to have loved one like me. And besides, I was no longer able to keep the trail. My baby was born in October."

The baby does not stay for long:

> "And whenever the wind blows in the night . . . I wake and wonder if he is well covered."

With all else lost, the Walking Woman is able to keep the trail.

It was while living this story, then, that the Walking Woman got the three things she and Austin agree one cannot live without. They agree in their one moment of reported dialogue, in which Austin herself is allowed to speak the story's climactic words:

> "To work together, to love together," said the Walking Woman, withdrawing her hand again; "there you have two of the things, the other you know."
>
> "The mouth at the breast," said I.
>
> "The lips and the hands," said the Walking Woman. "The little, pushing hands and the small cry."

In this moment of "fullest understanding," in which author and character complete each other's stories, Austin at once confirms her mother's surmise and speaks the words that are for her an elegy for a lost maternal career.

It is the uncanny power of these two women to anticipate or remember each other's stories that raises this story up almost beyond the reach of words. It is a touching story, one in which the solidarity of women in their fate is expressed through their ability to give and accept the comfort of a hand. At the point where the Walking Woman speaks of her love for Filon, of "the look in the eyes," she places her hand on Mary's arm. A remembering Mary says that "I do not know why at this point the Walking Woman touched me." She wonders whether "in some flash of forward vision, encompassing the unimpassioned years, the stir, the movement of tenderness were for *me*." Given Austin's history of passion, the touch could scarcely have meant anything less. The Walking Woman's experience of love is thrown forward on the life of her listener as a foreknowledge of erotic loss. The years were to be "unimpassioned." Austin wrote "The Walking Woman" some years after she had lost both "the look in the eyes" and "the mouth at the breast," but she writes of the meeting as if it were happening *before*. She thus raises up and transforms her losses, through the illusion of prophecy, into a story that can be foreknown and perhaps even forgiven. What remains to both women is the distance ahead. Grief for a happiness briefly held is converted into the desire for option in space. Walking becomes a metaphor for grace under pressure, of imaginative gain despite natural loss. In first seeing, then following, and finally talking with the Walking Woman, Austin wrestles with and receives a blessing from the angel of her fate.

Both angel and questioner are left twisted by the struggle. There is no "twist" mentioned in the "Tejon Notebook," but when Mary refigured the Walking Woman in her story, she saw one. One of the rumors of the Walking Woman was "as to whether she was comely. . . . Report said yes, and again, plain to the point of deformity. She had a twist to her face, some said; a hitch to one shoulder; they averred she limped as she walked. But by the distance she covered she could have been straight and young." Mary returns to this surmise at the story's end:

> Far down the dim, hot valley I could see the Walking Woman with her blanket and black bag over her shoulder. She had a queer, sidelong gait, as if in fact she had a twist all through her.
>
> Recollecting suddenly that people called her lame, I ran down to the open place below the spring where she had passed. There in the bare, hot sand the track of her two feet bore evenly and white.

Is this an identification and a wishing-away? In *Earth Horizon,* Austin throws off a remark about her brother Jim's "incipient symptoms of lameness, traceable, as was believed, to the state of his father's health. One could say here that all the Hunter children carried—as did so many of their generation—the mark of that inheritance." Whatever the literal analogues in the life, the "twist" seems here merely figurative. It is a trait the Walking Woman ought to betray given the claims she has been caught between. Or rather it is an emblem of a conflict more consciously felt by her author, one that pulled her in two seemingly incompatible directions. Both lose everything but their work—their walking. Yet it is the way the Walking Woman loses—she walks on in a perfect trance of forgetting—that seems to put Austin in the wrong: "At least one of us is wrong. To work and to love and to bear children. *That* sounds easy enough. But the way we live establishes so many things of much more importance." It's being caught between "the way we live" and the things that matter that twists Austin. It's the Walking Woman's ability to take, love, and walk away that untwists her. Hers is an actual physical triumph:—"She had walked off all sense of society-made values, and, knowing the best when the best came to her, was able to take it." Austin's power to transcend losses comes rather through the perambulation of story, as she suggests in describing the effect of the tale on the teller. As she moves into her story, the Walking Woman's face heals visibly: "It was while she talked that I decided that she really did have a twist to her face, a sort of natural warp or skew into which it fell when it was worn merely as a countenance, but which disappeared the moment it became the vehicle of thought or feeling." In this moment of passionate identification Austin makes it clear that storytelling was the act that could recover for the twisted self the grace to traverse the distance ahead.

THE UNSTORIED LAND

The land in which Austin told her stories had "little in it to love:"

> This is the nature of that country. There are hills rounded, blunt, burned, squeezed up out of chaos, chrome and vermillion painted, aspiring to the snowline. Between the hills lie high level-looking plains full of intolerable sun glare, or narrow valleys drowned in a blue haze. The hill surface is streaked with ash drift and black, unweathered lava flows. After rains water accumulates in the hollows of small closed valleys, and, evaporating, leaves hard dry levels of pure desertness that get the local name of dry lakes. Where the mountains are steep and the rains heavy, the pool is never quite dry, but dark and bitter, rimmed about with the efflorescence of alkaline deposits. A thin crust of it lies along the marsh over the vegetating area, which has neither beauty nor freshness. In the broad wastes open to the wind the sand drifts in hummocks about the stubby shrubs, and between them the soil shows saline traces. The sculpture of the hills here is more wind than water work, though the quick storms do sometimes scar them past many a year's redeeming. In all the Western desert edges there are essays in miniature at the famed, terrible Grand Cañon, to which, if you keep on long enough in this country, you will come at last.

The drama of Austin's work flows from her discovery that she has been uniquely conditioned to celebrate the ways in which "this long brown land lays such a hold on the affections." It is a landscape out of hell, a country where water aggravates the aridity its fall ought to allay. "Squeezed up out of chaos," this unfinished creation reaches out toward an imagination famished for love. Sustained attention to such a place measures one's power to nurture an unsponsored thing. Austin adopts this landscape because it is empty, unclaimed, unstoried.

The early trilogy on landscape dominates Austin's career: *The Land of Little Rain* (1903), *The Flock* (1906), and *Lost Borders* (1909). Each book turns on what Thoreau calls "water privileges." (The abuse of these privileges will eventually drive Austin from California, though this is not yet her theme.) When Austin says of California that "the virtue of the land is the virtue that we love most to attribute to the mothers of men," she alludes to the sheltering power of the Sierra Madre (the Mother Mountain), its "aloof but solicitous care." In the eastern shadow of the Sierra, however, she was to discover in the land a more abiding maternal ambivalence. "She has denied to men the one instrument by which the desert could be mastered. Mighty as man is in transforming the face of the earth, he is nothing without the Rains." In the incapacity of the land of Lost Borders to generate a sustaining element Austin at once perceived and projected the drama of nurturance being played out in her own life.

Although each one of these books begins with a natural lack, each finds a compensating human behavior and locates in some act performed on the land a metaphor for its unique structure. *The Land of Little Rain* answers bareness with invention, *The Flock* counters dispersal with shepherding, and *Lost Borders* mends isolation with dialogue. In her first book, the rhythmic sentence becomes a measure of how far Austin will go in trying to reclaim the land with story. The repeated gesture that binds the book together is the act of annexation through naming. Setting out on a trail is at once the subject and shape of *The Flock,* a book that follows the fourteen meditations of *The Land of Little Rain* with an attempt at sustained epic. *Lost Borders* curtails such ambitions and returns to the notion of the collection as an adequate structure. Austin's earlier ambivalence about narrative here issues in a deep commitment to it. Piecing the broken pot together becomes the book's paradigmatic metaphor, and the reluctant dialogue acts as the rhetorical vehicle of and obstacle to a woman's attempt to create a vessel adequate to contain her experience.

The Land of Little Rain is a book of great sentences and untold stories. The rhythmic power of its syntactical structures works against their accretion into the more extended rhythm of the tale. "The Pocket Hunter" gets his chapter, but the whole of it slips from memory in the face of its crowning epiphany. Caught in a blizzard on Waban, he had come upon "the heavy breathing of the flock" and snuggled down among the warmth of packed fleeces:

> If the flock stirred in the night he stirred drowsily to keep close and let the storm go by. That was all until morning woke him shining on a white world. Then the very soul of him shook to see the wild sheep of God stand up about him, nodding their great horns beneath the cedar roof, looking out on the wonder of the snow.

If the image strikes us here, it is the sound that carries us away. The last sentence quoted signals its climactic position with an adverb, which then leads us through a rush of "s's" against which are poised the full stops of "k's" and "p's." The string of monosyllables – interrupted by "about" – at once quickens (the words are short) and retards (the words are discrete) our progress. The ecstatic tension between hurry and arrest then dwindles into two participial phrases that give us time to take the scene in. "Think of that to happen to a Pocket Hunter!" Austin exclaims, but it has also happened, by virtue of her command of sentence sound, to us.

Austin uses rhythm to disrupt the orderly flow of narrative because of her principled belief that the land resists the imposition of story. Stories obscure the land's fundamental indifference to human origins and ends. The residents of Austin's exemplary ghost town are "untroubled by invention and the dramatic sense." Their "emptiness" proves the appropriate response to the "rawness of the land." "Here you have the repose of the perfectly accepted instinct which includes passion and death in its perquisites." Austin says this in the last paragraph of "Jimville," an anti-romance that satirizes Bret Harte's disposition to impose a narrative logic on the indeterminacy and accident of life in frontier towns. When Jim strikes gold in the very gulch where he had rescued a "three days' babe nozzling" at the breast of a dying squaw, we prepare ourselves for a rewrite of Harte's great tearjerker. Austin even borrows Harte's pun in fancying "this piece of luck" as interposed for Jim's reward. But causality no more begins to surface than she breaks off the story: "Bret Harte would have given you a tale. You see in me a mere recorder, for I know what is best for you; you shall blow out this bubble from your own breath." The most she intends to offer is the derivation of a place name – the point of reciting these events is to explain the origin of "Squaw Gulch." The sheer act of conferring names on the earth sufficiently annexes it to human need.

Names dominated the period during which Austin began *The Land of Little Rain,* as she testifies in the "Tejon Notebook:"

> I am learning a lot about sheep herding. I am putting it in another book, keeping this one for plants and the landscape. I never forget the names of things and where I saw them but I forget what they make me feel and think. Also I forget the words that come with the first time the flower or the mountain speaks to me. It is like that – like someone speaking. I am starting a book for the words.

The book about sheepherding became *The Flock; The Land of Little Rain* was to remain a book that reconceived autobiography as lexicography. By putting names on paper Austin tried to recover a forgotten history of the self. The book never fully acknowledges its status as an indirect act of self-chronicle or its aspirations to replace given names with Austin's unique "words": "If the Indians have been there before me, you shall have their name, which is always beautifully fit and does not originate in the poor human desire for perpetuity." Austin consciously disdains an immortality founded on originality and chooses instead an "intimacy" with what is already immortal. She tries to stay true to the land by withholding names from it altogether, so as to keep it anonymous, unlocatable, and apart: "So by this fashion of naming I keep faith with the land and annex to my own estate a very great territory to which none has a surer title." In this very act of self-effacement Austin asserts the human will to fame through figuration. If the gap between material and spiritual power is here resolved through puns on "annex," "estate," and "title," it is because Austin has immersed herself in the double-minded words (see the opening of "Where I Lived, and What I Lived For") of Emerson and Thoreau. If the land teaches always and only resignation to the reality principle, Austin's literary tradition compensates for its suspicion of story with a bracing advocacy of style.

Strong sentence rhythm serves Austin not only as a counterweight to narrative but as an approximation of the underlying continuities of nature. Caught in a landscape of unfinished "essays," she appeals to syntax, like Wordsworth, for relief from a world of minute particulars. She has been climbing the streets of the mountains through the pines, and has just broken through their "locked ranks" to the vantage point of a "high, windy dome": "They troop quickly up the open ways, river banks, and brook borders; up open swales of dribbling springs; swarm over old moraines; circle the peaty swamps and part and meet about clean still lakes; scale the stony gullies; tormented, bowed, persisting to the door of the storm chambers, tall priests to pray for rain." Like the sentence about the mountain stream in "Water Borders," this sets out to imitate in its effect the natural process it describes. The spaced volley of active verbs – "troop-swarm-circle-part-meet-scale" – nearly overrides here the possibility of seeing the terrain. The half-stops of the semicolons allow us little time to shore up each movement before trooping on to the next. Just as the focus begins to blur, we pause at "tormented, bowed," and the rampant subject becomes an enduring object. We close with the participle "persisting," and so return to the underlying fact of the pines' continuous though rooted becoming. We move here through an attempt to describe the form of a motion, a persistent sentence on the persistence of the pines. Donald Davie might call this "syntax as music"; certainly *how* we move through this sentence matters as much as *what* we see. Yet Austin's sentences do not frequently achieve – she could not, after all, further the flow with repeated enjambment – Wordsworth's sense of untrammeled possibility. Her major effect, for all the suspension of differences along the way, is of authoritative closure. Austin's best sentences use measured breath to inspire the world. If they sound at times a little melodramatic, it is perhaps because they bear so much of the ambition toward amplitude that she will not yet allow herself to exercise over the length of a plot.

The one character in *The Land of Little Rain* who does get a plot is Seyavi, the Basket Maker. Despite its grim close in the blindness and

The Basket Woman from the Campody at Georges Creek

8. "The Basket Woman from the Campody at Georges Creek," a caption in
Austin's handwriting

immobility of old age, her chapter serves Austin as one of her most
satisfying versions of the amply lived life. Austin portrays Seyavi's
inexorable verge into sublimation—she loses her husband, raises her
child, turns to her baskets—as a human triumph. Hers is a life in which
all but her art, and finally even her art, gradually falls away. "Seyavi
made baskets for the satisfaction of desire." *Before* she so made baskets,

Austin tells us, "she danced and dressed her hair." What makes this a
story is that Seyavi has known, if only in sequence, all the seasons of a
woman's life. Each "satisfaction of desire" finds its appropriate substitute until art gives way to memory, and the blind basket weaver becomes the child of her own experience, as she "sits by the unlit hearths
of her tribe and digests her life, nourishing her spirit against the time of
the spirit's need." This final gift of self-nourishing is one Seyavi can
make herself because she has denied none of her desires in seeking to
fulfill any one of them. Hers is a career that gently rebukes one in
which desires are endured as mutually exclusive choices. Her story
intrudes into a book so wary of them as the one Austin could not help
but tell.

The Flock can be read as an expansion of Seyavi's story, a celebration of
the surprising "sufficiency of mother wit" on the womanless frontier. It
is a book about nurturant men trying to raise babies in the course of
their work – about shepherds and lambs on the long trail. *The Flock*
begins with the shepherd's lore for circumventing a rejecting ewe. In a
dry season the twin lambs allotted each mother force the shepherds into
ingenuities of adoption:

> Years of curtailed pastures she cannot suckle both and grow wool,
> and neither youngster will be strong enough to endure the stress
> of a dry season: the mother becomes enfeebled, and the too grasp-
> ing shepherd may end by losing all three. Much depends on the
> promptness with which the weaker of the twins is discarded or
> suckled to some unfortunate mother of stillborn lambs. Once a
> ewe has smelled the smell of her offspring the herder must take a
> leaf out of the book of the Supplanter in the management of
> forced adoptions. The skin of the dead lamb is sewed about the
> body of the foundlings, limp little legs dangling about its legs, a
> stiff little tail above a wagging one – all of no moment so long as
> the ewe finds some rag-tail smell of her own young among the
> commingling smells of the stranger and the dry and decaying
> hide.

More pathetic are the attempts of the wethers (male sheep castrated
while immature) to coax lambs to their sides. They learn to imitate the
"soft, shuddering cry" of nursing time and substitute it for the
mother's "accustomed bleat." Austin admits that "the return of these
unsexed brutes to the instinct of parental uses takes on the proportions
of immeasurable law." It is a law from which Austin presumably ex-
empts herself on behalf of her accustomed medium, language: "Every
now and then some inconsidered protest arises against the clipped and

mutilated speech by which a human mother expresses her sense of satisfaction in her young." Better to leave such attenuations of speech to the self-sacrificing, androgynous shepherds. *The Flock* becomes a study of the ways in which the insistent claims of motherhood can inhibit one's distinctive voice.

This world's constant preoccupation with nurturance inhibits Austin from realizing through it her central ambition, which is to shape it into epic story. The book promises a sequential plot dominated by the "going and coming" along the Long Trail:

> The great trunk of the trail lies along the east slope of the Sierra Nevadas, looping through them by way of the passes around Yosemite, or even as far north as Tahoe, shaped and defined by the occasions that in little record the progress from nomadism to the commonwealth. Conceive the cimeter blade of the Sierras curving to the slow oval of the valley, dividing the rains, clouds herding about its summits and flocks along its flanks, their approaches ordered by the extension and recession of its snows.

The trail here is appropriated to the metaphor of the flock; the flock is not put in motion on it. Instead of delivering a narrative sequence, the chapters in *The Flock* radiate from a central concern, as Austin seems to admit when she speaks of the way she came upon her stories: "One finds tales like this at every point of contact with the Tejon, raying out fanwise like thin, white runways of rabbits from any waterhole in a rainless land." Given an opportunity to assert her will over the narrative, Austin diffidently withdraws: "But one must really make an end of incident, and follow after the sheep." By portraying herself as a follower rather than a leader – "I suppose of all the people who are concerned with the making a true book, the one who puts it to the pen has the least to do with it" – Austin elects not to assert her speech over the distance of the trail.

So the promised epic of passage turns out to be a digression on care. *The Flock* unfolds as a repeated series of departures, of venturings out from the "home fold." This is the place from which all runways ray. The particular emotion we are asked to enjoy is the bittersweet thrill of leavetaking. The deepest theme of the book is separation, and Austin's fascination with it cuts athwart any intention to structure an "Iliad of adventure." The rhythm in which *The Flock* instructs us is one felt not only in "the parting of the flocks," but in the parting with a child.

The fourteen stories in *Lost Borders* deal with the dissolution of human bonds in the boundless desert wastes. "Love weaves the fascinating intricacy of story," and it is love that the life in this land makes impossible. The "deep-breasted" desert makes "men serve without desiring her": "It is men who go mostly into the desert, slack their ambitions, cast off old usages, neglect their families because of the pulse and beat of a life laid bare to its thews and sinews. Their women hate with implicitness the life like the land." Seduced into a passionless love of the elemental, the men of *Lost Borders* abandon their women to "the vast impersonal rivalry of desertness." Out where the law and the landmarks fade together, "the souls of little men fade out at the edges." Their women are left to weave and unweave the interrupted intricacy of story.

This is a book of stories about men and women told by women to a woman. The bond between the sexes gets replaced by a passionate and illicit bond between an intrusive female listener and her wary confidants. In *Lost Borders*, Austin fully distinguishes her ambition to story from the reserve she attributes to her sex. If "The Walking Woman" resolves this tension in its full and uncensored collaboration, the interplay between Austin's creative will and the reluctance of her sources makes the drama of the book.

Language as the special province of the male is a theme with which Austin opens her autobiography. The early pages of *Earth Horizon* celebrate the violation of a taboo. Mary's father invites her to transgress sex roles by proposing to make her a citizen in the uncensored community of words. Raised in a world "meticulously strict as to what could, and could not, be said to and before ladies," Austin develops with her father nonverbal strategies for sharing "Things that weren't to be said in front of Mothers." Such "things" pass "in a twinkle between Father and you, which must not even be admitted to have passed!" Through a complex of signs and gestures, Mary's father habitually assures her that he would speak frankly with her if he could. At times he inadvertently makes good on the intention. The memory of a freely uttered curse becomes one of Mary's most cherished: "It was worth remembering even with tears that Father never minded saying '*My God*' before Mary."

Austin fully inherits this legacy in *Lost Borders,* even while identifying with the opposite sex in her ambition to betray secrets. She has just listened to an unnamed male narrator tell the story of Catamenda, the Indian who saved him from death in the desert by walking him through a sandstorm. She had given him all her food and water, and dies in his arms by Black Mountain Spring. What he remembers and talks about are her loving ways.

> A man's story like that is always so much more satisfactory because he tells you all the story there is, what happened to him, and how he felt about it, supposing his feelings are any part of the

facts in the case; but with a woman it is not so. She never knows much about her feelings, unless they are pertinent to the story, and then she leaves them out.

A woman *cannot* tell her story, Austin intimates; there is something unspeakable at the heart of female experience.

Those who try to tell Austin their stories seem to agree. "The Woman at the Eighteen-Mile," when Austin finally finds her, makes her auditor promise not to repeat her words. Mary has tracked the story as she would a lost love: "All this time the story glimmered like a summer island in a mist, through every man's talk about it, grew and allured, caressing the soul. It had warmth and amplitude, like a thing palpable to be stroked." There is a suggestion here that a woman's relationship to her "story" can be as intimate as any she shares with a child or a man. These are women who, like Austin, have lost everything but their stories, and the sharing of them can compromise a trust. Austin want the Woman's story, but she wants as much to preserve their female solidarity:

> If it were not the biggest story of the desert ever written, I had no wish to write it. And there was the Woman. The story was all she had, absolutely all of heart-stretching, of enlargement and sustenance. What she thought about it was that the last lusive moment when she touched the forecast shadow of his destiny was to bind her to save his credit for his children's sake.

The irony of most of these acts of withholding is that they protect the integrity of an experience with a man.

Austin keeps a kind of faith with the Woman by structuring her story in such a way that it is not the Woman's testimony that convicts her man. She begins by telling us of her long-standing desire for a story of "Death Valley that should be its final word." She then meets a teamster who gives her a fragment of the story about Lang's murder, the most famous incident of the region. His is a pure act of *habeas corpus;* he cites the fact of the murdered body and nothing more. Left only with "the middle of an idea, without any definiteness as to where it began or ended," Austin tracks the story for seven years. She gradually shores up a host of fragments.

> There was a mine in it, a murder and a mystery, great sacrifice, Shoshones, dark and incredibly discreet, and the magnetic will of a man making manifest through all these; there were lonely water-holes, deserted camps where coyotes hunted in the streets, fatigues and dreams and voices in the night. And at the last it appeared there was a woman in it.

Austin knows the Woman, and remembers her as "one of the very few people I had known able to keep a soul alive and glowing in the wilderness, and I was to find that she kept it so against the heart of my story. Mine!" Austin finally tracks her to her lair, and there, halfway through the chapter, the Woman begins to tell her story.

"For her the heart of the story was the man, Whitmark." This is the man linked by common gossip to the murder, and Austin can feel the pieces falling into place: "I sat within the shallow shadow of the eaves experiencing the full-throated satisfaction of old prospectors over the feel of pay dirt. . . . It was as good as that. And I was never to have it!" Because she had promised not to "tell" (the double meaning of this verb – as in "to narrate" and "to snitch" – is a major theme of the book), Austin is reduced to giving us her reaction to the strike, not the gold itself. The focus shifts from Whitmark's guilt to his love, to the one moment the Woman feels able and privileged to tell: "The crux of the story to her was one little, so little, moment, that owing to Whitmark's having been taken with pneumonia within a week afterward, was rendered fixed beyond change or tarnish of time." For two years Whitmark and the Woman, each married to others, had known the happiness of the Walking Woman. They had worked side by side in a great venture in the mines. Now the time has come for his return home. As they ride together toward the point of departure, each seems caught in a mixture of triumph and gloom. The moment comes to say good-bye. It is Whitmark's prophetic statement on leave-taking that the woman feels compelled to report:

> " 'I have *missed* you so.' Just that, not good-bye, and not *shall* miss you, but 'I *have* missed you *so*.' "

The power of this farewell for Austin's imagination would be difficult to exaggerate. She has been searching for the "biggest story of the desert." By the time she finds it, she has promised not to tell it. Of course, she manages to tell it after all: The sheer juxtaposition of the teamster's report with the Woman's story conclusively links Whitmark to Lang's murder. Thus, Austin at once keeps and breaks faith with the Woman in a complex act of fidelity to the conflict that found her at once an artist and a woman. What she got beyond all expectation is not just another chance to suffer the conflict, but an unlooked-for parable about the shape her own life had taken and was to take. There is no more powerful summary in Austin of the message her work was continually carrying home to her experience, its steady foreknowledge, in which the Walking Woman also participates, of erotic loss.

Incomplete as many of these stories are, they do cohere into a repetitive pattern characterized by a movement of penetration, embrace, and withdrawal. The man is the thing that comes and goes, the desert – or the woman – what remains. Climaxes here are hurried through; the interest is not in action but in Austin's struggle to piece together the incidents leading up to the moment of sexual exchange. These moments usually take the form of a reported dialogue that resolves the tensions of the narrative, as when the dying Catamenda says to her uncomprehending beneficiary, " 'Vera good boy, mucha like,' " or in the question " 'Tiawa?' " and the answer " 'Great One,' " or in Turwhase's cry to the man who had thought he could take away her child: " 'Mine!' " "Mine!" is the very word Austin uses to describe *her* relationship to the Woman's story, and the repetition reminds us that it is such entities that she has, perhaps against the very experience of womanhood, chosen to nurture. Each fragmented story is here part of a large, fragmented structure that Austin strives to make whole. At the very beginning of the book, her friend Woodin brings her a potsherd. " 'You ought to find a story about this somewhere.' " She replies: " 'I will do better than that, I will make a story.' "

Each story forms a tessera of the vessel that Austin tries to bond together. Telling stories becomes emblematic of recovering lost borders. *Lost Borders* proves less a book about a localized threat to manwoman love than it does one about the power of story to counter the universal fragility of human bonds.

And yet Austin's breakthrough to adequate form continues to depend in good measure on the locality that inspired it. It was the arid landscapes of California that opened Austin to a sense of her history as one that could be intimated but never fully expressed. "The earth is no wanton to give up all her best to every comer." Austin likens the desert to a female "sphinx," to a presence whose riddling surface holds the key to our identity. The land became at once an emblem of reticence and revelation, an undecipherable text dying to be read. Facing its unstoried poverty, Austin was left free to appropriate its contours to her own unfolding story. Her departure for a landscape much richer in human associations marks the end of her power to decipher the figure hidden in the barren ground.

AFTER CALIFORNIA

In 1903 the United States Bureau of Reclamation began a survey of the Owens Valley. Dams and canals were planned to irrigate two hundred thousand acres of arid land.

All reports and estimates of costs demonstrated that the Owens Valley project promised greater results than any other for the cost. Individual owners made transfers of rights and privileges. And all this time the supervising officer of the Owens Valley project and Mullholland, chief engineer, had been working to secure a new water supply for Los Angeles. Suddenly it burst upon the people of Inyo that they were trying to secure the waters of Inyo. Everything had been done. The Reclamation Service had been won over. The field papers had changed hands. Transfers had been made. Sales had been effected. A Los Angeles man, Eaton, had been in the Valley all this time spying and buying; he and his fellows had represented themselves as representing the Government, when they had in fact been representing the city. There were lies and misrepresentations. There was nothing any of us could do about it, except my husband, who made a protest to the Reclamation Bureau. But the city stood solid behind Eaton as one man. . . . Mary did what she could. . . . She walked in the fields and considered what could be done. . . . She was told to go away. . . . There was nothing more for her in Southern California.

Austin left Inyo for Carmel in 1905. She was never to return to a permanent residence there, though Wallace, Register of the Land Office at Independence, was to stay and fight for many years. Muir died soon after losing Hetch Hetchy; after her expulsion Austin was to wander for two decades before settling in another garden, New Mexico.

Water had been so rich a psychological symbol for Austin that she foundered when trying to convert it into a political one. California would have to wait for Roman Polanski's film *Chinatown* (1974) before getting an adequate jeremiad on the politics of water; *The Ford* (1917), Austin's novel about the rape of the valley, proved little more than a disappointing wish-fulfillment. Having annexed to her "own estate a very great territory to which none has a surer title," Austin was unable to relinquish in imagination what she had already lost in fact. In this undoing of history, the people win. The heroine, Anne Brent, defies speculation with speculation and buys up not only her lost ancestral home but enough land to keep the rascals out. She sacrifices her sweetheart, Frank, in the process, and so, in an inversion of Austin's pattern, gives up love for a literal title to the land. *The Ford* becomes a fantasy of redemption through real estate.

California had appealed to Austin precisely because of its resistance to the encroachment of human desire. In Tejon she had fallen into a place without memory: "Her trouble was that the country failed to explain itself. If it had a history, nobody could recount it. Its creatures had no known life except such as she could discover by unremitting vigilance of observation." The actual "malnutrition" of the body Austin suffered during her first months in California had looked like a fate also in store for her mind. Her discovery that she could recover physical health with "something grubbed out of the woods" (wild grapes) corresponded with her discovery that it was the very poverty of the land on which she could feast her spirit. The imagination's strength came to be measured by its power to nourish the half-starved.

New Mexico presented itself as a place so aware of its human histories as to prove self-explicating. *The Land of Journey's Ending* (1924) surveys a region – between the Rio Colorado and the Rio Grande – where culture had for centuries enjoyed a thorough interpenetration with nature. The "overwhelming scale of things" in the Southwest can induce "a kind of twilight sleep on the sensuous faculties." What Austin did see was the Southwest as the next hearth for a world culture. But as Vernon Young argues, in her books about the region she "confused restoration with birth, intellectual synthesis with organic determinism. . . . Museums of anthropology and Indian ceremonial do not constitute the tools of new culture; they memorialize a vanishing culture." *The Land of Journey's Ending* acquires the character of a highly idiosyncratic expansion of those entirely respectable handbooks, the WPA Guides. The challenge here is to control an embarrassment of riches, not to breed life out of the dead land.

Had she arrived before the onset of its self-conscious cultural revival, Austin might have written as powerful a book about the Southwest as John Van Dyke's *The Desert*. Published two years after *The Land of Little Rain,* this book does for the Colorado and Sonoran deserts what Austin was to do for Tejon and Inyo. It succeeds because it casts a cold eye on the potentially sentimental claims to which Austin gave way as she moved from her first desert home to her last: "The secret charm of the desert is the secret of life triumphant." In *The Land of Journey's Ending,* Austin elevates the pleasure principle over its dark twin. Van Dyke's classic tells a sterner story, while giving full play to the belief that the desert sustains our will to survive.

Through the ordering of his chapters, Van Dyke allows for the play of the two principles. *The Desert* inclines toward the visionary and declines toward the substantive. We begin with sunrise and end with sunset. After opening chapters on human impressions and history, we move through appreciations of wind, water, light, and clouds. This first movement culminates in the book's central chapter, "Illusions." Here Van Dyke fully indulges his love of perception over fact: "The landscape that is the simplest in form and the finest in color is by all odds the most beautiful." But fact goes on to prevail as we proceed through chapters on flora and fauna, foothills and mountains. "The light is fading out." The book that begins by celebrating the freedom of the eye ends with an elegy for the inescapable mortality of man and his landscapes:

> Have we not proof in our own moon that worlds do die? Is it possible that its bleached body will never be disintegrated, will never dissolve and be resolved again into some new life? And how came it to die? What was the element that failed – fire, water, or atmosphere? Perhaps it was water. Perhaps it died through thousands of years with the slow evaporation of moisture and the slow growth of the – desert.

The desert that had been a stimulus to aesthetic rapture becomes by the end a metaphor for the end. The ubiquity of these great expanses of "sand and rock" leads Van Dyke to embrace them as the sites in which nature fully articulates our destiny: "For death may be the culmination of all character; and life but the process of its development." The immanence of the reality principle is, however, a conviction from which Van Dyke, as an artist rather than a moralist, generously protects his reader. By provisionally disguising a landscape of *memento mori* as an oasis of free play, Van Dyke converts our experience of *The Desert* into a happy dallying with "false perspective" – into a mirage.

Austin's last years were so richly endowed with life that she would scarcely have recognized Van Dyke's vision of her home. If walking was her metaphor for the ongoing artistic quest, she had perhaps stopped walking many years before. Now was the time to build the beloved house *La Casa Querida,* to bake her legendary pies, to entertain the D. H. Lawrences and to do her best to preserve the culture of the Pueblos. She filled her life with friends. Some years before, she had written, though never published, "The Lost Garden." She gave it a final revision in 1928. It is a kind of last judgment on the art of her life. In this revision of the myth of paradise, Austin becomes, by the very completeness of her will, the sole author of the fall. Only by fastening their love on places rather than persons can natures such as Austin's, she seems to say, escape the limiting history of identification with their halved precursor, Eve, and so win through to the self-nurturing company of the word:

> Within the Garden close I have built many houses which I have afterward abandoned. For this is the unfailing service of the Garden, that it does not insist upon itself nor compel the visitor to its frame. The house I have there now is very like the one I live in at home, but finer, and rubbed clear of every trace of toil and pain

which goes to the making of even the most loved home. It is filled
with friends, often, friends whose faces change, whose counte-
nances are all bright with gentle affinities of affection rather than
understanding. But this is most curious, that no one has ever lived
there with me, not even the Friend Who Never Was. That one
comes and walks sometimes in the Garden where we have those
long consoling talks of which no word is ever spoken. This is
curious, because most of my friends confess that they go to their
Garden to be with those from whom in their lives they find
themselves divided by death or distance or by the Flaming Sword
that kept the Gates of Paradise. . . . Once there was around this
emptiness, the faint edge of pain, and I would go through the
house, setting the doors ajar, looking for the tenant who was lost
when the Garden was lost and has never come back again. But
now I do not look. I know now that there was never anyone
there; that it is the fortune of some natures to be not halved, but
whole. It is perhaps in the dimension of the Garden that wholeness is achieved, and not in the mate, who is but a symbol of the
other half of ourselves, by the rediscovery of which is overcome
the last great schism of dying.

Chapter 5

Norris and the vertical

In the spring of 1899, twenty-nine-year-old Frank Norris (1870–1902) spent eight weeks on the San Anita Rancho, near Hollister, California. He went to the rancho to gather impressions for his next novel, *The Octopus*. The area around Hollister resembled the locale of the Mussel Slough affair. Norris planned to center his story around this bloody shoot-out, which had occurred between ranchers and agents of the Southern Pacific Railroad nearly twenty years before. During the 1870s, settlers had taken up land along the railroad's right-of-way with the pledge that they could someday buy it at $2.50 upward an acre. They improved the land and then, when the railroad finally acquired clear title, saw it offered for sale at prices between $17 and $40 an acre. After losing ejectment suits, members of the Grand Settlers' League confronted a U.S. marshal and would-be purchasers of their land near the town of Hanford in the Mussel Slough district of Tulare County. Firing broke out, and after the dust settled, one railroad agent and four settlers lay dead. Two settlers died thereafter, five were sentenced to prison, and others hunted down and killed another of the railroad's hired guns. After losing one more court battle, most of the settlers moved away, and those who stayed accepted the railroad's terms.

Mussel Slough, now part of Kings County, lies some 120 miles southeast of Hollister in the lower San Joaquin Valley. Norris went to Hollister the way John Ford went to Monument Valley, in search of a site that would provide his story with an answerable if enlarged historical scale. He may have bagged wheat on the threshing platform of the San Anita; he certainly set about to conflate its landscapes with those of the great valley. Hollister was in the rolling earthquake country between spurs of the Coast Range; Tulare was flat, arid country with distant horizons. Farmers in Tulare worked the land in small holdings, and without the convenience of Norris's fabulous "irrigating ditch." The rancho at San Anita still had more than five thousand acres of wheat under cultivation, and Norris reconceived the lives of the valley people by way of its epic proportions. If Tulare lacked the romance of antiquity, Norris could supply it by importing a copy of the mission a few miles west of Hollister, San Juan Bautista. The Morse Seed Ranch nearby, an agricultural impossibility in the San Joaquin, became the magical seat of Angéle Varian. And the coast live oak migrated over the mountains to shed in Tulare its welcome shade.

The vast plows that crawl across the earth, the carpet of the land unrolling to infinity, the heat rising in waves toward an unanswering sky – this familiar Norris landscape arose from careful observation of time and place. But the eventual function of setting in the novel is as symbol rather than as document. Norris did not much trouble himself about accuracy of geographic and historical detail. He superimposed two California places to create a nowhere land in which his characters could play out a fable about survival in time. He thus marks a new stage in the development of imagination in California, one that seeks out the representative within the unique. "I think there is a chance," he wrote, "for somebody to do some great work with the West and California as a background . . . which will be at the same time thoroughly American." The discovery of California still unfolds in his work, but the larger drama is that by persisting in such discovery we come up against a story of national and even universal significance.

The argument of the second half of this volume thus moves away from the particularities of landscape. With Norris, writing about place in California becomes increasingly allegorical. Not only is the Epic of the Wheat an announced attempt to discover the typical in the local, but *The Octopus* bristles with images that express a growing tendency to render experience in this place emblematic. The last such image offered is one of failure, as if Norris were reckoning the cost of regional self-consciousness. If the major tension in California is between figure and ground, what better way to lampoon its facile resolution than by identifying the vast geography of California with a human body. Norris does exactly this at the end of the novel. Frustrated in his attempt to find an adequate image for life in the state, a departing Presley learns from Cedarquist that someone at last has fashioned "a figure of California" that is "a real work of art." A monument of "heroic size," the figure, devised for a state fair, is in fact a statue made of "dried apricots." Culture here pays ritual homage to nature, but the upshot is one of those hollow fetishes of regional pride that can edge out serious attempts to take the measure of a place.

Norris and the writers that follow him do not all see California as figurative, but many of them do. The chapters that follow provide a selective account of five careers in which the impulse toward open appropriation of natural space for symbolic purposes is particularly strong. As argued in the Introduction, this way of thinking about landscape marks an alienation from it: Specific terrains are claimed as *materia poetica* because of the felt difficulties of living in them. In surveying the range of twentieth-century response, some hard choices had to be made; certainly the careers of Gertrude Atherton, Jack London, Wallace Stegner, and Joan Didion (to name a few) deserve further study. The voices that have summoned up California are rich and various, and the choir grows.

BODIES IN SPACE

Norris's effort is to raise a figure up above the ground. It is as if his characters struggle with a gravity pulling them back into the earth. His word for this resisted process might be "devolution," and his novels and stories take as their subject the threat to human stature posed by our career on an evolutionary ladder. Fascination with dynamic processes issues for Norris in a fiction of arresting images. The paradox of his work is that although its theme is motion throughout time, its plots appear to measure man within a space. Actions he initiates as dramas of development attempt to convert themselves, through his insistence on making fate visible, into dramas of position.

Two images recur in Norris's work with uncanny force: an isolated vertical figure and a vast, empty, horizontal space. Ur-images, they suggest a point of departure or a limit of regression. At the same time, they can operate in the work as images of a beatific state or transcendental goal. Norris achieves his first powerful overlay of these core images in the climax of *McTeague*. In the year before his death the exposed figure and the vacant space have become, in the short stories, an obsessive theme. It is while sustaining a superimposition of figure and ground over the span of an entire novel, however, that Norris fully releases his imaginative powers. This happens in *The Octopus,* a book built out of body and landscape.

Vandover the painter anticipates Norris the novelist:

> His finished pictures were broad reaches of landscape, deserts, shores, and moors in which he placed solitary figures of men or animals in a way that was very effective – as, for instance, a great strip of shore and in the foreground the body of a drowned sailor; a lion drinking in the midst of an immense Sahara; or, one that he called the Remnant of an Army, a dying war horse wandering on an empty plain, the saddle turned under his belly, his mane and tail snarled with burrs.

9. Frank Norris

Vandover's designs betray Norris's self-consciousness about a theme
that, although it everywhere informs Vandover's story, has not been
given full expression through a structure of imagery. The painter's
story, like McTeague's, is of a fall, but only in the dentist's case will
Norris deploy a background sufficient to dramatize his hero's carefully
foreshadowed failure to remain erect. Vandover's failure "to pull up"
remains one imaged primarily through the literal degeneration of his
figure: He becomes "a thing four-footed." Norris's moralizing tone
expresses throughout his impatience with a character engaged in a melodramatic act of autodestruction rather than in an epic struggle with
forces – in spaces – greater than himself.

Norris expands on Vandover's "feeling for desolate landscapes" in
two late stories, "A Memorandum of Sudden Death" and "The Ship
That Saw a Ghost." Both are about men cast away, perhaps to die, in
sandy or watery deserts. The author of the memorandum flees the
pursuing Indians into "an absolutely flat piece of country." Here the
human assumes an ominous verticality:

> The desert hereabout is vast and lonesome beyond words . . . the
> abomination of desolation; and always – in whichever direction I
> turn my eyes – always, in the midst of this pale-yellow blur, a
> single figure in the distance, blanketed, watchful, solitary, stand-
> ing out sharp and distinct against the background of sage and
> sand.

So far, Norris has simply reproduced Vandover's painting. But a later
meditation reveals that Karslake's "last stand" is caught up in the drama
of creation itself:

> Even the sage is sparse – a bad place even for a coyote. The whole
> is flagellated with an intolerable heat and – now that the shooting
> is relaxed – oppressed with a benumbing, sodden silence – the si-
> lence of a primordial world. Such a silence as must have brooded
> over the Face of the Waters on the Eve of Creation – desolate,
> desolate, as though a colossal, invisible pillar – a pillar of the Infi-
> nitely Still, the pillar of Nirvana – rose forever into the empty
> blue, human life an atom of microscopic dust crushed under its
> basis, and at the summit God himself. And I find time to ask
> myself why, at this of all moments of my tiny life-span, I am able
> to write as I do, registering impressions, keeping a finger upon
> the pulse of the spirit.

Here the scene of Karslake's death dissolves into the Primal Scene.
The attempt to stand against the Indians in this godforsaken place is like
life's attempt to rise above the horizontality of its origins. He writes as

he does in order to answer the silence of the landscape and so to rise
above it and thus to connect his end (the death of an articulate man)
with his beginning (the struggle of life to articulate itself). It is not for
nothing that Karslake concludes his meditation by comparing himself
to John on Patmos, for in his struggle against space and silence he has
discovered on the pulses of his own spirit that in the beginning was the
word.

The narrator of "The Ship That Saw a Ghost," at sea in the South
Pacific, must also fend off an oppressive vacancy:

> Forever and forever, under the pitiless sun and cold blue sky
> stretched the indigo of the ocean floor. The ether between the
> planets can be no less empty, no less void.
>
> I never, till that moment, could have so much as conceived the
> imagination of such loneliness, such utter stagnant abomination of
> desolation. In an open boat, bereft of comrades, I should have
> gone mad in thirty minutes.
>
> I remember to have approximated the impression of such
> empty immensity only once before, in my younger days, when I
> lay on my back on a treeless, bushless mountain side and stared up
> into the sky for the better part of an hour.
>
> You probably know the trick. If you do not, you must under-
> stand that if you look up at the blue long enough, the flatness of
> the thing begins little by little to expand, to give here and there;
> and the eye travels on and on and up and up, till at length (well
> for you that it lasts but the fraction of a second), you all at once
> see space. You generally stop there and cry out, and – your hands
> over your eyes – are only too glad to grovel close to the good old
> solid earth again.

What links these passages – beyond the shared phrases ("abomination
of desolation") and the shared peril – is the repeated play ("trick") of
mind. The narrators take control of their fear by turning a sense of
encroachment from without into a projection of a vision from within.
It is a kind of ironic troping that sees flatness as if it were height. The
fantasy of a shape (a "pillar") or dimension of uprightness expresses
Norris's sense that man's unique power is to convert the horizontal into
the vertical, to say matter in terms of spirit.

If acts of vision are here the best defense against agoraphobia, its true
contrary is the upright human figure. Strictly erect characters fill Norris's work. His first impulse is to define character through posture; it is
Travis Bessemer's "carriage" with which Condy Rivers falls in love.
Ross Wilbur also opts for a woman of distinctive stance, one "Huge,
blonde, big-boned." And it turns out that the only way he can stand up

to his beloved is to knock her down. "Grettir at Drangey" is a story about standing tall and alone. It offers the best pure example of Norris's fascination with the body physically upright and its will to resist the grave. Grettir and his brother have stolen the island of Drangey, and now the last battle for it is engaged:

> Twice Grettir, dying though he was, flung the fight from him and rose to his full height, a dreadful figure, alone for an instant, bloody, dripping, charred with ashes, half naked, his clothes all burning; and twice again they flung themselves upon him, and bore him down, so that he disappeared beneath their mass.

Dying men crawl from the huddle. Grettir begins to fail:

> For a moment in that flicker of fire he seemed to grow larger. Alone, unassailable, erect among those heaps of dead and dying enemies, his stature seemed as it were suddenly to increase. . . . There he stood already dead, yet still upon his feet, rigid as iron, his back unbent, his neck proud, while they cowered before him holding their breath, waiting, watching. Then like a mighty pine tree, stiff, unbending, he swayed slowly forward. Stiff as a swordblade, the great body leaned over farther and farther; slowly at first, then with increased momentum inclined swiftly earthward. He fell . . .

As if filming the scene in slow motion, Norris manages to prolong the fall (I have quoted less than half of it) to the point where "fell" becomes anticlimactic. A story about standing *through* death, "Grettir at Drangey" carries to the limit Norris's fantasy that a true hero cannot be brought low. The extremity of the rhetoric here registers the fragility of the hope.

For what happens to Norris's characters is that they fall. "Fall" in fact seems to be the fate of anything erect; it is difficult to remember a hero whom Norris leaves standing. Our last sight of Vandover finds him "on his knees." The will to stumble can be expressed as casually as it is in "Little Dramas of the Curbstone," where the narrator remarks a girl's collapsing knees, due perhaps to "some weakness of the joints, that smote upon her like this at inopportune moments." Or it can take an overtly allegorical dimension as it does in "Dying Fires," where the young writer's imminent compromise of his talent in New York is foreshadowed in his muttered threat to the city – "I must down you . . . or you will down me." Revivalist Dick Nickerson's sudden collapse – "he was holding forth one blazin' hot day out in the sun when all to once he goes down, *flat,* an' don't come round for the better part o' two days. When he wakes up he's *another person;* he'd forgot his name, forgot his job, forgot the whole blamed shooting-match" – completes itself in a second fall that restores him to his moral, methodist self. So in "A Reversion to Type" floorwalker Paul Shuster "bolts" from his everyday self into a career of profligacy and crime, only to return six weeks later to the comfort of routine. "Such he was at forty. At forty-one he fell." His horizontal flight away proves actually a vertical descent, back down the ladder of his ancestry, into "inherited tendencies." At stake in these falls into amnesia and error is not loss of life but loss of self, integrity rather than survival. Norris thus gathers his "falls" into an iconography capable of figuring forth complex moral as well as physical and imaginative dilemmas.

The ending of *McTeague* acquires its resonance from the acts of foreshadowing, some almost subliminal, with which Norris prepares us for the final scene. (It is of a man trying to rise to his full height, handcuffed to his archenemy in the middle of a flat expanse.) Readers of the novel often register the contrary impression: The shift after Trina's murder to the landscape of the Sierra and the deserts beyond strikes many as an unearned leap. Franklin Walker reports that Norris broke off work on the novel after "reaching the point at which the dentist murders his wife," and we might therefore correlate the discontinuity in setting with the discontinuity in the act of composition. (Norris resumed work on the novel in the very place to which he would shift its action – the Big Dipper Mine in Colfax, California.) His Harvard plot summary of the novel, written in March 1895 and thus more than two years before the final stint, lays out, however, the sequence he had in mind:

> McTeague goes from bad to worse and finally ends by killing his wife. He manages to escape and goes back to the mines where the first part of his life has been spent. The facts concerning him come to light here and he is obliged to run for it. His way is across an arm of an Arizona desert, here he is ridden down by a deputy sheriff. The two are sixty miles from the nearest human being and McTeague determines to fight, he kills the sheriff and is about to go on when he discovers that even in the fight the sheriff has managed to hand-cuff their wrists together. He is chained to the body sixty miles from help.

Norris's devotion of more than half of the summary to the final three chapters of the novel suggests that he was above all compelled by its ending. And, from the beginning, Norris's story demanded that its hero be plunged back into aboriginal space.

Donald Pizer has argued convincingly that *McTeague* is the parable of

our sexual fall. "In *McTeague,* sex is not simply a step toward degeneration, as it is in Vandover. It is rather that which comes to all men and
women, disrupting their lives and placing them in relationships which
the sanctity of marriage cannot prevent from ending in chaos and destruction." Uncomprehended desire certainly brings McTeague low.
What interests me rather is not the content but the form of his fall, the
ways in which Norris directs attention to the sheer human tropism
toward the horizontal. This is the action of all his serious novels and
one that compels him as much or more than the various causes for fall
that can be adduced. Because this process involves issues of position
and relationship, it is hardly surprising that much of the key action in
McTeague turns upon the prepositions "up" and "down." The play of
these little words helps to map out the novel's psychic terrain.

McTeague's first conversation shows him as the thing caught
between:

> "Oh, Mac!" he called. McTeague came to his door.
> "Hullo! 's that you, Mark?"
> "Sure," answered Marcus. "Come on up."
> "You come on down."
> "No, come on up."
> "Oh, you come on down."
> "Oh, you lazy duck!" retorted Marcus, coming down the stairs.

This conversation initiates what will become an incessant struggle between Marcus and McTeague over status and stature. The novel is, in
its own words, a study in "relative positions," and the ways in which
they become inverted or perverted constitute its central action.

The story begins with a man falling asleep in a chair: "By and by . . .
he dropped off to sleep." Yet he is also a man on top of his world, and
the full promise of his situation Norris captures in one sentence. "Bull-
like, he heaved himself laboriously up, and, going to the window,
stood looking down into the street." In the contrary motions of this
sentence, McTeague displays a physical mastery of himself (though not
without effort) and a visual mastery of the world. His second-floor
office proves for him "a point of vantage" from which he watches the
world below go by. Elevated above the perpetual movie of the street
("Day after day, McTeague saw the same panorama unroll itself"), he
stands above and aside from the endless horizontal flow. Desire will
draw him down.

Trina comes to McTeague after a fall. Courtship begins with the
woman reclining beneath a standing man. As he bends over her broken
tooth, the brute "leaps" up in him but the "better self" cries "Down,

down." He compromises the claims of both with an abrupt kiss. He then proposes, and Trina declines by throwing up. Trina and McTeague now find themselves caught in a sliding scale of power and esteem: "In spite of themselves they were gradually resuming the same relative positions they had occupied when they had first met." He wins her with a second kiss after crushing "down her struggle with his enormous strength." Marcus vacates the triangle as one would leave a room. "Mac, I'll give her up to you. I won't stand between you." For the two men, soon estranged, the struggle for dominance remains one of relative size and proximity. McTeague: "He can't make small of *me*." Marcus: "I'll not stand up with um." The feud culminates in the wrestling match where Marcus bites through McTeague's ear only to have his footing taken away: "He swung him wide, as a hammer-thrower swings his hammer. Marcus's feet flipped from the ground, he spun through the air about McTeague as helpless as a bundle of clothes." By upending Marcus, McTeague seals his own public fall, for the enraged friend will tattle on the unlicensed dentist and so remove the central prop to his social and economic status. Initial resistance to fate gives way to insistent slippage: "At first these deprivations angered McTeague. Then all of a sudden, he slipped back into the old habits." And slippage gives way to sinkage: "The McTeague's now began to sink rapidly lower and lower." The move into Zerkow's den puts them directly below the site of their beginning. The action culminates in a final shift of relative positions; McTeague invades the kindergarten and murders Trina while she scrubs away "down on her hands and knees."

In Chapter 20, McTeague falls out of cityscape and into landscape. (Chapter 19 ends with the school children about to stumble across the dead Trina.) The effort to rise morally and socially is here transposed into the sheer struggle to survive and evolve:

A tremendous, immeasurable Life pushed steadily heavenward without a sound, without a motion. At turns of the road, on the higher points, cañons disclosed themselves far away, gigantic grooves in the landscape, deep blue in the distance, opening one into another, ocean-deep, silent, huge, and suggestive of colossal primeval forces held in reserve. At their bottoms they were solid, massive; on their crests they broke delicately into fine serrated edges where the pines and redwoods outlined their million of tops against the high white horizon. Here and there the mountains lifted themselves out of the narrow river beds in groups like giant lions rearing their heads after drinking. The entire region was untamed. In some places east of the Mississippi nature is cosy, intimate, small, and homelike, like a good-natured housewife. In Placer County, California, she is a vast, unconquered brute of the Pliocene epoch, savage, sullen, and magnificently indifferent to man.

Sierra landscape becomes a vast emblem of McTeague's failure to uplift himself. If it is indifferent, it is nevertheless stubbornly on the rise. And if the narrator finds it uncanny, McTeague feels almost enwombed, a man cozily at home. "He recognized familiar points at once." This is the place McTeague started from, as a human and an organism. Once again a creature of instinct, McTeague regresses toward the ground and even, as a miner, into it. The sequence in the mines convincingly renders the devolution of this "returning prodigal." But Norris pushes on into a landscape even more stark within which to measure McTeague's fall. What his imagination requires is a site – Death Valley – in which the drive for self-sufficiency can declare its intimacy with the longing for the undifferentiated.

"There was no longer any shadow but his own": This is the precarious condition toward which McTeague's journey instinctively leads. To be the one upright thing, to reduce identity to pure stature, to jettison community and relationship – the pathos of these drives is justly figured in the novel's final scene. In this novel so full of doubles, McTeague meets, on the train through Owens Valley, a pathetic image of his end: "The dentist looked back and saw him still standing motionless between the rails, a forlorn and solitary point of red, lost in the immensity of the surrounding white blur of the desert." It is the receding figure of the Indian buck who had presented McTeague a letter attesting to his qualifications for charity. The image of the man against the sky is here openly emptied of any tragic grandeur. But such a possibility has in any case been compromised away by the stolid incomprehension with which McTeague has met his fate; there is no chance that he will fuse uprightness with insight. What remains is that McTeague's romance with the vertical, so often a matter of discreet verbal repetitions, be fulfilled in a final panoramic tableau.

The calm of the last shot closes down on an irrepressible skirmishing for relative position. While fleeing across a "flat, dazzling surface," McTeague is suddenly arrested by a shout:

"Hands up. By damn, I got the drop on you!"
McTeague looked up.
It was Marcus.

This is the second time Marcus has urged McTeague up, and this time he succeeds. But after the chase of the mule ends in a squashed canteen, the two men abandon the quest for hierarchy as they acknowledge the overwhelming fact of their common location. They are lost in the middle of nowhere.

> "Well, let's – let's be moving along – somewhere."
> "*Where*, I'd like to know? What's the good of moving on?"
> "What's the good of stopping here?"

In the horizontal mode to which they are confined, it scarcely matters that their voices have become indistinguishable. Mere momentum across is seen as literally pointless. What rescues the characters from paralysis and collapse is hatred, a hatred that their attraction throughout has shown to be the other side of love. The old enmity flames "up again," and they fight their last fight:

> As McTeague rose to his feet, he felt a pull at his right wrist; something held it fast. Looking down, he saw that Marcus in that last struggle had found strength to handcuff their wrists together. Marcus was dead now; McTeague was locked to the body. All about him, vast, interminable, stretched the measureless leagues of Death Valley.
> McTeague remained stupidly looking around him, now at the distant horizon, now at the ground, now at the half-dead canary chittering feebly in its little gilt prison.

Has any novel ever imaged more literally our powerlessness to escape our buried selves? The intimacy between McTeague and Marcus (they have, after all, mouthed the same billiard ball) here achieves its ecstatic *liebestod*. This is the final use of landscape in *McTeague* – to disappear. Death Valley provides a background so empty that nothing distracts us from the hero's isolation with his fate. Relative positions are reversed again in an inversion of the first exchange, but position – the two men occupy the same psychic space – has clearly ceased to matter. The pattern of expectation is fulfilled, and the other's shadow is his own.

Norris ends *McTeague* by representing his hero's story as a picture. Although the content of this picture invites analysis (it is a pure reduction of "The American Sublime," "the empty spirit in vacant space"), the fact of the closing tableau has the most significance for Norris's career. *McTeague* has dealt with steady devolution in time, but it registers that process as failed transcendence in space. Attention to the self in landscape diverts us from the fate of the self in history, and the strategy of the ending, as of the whole, is to imagine human actors as bodies "in space." If the books written before *The Octopus* aspire to the condition of painting, *The Octopus*, for all its fascination with figure and ground, attains its unique power by directing more attention to narrative sequence than to pictorial representation. In his best novel Norris thus increases the reader's liability for loss by recurring to the special province of an art that, as Lessing argued, unfolds in words: actions "in time."

ACTIONS IN TIME

The Octopus begins with a man mapping out a landscape. He does so by moving through it with his body. Presley's bicycle ride accomplishes two clear narrative functions; it acquaints us with the territory and introduces most of the central characters. Exposition becomes the simple function of what a man in motion meets along the way.

The Octopus actually begins with a map. The great square faces the opening page as if to announce that this will be a story about circumscribed space. It is a land of angles and intersections. The one strong straight line is dictated by the bed of the railroad. A huge trapezoid crowds out a maze of smaller polygons. That the novel was inspired by Millet does not prevent it from aspiring to the condition of a Diebenkorn. Freestanding character will struggle throughout to reclaim itself from a landscape in which the human presence has been abstracted into linear patterns.

But in Chapter 1 space serves the definition of character. As Presley rides down the County Road from Bonneville and then across Los Muertos, he encounters the name of S. Behrman and the actual persons of Hooven, Harran Derrick, and Dyke. After his meal in Guadalajara, he cycles on to meet Annixter, Vanamee, and Father Sarria. As we read into the chapter, location begins to imply function. Characters closer to the center of the journey – Dyke and Annixter – will play parts central to the action. The most life abounds where the most lines meet, at Annixter's Home Ranch. "It was traversed in all directions." Presley's singular commitment to motion (all others take up a station along the way) suggests a corresponding extravagance of mind. These men are points on a map of his own making, and what connects them and gives shape to the chapter is Presley's "turn through the country."

But the landscape is not all person. Presley moves through a space distinctive in its very vacancy. "All about him the country was flat. In all directions he could see for miles. The harvest was just over. Nothing but stubble remained on the ground." It is a space at once vulnerable and immune to impress. Vacancy throws up an occasional "landmark" – Hooven's oak, the county watering tank. Norris's repeated simile for the landscape is "a gigantic scroll." (The chapter is full of horizontal metaphors for experience – threads, scrolls, roads.) Its horizontal "reach" seems "infinite, flat, cheerless, heat-ridden." But for its freestanding human landmarks, movement across it would generate the sensation of arrest.

But the movement of the chapter is not only across, but up. Place does afford one natural point of vantage, and Presley directs his journey toward it, the crest of wooded hills above the mission. By chapter's end he has not only traversed the territory but gained a prospect on it. His first act at the summit is to take his ease, "prone upon the ground." Then he rises to his feet. "As from a pinnacle, Presley, from where he now stood, dominated the entire country." Presley has already half-listened to Vanamee's verbal map of his travels, and now he constructs one of his own. Blind at first to the horizontal dimension, his gaze fastens only on verticals: the "campanile," the "tower" of Annixter's artesian well, the "roofs" of Guadalajara, the "dome" of the courthouse, Hooven's "live oak," the "eucalyptus trees," the "watering tank," the "long wind-break" of poplars. Then "the eye of the mind," fortified by the sight of so much uplift, expands to acknowledge "the great sweep of landscape." As ranch after imagined ranch dissolves itself and disappears over the shoulder of the world, Presley experiences a fantasy of incorporated space. "A sudden uplift, a sense of exhilaration, of physical exaltation appeared abruptly to sweep Presley from his feet. As from a point high above the world, he seemed to dominate a universe, a whole order of things. He was dizzied, stunned, stupefied, his morbid supersensitive mind reeling, drunk with the intoxication of mere immensity." Presley is undercut here by his own will toward inclusion; uplift ends with lost footing. Presley's epic ambitions dangerously amplify, to the point of parody, what his physical journey had just modestly enacted: the figure of a man who is the measure of his world. Despite its final excesses, Presley's encounter with landscape nevertheless establishes one of the novel's key experiential sequences. In the world of *The Octopus,* immersion in space culminates in a dominating act of vision.

If Chapter 1 celebrates the potentiality of space, it also registers the pressure of time. Landscape may look like a scroll, but it is also experienced, after all, as a rhythm. This becomes clear as Presley listens to Vanamee talk about the Long Trail: "His brain had been swiftly registering picture after picture that Vanamee's monotonous flow of words struck off, as it were, upon a steadily moving scroll." Here Norris puts the scroll image in motion. Presley's attempt to apprehend a narrated landscape – to visualize by way of a "flow of words" – reminds us of the temporal experience we have been having. We have been reading. However strong the desire of author, character, and reader to convert motion into vision, action in the story and apprehension of it demand immersion in time.

A man "in a hurry," Presley is late from the start:

10. What Presley saw: the model for Guadalajara in *The Octopus*, San Juan Bautista as seen from the heights in the 1880s

Just after passing Caraher's saloon, on the County Road that ran south from Bonneville, and that divided the Broderson ranch from that of Los Muertos, Presley was suddenly aware of the faint and prolonged blowing of a steam whistle that he knew must come from the railroad shops near the depot at Bonneville. In starting out from the ranch house that morning, he had forgotten his watch, and was now perplexed to know whether the whistle was blowing for twelve or for one o'clock. He hoped the former. Early that morning he had decided to make a long excursion through the neighboring country, partly on foot and partly on his bicycle, and now noon was come already, and as yet he had hardly started. As he was leaving the house after breakfast, Mrs. Derrick has asked him to go for the mail at Bonneville, and he had not been able to refuse.

Those details that here orient us in space may obscure the careful notation of Presley's career in time. Cartographic information crowds into the first sentence in the form of a parenthesis between commas. The core sentence deals instead with Presley's awareness of time, with his passing the saloon and hearing the whistle. What we see here and hereafter is a man trying to impose clock time on the duration in which he moves, and failing – marvelously. The chapter unfolds, as we have seen, as Presley's attempt to confer meaning on his world by spatializing it. This is what we do when we make a map, but it is also what we do when we use a clock. To the immediate data of consciousness experience registers itself as a seamless flow; Bergson's metaphor for life in duration is a river in which we are all immersed. (Norris will later resort to an allied image for the subconscious and inescapable experience of duration: "The insistent flowing of the fountain seemed only as the symbol of the passing of time, a thing that was understood rather than heard, inevitable, prolonged.") In our attempts to order *durée,* we abstract a pattern of intervals from it that we call "time." Time is duration of which we have become aware and which we measure like a space. Mapping space and "marking the time" are for Presley allied functions by which he hopes to stay the confusion of his world. He will succeed in neither. Such ambitions are undermined from the start by instincts in Presley himself. If he shows a concern with temporal intervals – he has "forgotten his watch" – he has, after all, forgotten it. And his underlying decision to "make a long excursion" suggests that he is prepared, given the implicit open-endedness of such a project, to disregard such intervals altogether. Presley sets out to measure his world through the constructs "space" and "time," but his actions also register the pleasures and liabilities of life in an enduring flow.

The chapter's digressive style advances a subtle argument against the tyranny of temporal intervals. The protagonist's haste is more than matched by his author's patience. Presley's function is to cover territory and to encounter character; Norris's, to describe both. Presley's "turn through the country" proves the perfect vehicle for authorial turning aside. Within the long asides on the season and on Dyke, Annixter, and Vanamee, we nearly forget that our object is to get to the top of the promised hill. Norris thus establishes his style of narrative imagination, with its tendency to dally along the way, as the best antidote to the *Atropos* of temporal fate – to the unseeing haste of the railroad, in Thoreau's words, "that never turns aside."

As if the character somehow took a cue from the patience of his author, Presley's pace through the chapter gradually begins to slow. He starts as a man with a "plan." He wants "to get on as fast as possible." As much as Hooven, then, his haste makes him a man of "contracted horizon." Norris takes all the more care to preserve for Presley the option of peripheral vision. "But evidently it had been decreed that Presley should be stopped at every point of his ride that day." Norris comes close to admitting here that the demands of his story may be issuing such decrees. But such a comment also prepares us for the recognition that the digressive style answers the imperative fullness of this world. Presley must listen to a number of stories, just as the reader is asked to pause to take in Norris's biographies. It is his growing willingness to listen (compare his initial reluctance to convey Hooven's message to his eventual solicitation of a story from the centenarian) that prepares him to meet the character with the longest story: Vanamee.

By the time Presley gets to Vanamee, he has lost any strong linear momentum: "Presley turned sharply aside." He does so, Norris indicates, in response to a kind of mental telepathy, and Vanamee's role throughout will be to test and challenge the normal boundaries of experience. Vanamee is at first distinguished by his location in space. "On the far side of the herd, erect, motionless – a single note of black, a speck, a dot – the shepherd stood." He proves even more remarkable for his stance toward time. "Here was a man whose whole being had been at one time shattered and riven to its lowest depths, whose life had suddenly stopped at a certain moment of its development." Father Sarria notes that after a six-year absence Vanamee's "beard had not grown an inch." His face and bearing remain "the same." Vanamee's story promises to mark the climax of the chapter, and in achieving transcendence of both the spatial and temporal worlds, Vanamee would seem to resolve the pressures and dilemmas that weigh on Presley. But Norris provides one last scene that deflates Vanamee's ambition to abstract himself from specific location and duration. While he reviews his story, his sheep wander off and get killed.

Vanamee's story is of a sudden intrusion into a peaceful landscape. Sixteen years before, he had loved Angéle Varian. Each summer night they had met in the deep shade of the pear trees of the mission. "Then one night the tragedy had suddenly leaped out from the shadow with the abruptness of an explosion." On a moonless night, Angéle arrived in the garden earlier than usual and "found the apparently familiar figure waiting for her. All unsuspecting she gave herself to the embrace of a strange pair of arms, and Vanamee, arriving but a score of moments later, stumbled over her prostrate body, inert, and unconscious, in the shadow of the overspiring trees."

The "Other" is never found. He leaves behind "a track of terror." The "thread" of Vanamee's life has "been snapped," and he lives on to haunt, in body and in spirit, the site of Angéle's grave. So victimized has he been by time that he withdraws from it to brood on his unavenged loss. Since this story presents itself as the first chapter's one "impenetrable mystery," readers naturally expect that the novel will set out to solve it. But Vanamee's is a story that goes nowhere, an obsessive running in place. The solution, when it comes, occurs to the side of and as a symbolic complement to the action about which we have been made to care. The true hero will be Annixter, a man immersed in landscape and duration.

The shepherd's story is actually told by way of Presley; Vanamee's talk of the Long Trail provides the prolonged murmur above which Presley remembers it. His willingness to recall story measures his growing patience with life in time. This movement culminates in an orgy of remembering. Presley's scansion of the landscape is followed by a second overview in which he gains a retrospect not on actual space but on the stories he has been told or has remembered that day – of De La Cuesta, "Vanamee's strange history," and "the story of the Long Trail." No longer seeing (the valley is now "shut from sight"), he falls back on an inward rehearsal of "the component parts of his poem, the signs and symbols of the West." What he returns to are those verbal sequences – stories – that will allow him, in the "epic" project to which Vanamee has given the name, to impose a suspenseful rhythm on space.

"But suddenly there was an interruption." Just as Presley is about "to grasp his song in all its entity," his revels are ended by a shock from the world that goes on. Abstracting stories from time must give way to his own story in time. The roar of the engine shoots by. "Abruptly Presley remembered." "Abruptly" the sound will diminish. And "abruptly" he will pause before the sight of the sheep slaughtered along the rails. If

McTeague is a novel of prepositions, *The Octopus* is one of adverbs. This is consonant with its ongoing concern with the quality of a motion. One adverb dominates the action: *abruptly*. If there is any one way in which experience in time comes in this fictional world, it is as, in Frost's term, an "abruption." The quietude of the day, the careful mapping of topographical and compositional possibilities, the growing patience to wait upon the moment – all this is disrupted by a violent suddenness. Not only Vanamee's life has been crossed by a "track of terror." (His tendency "to drop down" "without warning" – a description twice repeated – ominously links Vanamee to the explosiveness of the Other *and* the railroad.) In the face of this abruption, the shock is too great; Presley's last act is not to turn aside, but to turn "away." In the world of *The Octopus,* immersion in time culminates in an overwhelming experience of surprise.

Chapter 1 unfolds as a brilliant essay on human scale. The brilliance inheres in its power to enforce conclusions without stating them: that the meaningful points in our lives are those we can connect in the motion of a day; that identity consists in an insistent vertical thrust against the anonymous horizon of the earth; that to be human is not to keep an unwavering schedule but to pause and turn aside; that the familiar worlds and stories we map out are also scored by "tracks of terror." Man strives and fails to be the measure of his world.

Norris's work is highly "figural"; its scenes, images, phrases, and even single words anticipate and echo each other in a complex pattern of deepening repetition. If we cut into this figural procession to separate its components into frames, what we get may seem like a set of melodramatic paintings. (Norris's training as a painter in the French academic tradition impressed on him, according to William Dillingham, the values of "accuracy of fact, precision of detail, self-discipline, and objectivism.") Richard Chase seems to have done just this in his reading of the novel: "Like many American novels, *The Octopus* is all 'picture,' and the few 'scenes' we are given are perfunctory, with the exception of one or two that stick in the mind, like the ranch festival and accompanying jack-rabbit hunt, though even here everything is done with the wide brush." Although Chase sensibly observes that his "scenes are more successful in telling us about the characters than are Norris's theoretical devices," he goes on to illustrate this claim in the style of a New Critic, and so treats Norris's scenes as simultaneously arrayed in space rather than as unfolding in a significant sequence. He pays more heed to the content (people as "animals" in *McTeague*) than to the syntax of Norris's fictional strategies, and so overlooks the fact that in *The Octopus,* meaning also emerges through devices of repetition, pacing, and juxtaposition.

Foreshadowing operates throughout *The Octopus* to draw us into an action about which we care. The genius of Shakespeare, Coleridge argues, lies in his ability to produce "Expectation in preference to surprise." The genius of Norris lies, in his own words, in "preparations of effect." By extending to us the opportunity to recognize pattern and so to anticipate events, Norris confers on us, in the manner of the great tragic dramatists, a sense of implication in and responsibility for the promised end. Our foreknowledge is, of course, purchased by a lack of power; the characters are dignified by suffering a surprise that we are asked to witness as an expectation fulfilled. When the climax comes, it comes with an excruciating emphasis on the outline of the individual figure, and so reminds us that our concern for human loss will always loom larger than any interest in the ground. *The Octopus* is a novel that transcends its ostensible subject (standing in space) to become instead a parable about readiness in time.

The novel orders suspense through its repeated foreshadowings of an inevitable fall. In one half-sentence, Norris advances a formula that sums up the novel's three key incidents and hearkens toward the fourth and climactic one: "that abrupt swoop of terror and impending death dropping down there from out the darkness, cutting abruptly athwart the gayety of the moment, come and gone with the swiftness of a thunderclap." What does this describe but the invasion of the Other, the collision with the sheep, and Delaney's abruption into the dance? And what does it anticipate but the final felling of men on the Lower Road? These three acts of foreshadowing are characterized by their abruptness. Loss comes suddenly in this world; what dawns gradually, through this pattern of mounting repetition, is our awareness that loss will come.

Attention is everywhere drawn to the way men rise and fall. "Abruptly Vanamee rose." "The fall was a long one." "Annixter stood suddenly upright." "At ten o'clock Mrs. Hooven fell." Broderson is "bent earthwards." Magnus Derrick lives a life "rigidly upright." Defeat is seen as a giving in to the horizontal; without Hilma, Annixter admits, "I'd quit. I'd lay right down." (She is, after all, Hilma *Tree*.) Dyke is brought "down" in a wrestling match in which his defeat is offset, like that of Faulkner's Old Ben, by his arresting his attackers in a tableau in which he "stood nearly free." And if we miss this, there are the overt literary allusions to famous disasters; Vanamee's reference to Waterloo complements Presley's taste in epic, for when he picks up the *Odyssey,* he turns to the felling of the suitors. Victory is above all a matter of maintaining the vertical. "Let's stand in with each other in *one* fight." This last, spoken by Annixter, precisely anticipates the climax of the novel as a literal crisis of stature. It is the stubborn desire of all these characters to stand firm that makes the flatness of the San Joaquin and the linearity of the railroad the perfect background for and agent of their fall. The landscape of the Central Valley and the struggle of the ranchers to stand against the policies of the Southern Pacific were not aspects of the West that (in a phrase directed at Presley) Norris caught at "in passing"; given his consistent devotion to the theme of apotheosis, the place and the antagonist can be said to have chosen him.

What mirrors the mind's capacity to expect is its capacity for replay. This is the complementary device by which Norris binds temporal experience into story. As Vanamee says, "Hope, after all, is only memory seen reversed." Presley replays his experience twice at the end of Chapter 1. Vanamee rehearses his embracing of Angéle ("she came to him again") so often in fantasy that he conjures up a surrogate in fact. But the character with the most striking capacity to roll back the film is Annixter. Chapter 5 ends with a "series of pictures of the day's doings" passing "before his imagination like the roll of a kinetoscope." And in the very midst of his duel with Delaney, Norris suspends the action with a prediction of the way Annixter will remember it:

> Long after, Annixter could recall this moment. For years he could with but little effort reconstruct the scene – the densely packed crowd flattened against the sides of the barn, the festoons of lanterns, the mingled smell of evergreens, new wood, sachets, and powder smoke; the vague clamor of distress and terror that rose from the throng of guests, the squealing of the buckskin, the uneven explosions of the revolvers, the reverberation of trampling hoofs, a brief glimpse of Harran Derrick's excited face at the door of the harness room, and in the open space in the centre of the floor, himself and Delaney, manoeuvering swiftly in a cloud of smoke.

Norris establishes Annixter's imaginative authority by presenting his recollection with the concreteness and rhythmic power of the narrative voice. The formal device of replay also displays the author's skill at retrospective as well as prospective temporal patterning. Above all, such moments testify to the mind's capacity to range freely in time, whatever the body's liability to fall.

Chapter 1 not only organizes the novel's recurring themes and images; in its rhythm it acts as an exemplum of the rhythm of the whole. It moves slowly toward a big bang. The pivotal event is "prepared for . . . from the novel's initial chapter." So Norris argues in "The Mechanics of Fiction," an essay that makes it plain that the novelist's main concern is with timing. "No one who sets a thing in motion but keeps an eye and a hand upon its speed." In a metaphor that aligns him with the momentum of his plot rather than the aspirations of his characters, Norris identifies the author with an engineer guiding a train. He experiences the pivotal event as "the sudden releasing of the brake to permit for one instant the entire machinery to labour, full steam, ahead. Up to that point the action must lead; from it, it must decline." This is an ominous association, although it is one Norris embraces as he describes the momentum that gathers in a novel's final third:

> Now the action begins to increase in speed. The complication suddenly tightens; all along the line there runs a sudden alert. An episode far back there in the first chapter, an episode with its appropriate group of characters, is brought forward and, coming suddenly to the front, collides with the main line of development and sends it off upon an entirely unlooked for tangent. Another episode of the second chapter – let us suppose – all at once makes common cause with a more recent incident, and the two produce a wholly unlooked-for counter influence which swerves the main theme in still another direction, and all this time the action is speeding faster and faster, and complication tightening and straining to the breaking point, and then at last a "motif" that has been in preparation even since the first paragraph of the first chapter of the novel suddenly comes to a head, and in a twinkling the complication is solved with all the violence of an explosion, and the catastrophe, the climax, the pivotal event fairly leaps from the pages with a rush of action that leaves you stunned, breathless, and overwhelmed with the sheer power of its presentation.

Norris wrote this essay in 1901; he finished *The Octopus* in December 1900. He simply admits here to knowing what he had been about: His description reads like an abstract of the novel's action. (In a letter to Isaac Marcosson written in September 1900, Norris characterized his novel-in-progress: "With the first pivotal incident it quickens a bit, and from there on I've tried to accelerate it steadily till at the last you are – I hope – just whirling and galloping and tearing along till you come *bang!* all of a sudden to a great big crushing END, something that will slam you right between your eyes and knock you off your feet.") In *The Octopus,* Norris found an image (the railroad) adequate to his conception of novelistic form, though the logic of his analysis identifies the essential momentum of story with the motions of the Octopus itself. This is a profoundly tragic conception of plot – it conceives all plots as tragedies. For Norris, plot is the thing that knocks character down.

Two characters in particular define themselves in relation to the momentum of the plot: Vanamee, by standing aside from it, and Annixter, by standing up to it. Heroes of escape and resistance, each is tempted into time by love. The erotic tensions in the novel resolve themselves in a moment the two men share, one that retroactively confirms that Norris has committed his attitudes toward love to a running comparison between their two stories.

Vanamee consistently takes the long view in which human loss recedes beyond the vanishing point. The man who is first seen as a "dot" resolves all others, and their deaths and griefs, into "little things." This is, of course, the other side of an obsessive grief that keeps Vanamee riveted to a tiny patch of earth. The one struggle he gets close to is his own with lost love, and the sharpest irony of Vanamee's story is that he magnifies in his own life what he telescopically distances in the lives of others. His power to sublime the "material world" into "Vision" ("Reality dwindled to a point") thus proves compensatory rather than principled, and his story culminates in the lovely romantic irony of a thoroughly material kiss on the mouth. The man who argues for a compensation beyond human scale must and will accept as the answer to his visionary labors "a simple country girl coming to meet her lover." Having lost Angéle, he gets Angéle's daughter. His psychomachia concludes in a recognition of what had been there all along. That women have children (even the children of rape) and so carry life on is a fact whose recognition garners no laurels. That the consolation seems unearned (he has won her by standing still) does not seem to bother Norris; that it feels incestuous and emotionally false certainly bothers us.

Annixter's love story begins with a kiss; Vanamee's ends with one. Annixter's is a sudden, bungled kiss; he steps on Hilma's toe and ends up connecting with her shirtwaist. He takes no time. So the fight is engaged: The "devil of a driver" Annixter only will come to himself once he consents to "waste his time" in love. Annixter's story is of a man who learns to submit himself to a resisted element – time – and to an alien stance – supplication. Introduced as a set of binary oppositions, he integrates his "cross-grained" self by learning to embrace what he has opposed. His clumsy courtship unfolds through three proposals that subject his "hardness" to mounting humiliation. Annixter is the only character who manages to transform the fight against the railroad into a continuing reality in his private life: "I'm tired of fighting for *things* – land, property, money. I want to fight for some *person* – somebody besides myself." By loving Hilma he thus risks himself in two "fights" where he may be brought low. And love will, in fact, alter his stature, although in a way that undoes the hegemony of Norris's central structure of imagery. On the night when Annixter battles across "measureless distances" to a belief in love, his insight is imaged as an abrupt act of self-elevation. "Annixter stood suddenly upright." This is entirely consonant with Norris's mode of representing physical and spiritual victories. But it represents small

triumph for Annixter, who has his feet all too solidly on the ground from
the beginning. Instead he will discover the power of love to bend him to
its service. One night he returns from the city to come upon Hilma
asleep. "A realization of his boundless happiness in this love he gave and
received, the thought that Hilma *trusted* him, a knowledge of his own
unworthiness, a vast and humble thankfulness that his God had chosen
him of all men for this great joy, had brought him to his knees for the
first time in all his troubled, restless life of combat and aggression." Love
brings Annixter to his knees. This compromise of his physical stature
signifies the most striking act of self-transcendence in the novel as well as
its author's awareness that the motions of the spirit can redeem the
motions of the body.

Love materializes before Vanamee on the same night that Annixter
discovers love in himself. The rancher internalizes feelings that the
shepherd must objectify. Annixter will lose everything while gaining
his own soul; Vanamee abandons soulfulness in a comedy of literal
consolation. In every way, their erotic careers invert each other. Why,
then, does Norris superimpose their two moments of deliverance? To
advance his most powerful argument, I think, against ideologies of fate.

The birth of love in Annixter corresponds to the birth of the wheat in
the ground. "The little seed . . . suddenly in one night had burst upward to the light." Chapter 2 of Book Two ends with the changed man
illuminated against the changed earth: "The morning abruptly blazed
into glory upon the spectacle of a man whose heart leaped exuberant
with the love of a woman, and an exulting earth gleaming transcendent
with the radiant magnificence of an inviolable pledge." This is a coincidence of an order beyond the coincidences Naturalism allows. And, of
course, it occurs on the night of the novel's other great coincidence – the
appearance of Angéle's daughter to Vanamee. The two coincidences
coincide. "For a moment the life-circles of these two men, of so widely
differing characters, touched each other, there in the silence of the night
under the stars." Norris repeats this in the middle of Chapter 3, Book
Two, at the moment when Vanamee happens on Annixter gazing
"upon the flat, sombre land." Vanamee then walks to the cloister
garden and lies upon the ground. At this point Norris launches into an
extended retrospect. The story of that entire spring of hoping now
unfolds as Vanamee's sense of something out there advances with the
oncoming bloom. At the moment when the blooming cycle completes
itself the "something" catches Vanamee's eye. And at this moment
Vanamee's story again catches up with Annixter's: "It was the same
night in which Annixter out-watched the stars, coming, at last, to
himself." Angéle's daughter then sleepwalks forward, and Vanamee has
his "Answer of the night."

Wishes can be fulfilled: To what else do these two stories testify but the willingness of matter to "answer" mind? The correspondence between natural and mental processes rises here to that uncanny level of coincidence Jung calls "synchronicity." ("Such phenomena demonstrate that premonitions or visions very often have some correspondence in external reality.") Events such as these do not occur in fictional universes governed by the play of material circumstances. We may wish to object that the resolutions offered here are merely symbolic, meant to amplify the force of an emotional conversion without asserting the collaboration of a natural fact. But what are we to do with the literal appearance of Angéle's daughter in response to the same telepathic will that summons Presley to Vanamee in Chapter 1? And what are we to make of Norris's decision to assign these breakthroughs to the same night? The formal patterning of the episodes betrays Norris's belief in the shaping power of the imagination as much as do the two acts of vision superimposed. In *The Octopus,* Norris assumes the freedom to manipulate episode and image apart from all notions of determinism or standards of verisimilitude.

He even gets us to take sides. His interview with Huntington may have sent him back to the novel determined to give the railroad its due, but the fact remains that the ranchers are individuated through the pattern of expectation in ways that make them the primary objects of our concern. (It is difficult to imagine how we could ever balance our sympathy, against the force of the book's moralized imagery, in favor of a cause headed by the "round-topped" and "protuberant" S. Behrman, a man wider than he is tall. He literally has no stature.) Like Presley, Norris is finally "more interested in his poem, as such, than in the cause that had inspired it," and precisely this interest leads him to project the possible success of the ranchers *as* a cause. If plot is that that knocks character down, the willingness of character to stand up to it is what makes conflict and story possible. The reader duplicates such acts of resistance when he engages himself with the characters' fate. The concern we feel for the ranchers' specific act of resistance is one we feel for ourselves in any story in which expectation prepares us for a fall. Norris's arousal of sympathy for the ranchers thus fulfills formal imperatives as much as it expresses an ideological bias.

Presley's superficial command of the issues of authorial distance and concern makes him the consistent foil for Norris's successfully realized artistic intentions. We see Presley making the choices Norris has already made. Presley's tendency is to run to extremes. His initial impatience with his fellow characters and his attempt to distance himself through vision eventually invert themselves in a "frenzy" of earnest concern. "He had not then cared for the People"; now, in composing

"The Toilers," he moves toward becoming their terrorist avenger. His ambition to write an *"impersonal"* Song of the West gives way to an angry short poem. The failure of epic becomes the success of lyric.

If Presley's actions and reflections recapitulate many of the choices Norris faced while writing *The Octopus,* Presley usually chooses for better or worse without knowing why, and it is in his degree of self-awareness that he can be distinguished from his author. From the start Norris succeeds in suspending the claims of distance and concern through a passionate negative capability. Commitment to any cause is kept from becoming ideological by a continual awareness of the story as a fiction that interrogates and comments on its own procedures. If "Naturalism" is a reduction to which one is repeatedly drawn, invent an episode in which the engaged and distanced heroes simultaneously discover a harmony between the motions of nature and the motions of their minds. And if "indifference" toward character is a temptation to which one is liable to succumb, invent a character so much less "a character than a type" that he defines the ways in which so many others are so much more. This is just what Norris does with the mysterious Dabney.

Had Norris written a story "dealing with forces . . . not with men" (the words are that arch-Naturalist Shelgrim's), Dabney would have been its fitting exponent. He is first introduced while arriving with the Brodersons at the barn dance: "And with them came a certain Dabney, of whom nothing but his name was known, a silent old man, who made no friends, whom nobody knew or spoke to, who was seen only upon such occasions as this, coming from no one knew where, going, no one cared to inquire whither." This is all we need to know in a fictional world that subscribes to Shelgrim's interpretation of our story – nothing. In such a world no one cares "to inquire" whence or whither because character – the term itself would be a humanistic nostalgia – has no power to transcend its origin or affect its destination. (Norris recurs to these questions in the last description of Dabney as a man "who had come from no one knew whence and who went no one knew whither.") Norris presents Dabney as an undeveloped character whom we are free to wonder at or ignore, and so places the burden of "developing" Dabney on the reader himself.

Dabney is mentioned a dozen times in the novel, and nearly always with the same character signatures. He neither says a word nor does a significant thing. We know nothing about him except his demeanor; he is a psyche reduced to a shape. He is someone about whom we simply know, but about whom it is difficult to care. We are led to the conclusion that Dabney's presence is meant to remind us of how readily Norris has, with Vanamee and Annixter, provoked us to inquire "whence" and "whither." He has raised his central characters beyond the level of a type.

Having used Dabney in this fashion – having deployed him as an example of the way *not* to "use" character – how can Norris escape the charge that he has sacrificed Dabney to a force (his novelistic plan) as merciless as that invoked by Shelgrim? By giving him his role in the unfolding drama of expectation. His doing nothing prepares us, through the quietest of ironies, for the one thing he will *do*. In a full measure of his generosity, Norris extends to this man of whom nothing has been asked the privilege of recapitulating, in its "pivotal event," the novel's central theme. It is given to Dabney to body forth, with an economy almost terrifying, the concerns and movements of the whole.

The fall arrives as something heard:

> Instantly the revolvers and rifles seemed to go off of themselves. Both sides, deputies and Leaguers, opened fire simultaneously. At first, it was nothing but a confused roar of explosions; then the roar lapsed to an irregular, quick succession of reports, shot leaping after shot; then a moment's silence, and, last of all, regular as clock-ticks, three shots at exact intervals. Then stillness.

It unfolds as something seen:

> Delaney, shot through the stomach, slid down from his horse, and, on his hands and knees, crawled from the road into the standing wheat. Christian fell backward from the saddle toward the buggy, and hung suspended in that position, his head and shoulders on the wheel, one stiff leg still across his saddle. Hooven, in attempting to rise from his kneeling position, received a rifle ball squarely in the throat, and rolled forward upon his face. Old Broderson, crying out, "Oh, they've shot me, boys," staggered sideways, his head bent, his hands rigid at his sides, and fell into the ditch. Osterman, blood running from his mouth and nose, turned about and walked back. Presley helped him across the irrigating ditch and Osterman laid himself down, his head on his folded arms. Harran Derrick dropped where he stood, turning over on his face, and lay motionless, groaning terribly, a pool of blood forming under his stomach. The old man Dabney, silent as ever, received his death, speechless. He fell to his knees, got up again, fell once more, and died without a word. Annixter, instantly killed, fell his length to the ground, and lay without movement, just as he had fallen, one arm across his face.

Given his consistent valorization of the vertical, Norris could have shown no greater respect for his characters than in this careful notation of the way each falls. This is very hard to take, however well we have been prepared. There is, for me, no more moving scene in American fiction, and its power is due to the skill with which Norris has included me as a *bystander*. I have been preparing myself to stand in with these characters in one fight, but when the fight comes, the fact of its suddenness is belied by the deliberate slowness with which we are asked to take it in. Having been ready, I had thought the readiness all. The gap between my stunned sense of dispossession and the author's calm disposition of the plot suggests, instead, that not the readiness, but the ripeness, is all.

The fact of the deed is established first through the ear. Sound must penetrate in order to be heard; by opening ourselves to these roars and reports we are compelled to acknowledge the event as literally internalized. The vulnerability of the ear then gives way to the distancing power of the eye. The trouble here is that we have not *seen* the fight and get only its carefully visualized aftermath. Whatever those sounds meant, the eye sees that it has opened too late. We are left looking on – standing by – without being able to help. What good then does it do to be ready? Norris's climax reminds us, in its structure and in its effect, of the way we always must read or watch a tragedy – that the greatest power its audience ever has is the power to care and wish, and that it is the powerlessness of these feelings to affect events, when they have been aroused, that makes them arouse in turn a sense of pity and fear.

Dabney falls, rises, and falls. He recapitulates the struggle of Dyke, Presley, Harran, and Annixter to discover the meaning of their uprightness within what increasingly proves tragic time and alien space. But the two sentences given Dabney achieve more than a brilliant plot summary of the lives of Norris's heroes. They sum up not only what Norris's novel means, but the ways in which he has been able to bring his art of expectation to bear on even the slightest detail so as to *make it mean*. Dabney receives his fate wordlessly, as if it were something about which it would be fruitless to complain. "He fell to his knees, got up again, fell once more, and died without a word." The three-part structure followed by "and" suggests the pattern beginning, middle, end – and epilogue. Dabney embodies in one sentence the story that we, as humans, are sentenced to. We come from and return to the earth. In between our "whence" and "whither," we try to rise.

Chapter 6

Steinbeck's lost gardens

================

Steinbeck's (1902–68) recurring hope was for happiness in a garden. He cultivated many plots along the way – in Los Gatos, Monterey, Sag Harbor, Somerset – but there was one to which he returned. The hope flourished in a cottage in Pacific Grove. The three rooms under the big pine had been the family's summer retreat since John's infancy. "This was the 'home' to which Steinbeck kept returning throughout his life." These are the words of his third wife, the one with whom he would succeed in making the cottage a home, and, in succeeding, surpass the need for it. In times of crisis (the year is 1948) it had been a place to come to:

> The thing makes a full circle with 20 years inside it. Amazing, isn't it? And what wonderful years and sad ending ones. I am back in the little house. It hasn't changed and I wonder how much I have. For two days I have been cutting the lower limbs off the pine trees to let some light into the garden so that I can raise some flowers. Lots of red geraniums and fuchsias. The fireplace still burns. I will be painting the house for a long time I guess. And all of it seems good.

Steinbeck was to call one of these big pines the "repository of my destiny," and it would overarch his experience in ways he could not have foreseen. He was to find and lose this garden many times. The rhythm of repossession and eviction so characteristic of his life was one that also came to shape the energies of his work.

This garden that Steinbeck loved and so carefully tended was to find, however, no direct description in his work. Instead its felt significance for him was caught up into what he called his "storytelling imagination." Robert M. Davis reminds us that Steinbeck was a fabulator committed to "fictional" rather than "empirical" forms, and he does not write of places, real or imagined, except insofar as it moves the

11. The pine tree in the backyard of the cottage at Pacific Grove, the tree John Steinbeck called "the repository of my destiny"

fable forward. Unique California landscapes offered him constant energy and renewal, but when he came to imagine them, they proved less a place than a stage. The service he performs his native state is to elevate it to a locale where two central and competing stories of his culture can again be played out. By touching only lightly on the local in what follows, I hope to show that it is the power of Steinbeck's work to transcend region that makes it such a successful tribute to its unique time and place.

Steinbeck's hope was for happiness in a garden, and "ecstasy" was the kind of happiness Steinbeck sought. This is his word, one on which his work confers two precise meanings. Steinbeck loved etymology (the *OED* was his favorite book), and so would probably not be surprised to learn that his vision of human happiness lodges itself in the tension between the conventional and literal meanings of a word. By "ecstasy" we ordinarily mean the passionate transport to loss of self with another in sexual love. When Steinbeck's work invokes this sense of ecstasy, it usually does so, as in "The White Quail," by insinuating it as a haunting, lost possibility. The kind of ecstasy reserved for those characters who cannot rise to sensual self-abandonment is the literal kind, *ec-stasis*. To stand beside the self, to be self-conscious, to be the self's own best companion – this is the fate of Mary Teller and, in less obvious ways, of most of the members of Steinbeck's erotic partnerships. There is a continual displacement in Steinbeck of the shared ecstasy of love by the solitary ecstasy of self-consciousness.

He typically images this impasse as the failure to share love in a garden. His men and women find themselves isolated together in appallingly beautiful California enclosures. The shadow that stays their coming together is something fundamentally self-possessed – even auto-erotic – at the heart of a woman's experience. It is as if Milton's Eve had never turned away from her face in the pool. The challenge to Steinbeck is to recognize the temptation to withdraw into a space of one's one cultivation as not a female but a human bequest. In *The Grapes of Wrath* he reconceives self-consciousness as sympathetic imagination, and so endows his characters with the power to relocate and share in vision those natural spaces in which they had seemed destined to loss and divorce.

THE FLIGHT FROM ECSTASY

Steinbeck's career tells many stories: of the dance between the one and the many (the "phalanx" theory); of the primacy of middles over ends ("nonteleological thinking"), of the "warring qualities," not of light and darkness but of different kinds of light (see the last page of his last novel). These are themes set in motion, embodied in patterns of plot and imagery that we are asked to locate in no single work but to follow through the sequence of the whole. Steinbeck called the emergent patterns in a career "the long structure." Work flowed into work in an "inevitable stream." The image claims for continuity what it relinquishes about control. A man works toward, not from, any awareness of design: "A man has only a little to say and he says it over and over so it looks like a design. And the terrible thing is that I still don't know what it is I have to say, but I do know it isn't very complicated and surely it isn't new." Steinbeck's career tells, however consciously, many stories. The one I want to trace in this section of the chapter is the prolonged fantasy through which he sought to escape one of his deepest themes.

Steinbeck's best books try and usually fail to establish a place where ecstasy can be shared by the sexes; the lesser works are linked by their will to literalize a paradise of men. Wanderlust is the option by which his strong characters are repeatedly tempted; the choice is between home and the road. His lesser characters so easily resolve this tension – in favor of home – that we may doubt the offered resolution. What their stories give us, in fact, are pseudo-homes, places in the sun empty of the women who could give them eros, and tension, and continuity. From *Cup of Gold* (1929) to *East of Eden* (1952), Steinbeck produced a series of books that parody the story he had to tell, one that he does tell in four honest and painful books of the thirties.

Cup of Gold begins with the homecoming of a man cast out of his native valley by the cruel fruits of wanderlust:

> Maybe the telling will ease me, and maybe I can speak it out and forget about it for one night. I must go back to the damned place. I can never stay away from the jungle anymore, because its hot breath is on me. Here, where I was born, I shiver and freeze. A month would find me dead. This valley where I played and grew and worked has cast me out for a foul, hot thing. It cleans itself of me with the cold.

What he has been cast into is the New World, the continent across which the emigrating Steinbecks and Hamiltons would wester until reaching California. Settling there in another valley, they would meet and cross and raise a boy who would ease the selfsame loss with telling. Dafydd's tale of exile sends Henry Morgan out and away, although he promises to "be coming back very often for my blood's sake." He never returns, banished by his piracy from his beloved Wales. He fancies that he has centered his wanderlust on an object, the fabled La Santa Roja. "This woman is the harbor of all my questing." Once captured, she spurns him easily, for it is only *as a fantasy* that he has longed for her, or lost home. "There was no desire in him for a state or condition, no picture in his mind of the thing to be when he had followed his longing; but only a burning and a will overpowering to journey outward and outward after the earliest risen star." Henry's education ends in the loss of the two things (home and a woman) he thinks he wants; his author's begins when he learns that Henry's insidious appeal lies simply in his wanting no wants.

A recurring event in Steinbeck is the inheritance or willing of a house. This is the action of *Tortilla Flat* (1935), *Cannery Row* (1945), and *Sweet Thursday* (1954), although it surfaces as well, and with much different effect, in the boxcars and barns of *The Grapes of Wrath,* the lost family seat in *The Pastures of Heaven,* and the broken dream of homestead in *Of Mice and Men.* In the parodic novels, the house is found to be extraneous to true happiness, and a kind of moral credit accrues to those who outgrow the need for one, as crabs out of their shells. A happy man needs no localized home – this is the glib conclusion enforced by Danny's relief at the fire that destroys his inheritance. *Tortilla Flat* celebrates all of the prejudices that encouraged Steinbeck's lifelong dismissal of a domesticity about which his serious books would at least summon a considered ambivalence.

Steinbeck admitted that the book was written in "direct rebellion against all the sorrow of our house." John and Carol had recently moved back to Salinas to take up a prolonged deathwatch over his mother. As he wrote and waited, his father suffered a collapse from which he, too, would never recover. *Tortilla Flat* projects a world in which there are no mothers or fathers, no wives, no children, no work or property – in short, nothing to lose. Humor results here from the avoidance rather than the sublimation of pain. In *Tortilla Flat,* Steinbeck first deploys an Arthurian superstructure in order to valorize the extravagance of knightly quest. But he omits the cycle's countervailing emphasis on disciplined cultivation of a center, and so omits the essence of Arthur himself. Despite his contempt for Tennyson, Steinbeck's vision of Arthur falters for the lack of what that poet so convincingly voices, a healthy skepticism of quest:

> And some among you held, that if the King
> Had seen the sight he would have sworn the vow.
> Not easily, seeing that the King must guard
> That which he rules, and is but as the hind
> To whom a space of land is given to plow.

Who may not wander from the allotted field
Before his work is done; but, being done,
Let visions of the night or of the day
Come, as they will; and many a time they come,
Until this earth he walks on seems not earth,
This light that strikes his eyeballs is not light,
This air that smites his forehead is not air
But vision – yea, his very hand and foot –
In moments when he feels he cannot die,
And knows himself no vision to himself,
Nor the high God a vision, nor that one
Who rose again: Ye have seen what ye have seen.

Arthur chastens the returning knights with an experience their wanderings can neither produce nor comprehend. By staying home and doing
his work he wins through to a condition of grace much more enduring
than any glimpse of the Grail. The fallen world need not be given up
here – we notice the emphasis on the enabling parts of the body – in
order to achieve the light of vision. For the man who may not wander
from his field there lies always ready to hand the rooted ecstasy of the
domestic sublime.

Steinbeck followed *Tortilla Flat* with two books of formal brilliance
and moral vision. *In Dubious Battle* (1936) and *Of Mice and Men* (1937)
belong to the parodic sequence by virtue of participating in its central
fantasy; in their tragic sense of the fate of this fantasy in the world, they
forward the project carried out by Steinbeck's works of antithetical
imagination.

The story of a strike begun by a fall from an apple tree makes Steinbeck's most ambitious case for the power of male solidarity. Steinbeck
achieves this goal, as Howard Levant has shown, through a strict control of rhythm and image. His deployment of a "slow sullen movement" builds an overpowering suspense, while his figurative language
is so brilliantly focused (the recurring image is of a directed beam of
light) as to exclude awareness of the ranges of experience the story
omits. The book channels our anger toward injustices that transcend in
their urgency any sense that Steinbeck may also be avoiding a career
theme. While reading *In Dubious Battle* we are compelled by the sense
that economic reform must precede any further pursuit of happiness,
domestic or otherwise.

Of Mice and Men begins with two men walking into a peaceful
garden:

Evening of a hot day started the little wind to moving among the
leaves. The shade climbed up the hills toward the top. On the

sand banks the rabbits sat as quietly as little gray, sculptured
stones. And then from the direction of the state highway came the
sound of footsteps on crisp sycamore leaves. The rabbits hurried
noiselessly for cover. A stilted heron labored up into the air and
pounded down river. For a moment the place was lifeless, and
then two men emerged from the path and came into the opening
by the green pool.

This is a purified image of the utopia George and Lennie hope to set up.
The image and the hope are marred by the intrusion of a woman.
Curley brings a wife to the ranch. She is "trouble." Her sheer presence
haunts the story like a doom, and the book courts the gallantry of
Milton's Adam before Christ – she stands accused as not the co-author
but the agent of the fall.

Steinbeck has allowed, however, for a more complex vision of blame,
and one implicit from the book's opening pages. The primal intrusion is
not the female into the male world, but the human into the natural. The
"sculptured" peace into which George and Lennie first intrude itself
suffers a fall. For a moment, in the interval of transition between the
natural and the human order, the world becomes "lifeless." The human
is radically out of place, not at home in a deeper sense than George and
Lennie imagine. Displacement is the theme, and what distinguishes this
fantasy of male retreat from its counterparts is George's half-conscious
awareness of the fictionality of the hope for home. "I think I knowed
from the very first. I think I knowed we'd never do her." It is a fiction he
sustains out of love. He knows that the garden exists only in the head,
but unlike Crooks ("Nobody never gets to heaven, and nobody gets no
land. It's just in their head"), he does not convert this knowledge into
paralyzing irony. In its tragic awareness that promised "land" exists
securely only in the mind, *Of Mice and Men* anticipates the full exploration of this theme in *The Grapes of Wrath*.

The Log from the Sea of Cortez (written in 1941; expanded and
reissued in 1951) purports to record the events of a six-week scientific
expedition to Baja California. It is actually a careful fictionalizing of a
trip that omits the central fact that Steinbeck's wife went along. Steinbeck's letters praise Carol's shipboard behavior: "Carol is beginning to
be homesick for her garden. But she has been marvelous on this trip. I
don't know any other woman who could have done it." His exclusion
of her from the account of the voyage allows Steinbeck to tell instead
the story of a wandering fellowship. Although he had in fact taken
home along, he transforms the story into one of venturing out and
return. "Leave-taking" and "homecoming" arouse the deepest emo-
tions here. "It would be good to live in a perpetual state of leave-taking, never to go nor to stay, but to remain suspended in that golden

emotion of love and longing; to be missed without being gone; to be loved without satiety. How beautiful one is and how desirable; for a few moments one will have ceased to exist. Wives and fiancées were there, melting and open. How beautiful they were . . ." As if to complement this assertion, Steinbeck will later tell the story behind a "rough wooden cross" near the beach at San Lucas. "A man had come from a fishing boat, sick and weak and tired. He tried to get home, but at this spot he fell down and died. And his family put the little cross and the candle there to mark the place." The man's story becomes a lesson, "a slow painful symbol and a pattern of his whole species which tries always from generation to generation, man and woman, which struggles always to get home but never quite makes it." "Home" here is created out of the experience of absence. Even the life of Ed Ricketts, that least domestic of heroes, is redefined in *The Log* as a "deep and endless nostalgia-thrust and passion for 'going home.' " Missing home emerges indeed as the human condition, though, having brought along his wife and his best friend on the *Western Flyer,* it is presumably not a condition Steinbeck endured on this trip. In the words of its glossary, *The Log* proves a book about "Tropism" – the "Innate involuntary movement of an organism or any of its parts toward (positive) or away from (negative) a stimulus." The "stimulus" is a localized home, and the "organism" is an author caught up in an imaginative movement "toward" or "away from" a place whose effective presence he sets out to repress.

Cannery Row celebrates the instant canniness of temporary structures. "The Palace became a home." Mac and the boys reenact the story of *Tortilla Flat.* Settlement again proves a function of magic rather than work. When we call such novels sentimental, we mean, in Joyce's words, that they display the desire to enjoy without acknowledging the debtorship for a thing done. The thing enjoyed is a new concept of "home." The thing to be done is a testing of this concept over time. But clearly this has not been done. These books protect their characters from loss by walling them off from the world of contingency. The strain culminates in the gothic undiscipline of *East of Eden.*

In its fascination with the exaggerated displacements of desire, the gothic can achieve an unveiling of the wishes that underlie our social and psychological conventions. In Steinbeck's hands it becomes rather a mode for begging the hard questions. Instead of prompting him to interrogate the structures in which men and women try to live together, the gothic encourages him to create a woman so "monstrous" that shared ecstasy can only entail, for a man, spiritual suicide. *East of Eden* disappoints because we feel that in it Steinbeck has attempted a massive evasion of its promised theme.

The Edenic theme is explicit. "I mean to make a garden of my land.

Remember my name is Adam. So far I've had no Eden, let alone been driven out." This is an authentic facing up to a challenge already rendered moot. For Adam Trask and his author have collaborated in falling for an Eve with whom it is impossible, given her innate "tendencies," to share the garden. Since her "sexuality" is something her husband neither wants nor understands, the book becomes a story about an Adam who refuses to fall. He lives in the world but not of it, and his renunciation of desire is expressed through his ignoring of place. After losing his Eve, he refuses to farm. The novel proceeds to deal with the aftermath of this attenuated fall; attention shifts from the "Garden of Eden" to "Cain and Abel." It sees the latter story as the "father" of all stories, and the hell of parental rejection assumes imaginative priority, in Steinbeck's reading of the Bible, over the story of "original sin." So the anguish of descent replaces the anguish of sexual innocence and guilt as the novel reconceives the primal human story as an affair of fathers and sons. The final affirmation and forgiveness take place in a world in which the need for maternal love has been rendered extraneous. What we see here and throughout the line of novels that preceded it is an attempt to start history over, to undo the fall by avoiding the problem of sexual division. Steinbeck struggled all his life not to tell the story he was born to. He thought it was the cycle of a brotherhood (the fall of Camelot), but it was simply the Fall of Man.

LOSS OF EDEN

Steinbeck's best work naturalizes in his home state the central Western legend of loss. During the thirties he wrote four books that deal, in sequence, with the acts of settlement, corruption, fall, and eviction. California is the garden lost. Steinbeck treats his birthplace as a natural and an imaginative fact. Although its specific locales and landscapes shape the course of a story's action, its location on a map of the mind converts it into a kind of national or even racial destiny, the end point of man's incessant "westering." Steinbeck's contribution to the literature of region is to discover ways in which the unique features and history of a place can be discreetly raised up toward the status of myth.

Claiming the garden

Near the end of *To a God Unknown* (begun in 1928; published in 1933), Joseph Wayne and his brother journey from the drought-ridden Jolon Valley over the hills to the seacoast. In this foray toward the edge of things, Steinbeck entertains the possibility of a different career. *To a God*

Unknown is a book about the inability of California's interior valleys to sustain continuous life. It deals with the pressures unique to cultivated life in a bounded space, and one subject to violent fluctuations of weather. (One of the first important observations about Steinbeck, by Harry Moore, was that he habitually locates his action in a valley.) Survival in such places demands a collective effort, or at least a solidarity between two. But here, in this country of mist, shade, rock, and tide, Joseph comes upon a solitary with no interest in realizing himself through "plotted . . . squares of green." Weather here obscures form, and the landscape urges meditation rather than shared labor. Nature invites lapsing out, the transgression rather than the cultivation of boundaries. It is the landscape of Robinson Jeffers. Joseph Wayne wants to found and share his happiness in an arable space, and so this journey to the end of the West proves a vacation, not a turning away. He rides back to his dying ranch and plants himself there as a sacrifice to the potential fruitfulness of the land. His last act is a measure of his author's determination not to wander, as he sets out on his imaginative career, from his allotted field.

As the century turns, Joseph Wayne receives the blessing from his father and rides west from his native New England. The grass is green on the hills in California when he arrives. He settles in one of the little corridors that branch northward into the Coast Range from the Salinas Valley. Soon his brothers join him. Two spots concentrate Joseph's sense that this land is "holy" – the oak tree by the house, and the boulder in the glade. He and schoolteacher Elizabeth fall into sudden love, and he brings her as a wife to the valley. Burton, the pious brother, fearful of Joseph's easy pantheism, girdles the tree. Drought sets in, and Elizabeth slips and kills herself in a fall from the boulder. Joseph spills his will for planting into his brother Thomas's wife, and then gives her Elizabeth's child as the families flee the dying land. Alone on the ranch, he opens his wrists and, as his body grows "huge and light," rises up to become the oncoming rain.

This is a book torn between belief in what Blake would call natural religion and Poetic Genius. The novel's suppressed motto is voiced by Elizabeth, after she visits the boulder in the glade: "Nothing was in that place except my imagination." Its announced theme is rather that imagination and place interpenetrate each other with almost jealous possessiveness. Joseph openly believes that the land inspires him, but his actions suggest as well that he inspires the land. What brings on the drought? Burton's act of malice, itself answered by the malice of nature, or the cycle of the California seasons, indifferent to and unaware of human hopes? Steinbeck's narrative allows for either interpretation. His interest lies less in the object than in the experience of belief, and seen in this way, the book presents Joseph's conviction of the continuity between the human and the natural as generous and enabling. Steinbeck musters his verbal resources to Joseph's aid; the style sides with the hero. The narrative voice discovers symbols ("there was a curious femaleness about the interlacing boughs and twigs") as readily as the dialogue resolves into epigrams ("Everything's food"). The effect is of a looming portentousness, a sense that a subtext lurks everywhere had we but eyes to see it. Because the landscape here is the primary object of attention, we are directed toward it by the novel's style as a text asking to be read, as, in its own words, "a trail of innumerable meanings." The triumph of the Pathetic Fallacy is complete, but the question of whether man projects nature or nature man is kept precariously open.

Joseph establishes his garden, and then invites a woman into it. Steinbeck's quest for shared ecstasy begins in the scene where Joseph and Elizabeth, just married, cross into the awaiting home valley. She hesitates fearfully at the pass, face-to-face with a landscape that bodies forth the initiation to come:

> The mountain was split. Two naked shoulders of smooth limestone dropped cleanly down, verging a little together, and at the bottom there was only room for the river bed. . . . Midway in the pass where the constrained river flowed swift and deep and silently, a rough monolith rose out of the water, cutting and mangling the current like a boat prow driving speedily upstream, making an angry snarling whisper.

Joseph explicates the scene: "Here is a boundary. Yesterday we were married and it was no marriage. This is our marriage – through the pass – entering the passage like sperm and egg that have become a single unit of pregnancy." Elizabeth tries to fend off this ecstasy with a habitual autoerotic self-consciousness: "I'll have to go, but I'll be leaving myself behind. I'll think of myself standing here looking through at the new one who will be on the other side." The continuing threat to happiness in Steinbeck is that these two halves of the self can prefer the romance of doubling to the romance of coupling. Elizabeth chooses to walk on with her man. And she walks on into the valley of marriage with a foreknowledge Eve never knew: "It's a bitter thing to be a woman. I'm afraid to be. Everything I've been or thought of will stay outside the pass. I'll be a grown woman on the other side."

Life for Elizabeth can be said to begin in this moment: It marks her fall into identity, sex, and location in the world. For all of her fear, this coming upon herself as she walks through the pass is a pain not unmixed with pleasure: "The bitterness of being a woman may be an ecstasy." Joseph says this, and the "may" registers his and his author's hope that what they propose to do with and for women in taking them as wives is to help explore the space in which they can best become themselves. Penetration of this place corresponds, therefore, to Elizabeth's anxious awareness of the imminent reshaping of her bodily space. Steinbeck's profound insight, here and elsewhere, is that marriage consists of the mutual cultivations of an exterior space that reflects and gives public and permanent status to the shared ecstasy found in an inner one.

Joseph's urge to author a marriage in a garden does not go unpunished. The idea of an avenging natural catastrophe came to Steinbeck in early 1932, when the cyclical drought that had brought the actual Jolon Valley to its knees finally broke. These "recent" and "tremendous events" inspired Steinbeck to revise his novel. He decided to "cut it in two at the break and work only at the first half." The act of founding and cultivation in the novel's first half is thus answered, in the second and revised ending, by an act of natural undoing. Insofar as the drought can be taken to be an intentional act, the conclusion suggests that the Waynes are to be punished for violating their contract with a place. But it also allows Steinbeck to avoid having to elaborate on the role assigned to a man settled in a garden. *To a God Unknown* explicitly confronts the choices that must be faced in order to become "a woman," but remains evasive about what really must be given up in order to become a married man. California weather serves Steinbeck as an agent that suspends by destroying the author's uneasy experiment with domesticity. Home is broken up, and life returns to the road. Steinbeck has no doubt written here a novel about the tension between "imagination" and "place," but it is just as surely one in which the sedentary imagination is prevailed upon by the peripatetic. The difficulty of settled life in California will henceforth serve Steinbeck as a vehicle through which his deeply conflicted imagination explores the chances for happiness in any *place*.

Intrusion of the serpent

Steinbeck located his first short-story sequence in the Corral de Tierra, the small valley east of Carmel where he had spent weekends as a boy on his aunt Molly's ranch. He explained to Mavis McIntosh that the

valley was for years known as the happy valley because of the unique harmony which existed among its twenty families. About ten years ago a new family moved in on one of the ranches. They were ordinary people, ill-educated but honest and as kindly as any.

In fact, in their whole history I cannot find that they have committed a really malicious act nor an act which was not dictated by
honorable expediency or out-and-out altruism. But about the
Morans there was a flavor of evil. Everyone they came in contact
with was injured. Every place they went dissension sprang up.

On this legend Steinbeck builds his book.

The antagonist of *The Pastures of Heaven* (written in 1931; published
in 1932) is not a person but a curse. The book deals with the liability of
gardens to intrusion, and the ways in which the plots men cultivate in
space fatally attract a disrupting force from without. Each plot Steinbeck here cultivates in time enacts the same pattern; the twelve stories
betray a compulsion to repeat that suggests that the fate of man in this
"protected valley" is, simply, man's fate. "The damned serpent" always intrudes – this is the given of which the Munroes, hapless carriers
of misfortune, merely prove the local instance.

The sequence is distinguished by the apparent innocence of its surfaces. The characters betray little depth, inwardness, or capacity for
suffering, and the narrative issues from a distanced and mildly rueful
voice. The losses here memorialized include insanity, murder, prostitu-
tion, exile, fire, and sudden death, but under Steinbeck's hand all
"grow somehow pastoral, idyllic, seen through this amber light, as we
might watch the struggle of fishes and water snakes in the depths of a
mountain pool." T. K. Whipple's complaint that Steinbeck's style anes-
thetizes us to the very violence it conjures up hits home here. Consider
the scene in which the first snake strikes. John Battle, his mother insane
and his dour father recently dead, returns to his ancestral farm, convinced that it is haunted:

> One day in the deepening twilight John crept carefully upon a lilac
> bush in his own yard. He knew the bush sheltered a secret gather-
> ing of friends. When he was so close that they could not escape,
> he jumped to his feet and lunged toward the lilac, flailing his stick
> and screaming. Aroused by the slashing blows, a snake rattled
> sleepily and raised its flat, hard head. John dropped his stick and
> shuddered, for the dry sharp warning of a snake is a terrifying
> sound. He fell upon his knees and prayed for a moment. Suddenly
> he shouted, "This is the damned serpent. Out, devil," and sprang
> forward with clutching fingers. The snake struck him three times
> in the throat where there were no crosses to protect him. He
> struggled very little, and died in a few minutes.

This scene inverts the mode of *To a God Unknown*. The world of *The
Pastures of Heaven* is neither symbolic nor numinous; the hysteria of

character here is a pure projection into neutral space, and the tendency of life in this world toward disaster is simply bad luck raised toward the level of a causal principle. Steinbeck's interest is in the fact that evil will intrude, not in the losses it entails. In the face of this conviction, he adopts the icy calm of a fairy tale. To summon any emotion to the account of an inevitable abruption would express disarming vulnerability in the author himself.

If the curse of this "happy valley" is its liability to intrusion (the well-meaning Munroes do poison everything they touch), the dream it breaks is, again, shared ecstasy in a garden. These are dramas of invitation, and it is men who again try and fail to plant a wife in a prepared spot. "He kept the garden waiting for her." In the wake of his wife's insanity, John Battle's father sticks with his farm and makes his second try at love. "This farm was a poem by the inarticulate man. Patiently he built his scene and waited for a Sylvia. No Sylvia ever came." Pat Humbert refashions his home into the "Vermont house" that will win him pretty Mae Monroe. The very night he proposes to let her see it he learns of her engagement to another man. The pattern culminates in the story of Richard Whiteside. "I shall build a structure so strong that neither I nor my descendants will be able to move." He founds his Sutpen-like dynasty to see it wither into a chain of only children. When Bert Monroe accidentally sets fire to the "big, luxurious house," the loss simply confirms the dispersal of hope brought on by third-generation Bill, who has already glibly rejected his landed inheritance for a life with Mae in Monterey. The flaws that bring these people low are internal to the designs they project, however much Steinbeck draws attention to a violating force from without. The Munroes simply body forth the vanity of the human wish to rule out "accidents of blood," to control the space into which one invites the future. As in his first California book, the logic of his plot obscures the burden of his theme.

But the theme has at least been broached. In *To a God Unknown* and *The Pastures of Heaven,* Steinbeck courageously announces his hope for shared ecstasy and proposes the external threats to its fulfillment. In *The Long Valley* he will write a book that locates the threat to happiness in a garden squarely within the human heart.

The fortunate fall

The brilliance of *The Long Valley* (1938) consists in the way in which its structure comprehends and deepens, through a process of extension and revision, its initial themes. Though written over a period of six years, its fifteen sections cohere into a single story that culminates in "The

Promise." We enter the valley as a claustrophobic garden, swerve into male fantasies of self-sufficiency and escape, recur to the knowledge of "female troubles," regress to a boyhood of pure "longing," endure the distress of boyhood changing into man, and exit by way of the mythical past, where the pattern man describes on the land is not a plotted square but the sheer untrammeled movement called "westering."

Steinbeck asks us to participate here in a process of maturation in which his characters take up their stations with varying degrees of reluctance. This is a reader's book, one in which he is offered the chance to become the hero of a trial of recognition and growth. *The Long Valley* is built out of second thoughts. Reading here, as in the Good Book, becomes a matter of the ways in which an original bequest or testament is not denied but revised and fulfilled by a later one. And the story told, after all, is the same story: A garden made, given, and marred in the receiving has to be redeemed by an act of sacrifice that transvalues the human capacity for acceptance and the very nature of the gift.

The two opening stories in *The Long Valley* read like a script for "Eve's Revenge." In "The White Quail" the isolated female will objectifies itself in a garden as a compensation for the failure, so touchingly rendered in "The Chrysanthemums," to achieve ecstasy with a man. The sexual impasse enjoys a brief suspension in "Breakfast," but not until the collection's penultimate story does Steinbeck break through to a new vision of the life men and women can share. The third part of "The Red Pony" reconceives the relation of the sexes within the context of Steinbeck's first working nuclear family, and initiates a boy into the facts of life that Steinbeck's earlier characters had been unable to face or unwilling to accept. *The Long Valley* is the book in which Steinbeck finds a form that not only expresses his deepest conflicts but that attempts a resolution of them.

Steinbeck begins with "The Chrysanthemums" because of the power of its imagery and dialogue to establish, almost subliminally, this world's dimensions and conditions of being. He admitted that the story engages the reader in a discreet seduction: "He reads it casually and after it is finished feels that something profound has happened to him although he does not know what nor how." The action is simple enough. As Elisa Allen works in her garden her husband Henry strolls by to make a date for the evening to come. She chooses a movie over the fights. A tinker in a wagon then pulls into the yard. He offers to fix whatever needs mending. Elisa talks with him about gardening and life on the road. She offers him nothing to fix until he engages her about her chrysanthemums. She gives him some cuttings, and then finds some pans to mend. After he rides away she hurries indoors, washes herself vigorously, and dresses for the evening. As she and her husband ride toward town, she sees the discarded slips in the road. Suddenly she asks Henry about the fights, but now, "crying weakly," settles instead for a dinner with wine.

A husband fences himself off from his wife's desire. A stranger arrives who wants work but instead is offered a gift. A woman wants to give herself, but she is the only taker. Longing is called up only to be displaced again, into the ground or down the road.

The enclosure into which we are first invited offers a security akin to imprisonment. These are the opening sentences of *The Long Valley:* "The high grey-flannel fog of winter closed off the Salinas Valley from the sky and from all the rest of the world. On every side it sat like a lid on the mountains and made of the great valley a closed pot." Yet the land lies waiting, expectant that the fog will lift, hopeful of fertilization: "On the broad, level land floor the gang plows bit deep and left the black earth shining like metal where the shares had cut . . . the orchards were plowed up to receive the rain deeply when it should come." Place here images the isolation of character within the space of the self as well as the desire to break out of that space. A temporarily closed but potentially receptive world, the Salinas Valley participates in the unfolding drama of courtship for which it may seem the mere site.

Elisa Allen overpowers her flowers with an excess of desire. "The chrysanthemum stems seemed too small and easy for her energy." Although her femininity is obscured ("Her figure looked blocked and heavy in her gardening costume, a man's black hat pulled low down over her eyes, clod-hopper shoes, a figured print dress almost completely covered by a big corduroy apron"), power flows out through her "strong fingers." Elisa's zealous nurturance of her sprouts prepares us for the inattention with which she greets her husband. She starts at the sound of his voice, though he has been continuously within her view. He talks to her from the other side of a fence, speaking into a preserve "protected" from the ongoing activities of the farm. The formal way in which husband and wife praise each other further suggests that they keep and view their achievements as separate. Henry on her flowers: "You've got a gift with things." Elisa on his sale of the steers: "Good," she said, "Good for you." It is the "you" that hurts here; the success does not seem to belong to "us." But it is the word "good" that registers the real pain. Elisa repeats it thrice more in response to Henry's suggestion of dinner and a movie. It sounds like little more than a slightly automatic response to a mildly enticing prospect. But the word acquires a chilling resonance by the story's end, when husband and wife are left alone together after the tinker has gone. A stock response becomes, as she speaks loudly above the motor, a protesting too much: "It will be good, tonight, a good dinner." Given the crisis of emotion that Elisa has just undergone, "It will be good tonight" echoes back through her story and our sense of the history of the marriage as a hope desperately and repeatedly unfilled.

For what happens to Elisa Allen is that she reaches out toward the wandering tinker with a need he is no more able to fill than is her settled and uncomprehending husband. A man appears out of nowhere, pulling a "prairie schooner." He has the gift of language: he echoes ("When they get started"), jokes ("That's a bad dog in a fight"), makes similes ("Looks like a quick puff of colored smoke?"), and lies ("I know a lady down the road a piece"). He engages Elisa in a verbal rather than a physical exchange, and the crucial act of language is one in which she interrupts and completes his attempt to describe the passions of his nights. This allows for an intimacy deeper than anything she shares with Henry, though the mode of exchange and the tinker's eventual rejection of the gift posit a gap that is never crossed.

By taking a feigned interest in her act of nurturance, the tinker arouses Elisa's buried desire. (She has perhaps not noticed his horse and donkey, which droop "like unwatered flowers.") As she struggles to express the rhythmic ecstasy of "planting hands," her breast swells "passionately." The tinker hovers on the brink of falling for her:

> The man's eyes narrowed. He looked away self-consciously. "Maybe I know," he said. "Sometimes in the night in the wagon there – "
>
> Elisa's voice grew husky. She broke in on him, "I've never lived as you do, but I know what you mean. When the night is dark – why, the stars are sharp-pointed, and there's quiet. Why, you rise up and up! Every pointed star gets driven into your body. It's like that. Hot and sharp and – lovely."

Elisa is the first woman in Steinbeck to assume an understanding of what a man feels on the road, and she does it by assimilating those feelings to her own experience and capacities. This is an ecstasy of penetration in which actual loneliness in the event is compensated for by the shared imagining of it.

What makes "The Chrysanthemums" painful to read is our foreknowledge, gained by way of image and direct authorial asides, that the tinker cares nothing for Elisa at all. It is a story in which we watch a woman courageously reaching out to discover common ground with a man. But at the height of their apparent communion he quickly brings her down: "It's nice, just like you say. Only when you don't have no dinner, it ain't." Elisa is blocked not only by male insensitivity or wanderlust, but by the intensity of her own desire, which tends to close itself off from true discourse, of words or of the body. This is what happens after the tinker leaves:

> In the bathroom she tore off her soiled clothes and flung them into the corner. And then she scrubbed herself with a little block of pumice, legs and thighs, loins and chest and arms, until her skin was scratched and red. When she had dried herself she stood in front of a mirror in her bedroom and looked at her body. She tightened her stomach and threw out her chest. She turned and looked over her shoulder at her back.

If the recoiling male instigates this withdrawal into self-regard, it is an act consistent with the Elisa we meet before he arrives, who enjoys a self-sufficiency bordering on solipsism. She has a gift with "things," not presumably, with people, and there is no mention of a child. She nurtures a world she can control, just as the tinker follows a road of which he is the master. Elisa's appeal is that she seems to merge these male and female orientations in a capaciousness proof against the pathos of gender. But while she fantasizes about an unrooted life – "That's a bright direction. There's a glowing there" – she subsides back into a rooted one. By the story's end she is no longer feminine *and* masculine but a mere wife, willing to take on all the qualities that traditional role implies. "The Chrysanthemums" enforces the view that the fate of passionate men and women is to seek their fulfillment in different kinds of space, and that their ecstasies therefore remain radically separate.

If "The Chrysanthemums," as Steinbeck said, "is designed to strike without the reader's knowledge," "The White Quail" announces its themes with an explicitness unique in Steinbeck. It can be read in fact as an exemplum of the career. This is the story in which Steinbeck openly defines the two kinds of "ecstasy" (the story repeats the word five times) that govern his characters' emotional fates.

"The White Quail" moves toward the moment where "Mary Teller, Mrs. Harry E. Teller, that is," confronts the image of her doubled self. The story begins with a female god inviting Adam into her imaginary garden: "Would the garden like such a man?" She marries Harry because "the garden seemed to like him," and in Part Two realizes her dream in a place. Although Harry admires the completeness of her projection – "I like too much to see your own mind coming out in the garden" – he senses that he is only a creature in her creation. "You're kind of like your own garden – fixed, and just so. I'm afraid to move around." Though they squash the invading snails together, the Tellers cannot quell Mary's growing fears of an invading "enemy." The withdrawal of the body into a garden paves the way for the withdrawal of the mind into itself, where it safely becomes its own best company. Mary's world is a solipsistic creation in which the mind seeks to find only "its own resemblance," but, unlike the speaker of Marvell's "The Garden," she does not withdraw *in order* to return refreshed to the world of time, society, and relationship. The Tellers' individual bedrooms (Mary locks her door in "answer to a question, a clean, quick, decisive answer") preserve for Mary the possibility of the epiphany of separateness that occurs on the night she goes out to retrieve the shears:

> She went out into the garden and found the shears, and then she looked in the window, into the living room. Harry was still reading his paper. The room was clear, like a picture, like the set of a play that was about to start. A curtain of fire waved up in the fireplace. Mary stood still and looked. There was the big, deep chair she had been sitting in a minute ago. What would she be doing if she hadn't come outside? Suppose only essence, only mind and sight had come, leaving Mary in the chair? She could almost see herself sitting there. Her round arms and long fingers were resting on the chair. . . . "What is she thinking about?" Mary whispered.

This is Steinbeck's most theatrical staging of the psychological state that edges out shared ecstasy. " 'There were two me's,' " she thought. "It was like having two lives, being able to see myself." This "me" will even echo, though without Marvell's quiet irony, the self's wish to keep company only with its own semblance:

> Two paradises 'twere in one
> To live in paradise alone.

Or as Mary puts it, "How I would like to come to my garden for the first time. If I could be two people – 'Good evening, come into the garden, Mary.' " Mary gets her wish when she sees the white quail:

> Out of the brush ran a white quail. Mary froze. Yes, it was a quail, no doubt about it, and white as snow. Oh, this was wonderful! A shiver of pleasure, a bursting of pleasure swelled in Mary's breast.

A crescendo of ecstasy descends on Mary as she confronts her own purified image:

> "Why," Mary cried to herself, "she's like me!" A powerful ecstasy quivered in her body. "She's like the essence of me, an essence boiled down to utter purity. She must be the queen of the quail. She makes every lovely thing that ever happened to me one thing."

The white quail dipped her beak again and threw back her head to swallow.

The memories welled in Mary and filled her chest. Something sad, always something sad. The packages that came; untying the string was the ecstasy. The thing in the package was never quite –

The marvelous candy from Italy. "Don't eat it, dear. It's prettier than it's good." Mary never ate it, but looking at it was an ecstasy like this.

"What a pretty girl Mary is. She's like a gentian, so quiet." The hearing was an ecstasy like this.

"Mary, dear, be very brave now. Your father has – passed away." The first moment of loss was an ecstasy like this.

By perfecting her capacity for self-conscious hovering over potential experience, Mary rules out the time-bound experiences of sexuality and loss. Pleasure consists in holding off, in the self's awareness of incipient rather than consummated sensation. Mary's whole history of "ecstasy" culminates in a timeless garden of her own making, face-to-face with an image of a self poised forever on the brink of fall.

When Harry shoots the quail he tries to start the story of his marriage over, to restore the possibility of fall. But the husband who takes revenge on the image of the wife's self-sufficiency only discovers his own profound isolation. He has been living in but not of Eden. The story ends with Adam restored to his original status, voicing his primal cry: "Oh, Lord, I'm so lonely!" So we end at the beginning, with all the work still to be done, imprisoned in a garden with an Adam who has brought death into the world without having known the consoling sin of love.

The stories that follow "The White Quail" deal with the pursuit and avoidance of forbidden kinds of knowledge. Pepé's precipitous initiation into manhood ("I am a man now, Mama") coincides with his death, and the fatality of his ambition throws into question the matriarchy that sends him out and away. In "The Snake" a man tempts a woman with the gift of scientific knowledge ("A desire to arouse her grew in him"), but not before she has come to him with a veiled offer of sex. "Breakfast" begins with a sentence that might be spoken by a woman – "This thing fills me with pleasure" – though in fact the story is spoken by a man. More than the first-person narrative voice (rare in Steinbeck) here mediates the sexes; in its momentary fusion of home and the road, "Breakfast" insinuates that we really can have it both ways. It is the story of uncanny hospitality, of a man happening on a moment of domestic bliss in the middle of nowhere. A wanderer comes upon a tent and a stove tended by a young woman, a baby in the crook of her arm:

> I was close now and I could smell frying bacon and baking bread, the warmest, pleasantest odors I know. From the east the light grew swiftly. I came near to the stove and stretched my hands out to it and shivered all over when the warmth struck me.

He is welcomed like an old friend, yet no one knows or speaks any names:

> "Had your breakfast?"
> "No."
> "Well, sit down with us, then."

He arrives, eats, and leaves. "And I walked away down the country road."

It is the quality of his memory that puzzles the speaker here. "I don't know why, I can see it in the smallest detail. I find myself recalling it again and again, each time bringing more detail out of a sunken memory, remembering brings the curious warm pleasure." What he comes upon when he remembers is a universal human bequest liberated from location and history, a primal warmth innocent of identity and relationship. To establish this warmth in a place where people call each other by name – in a home – is the difficult task of Steinbeck's most courageous short story, "The Red Pony."

The two original sections of "The Red Pony" were written, according to Steinbeck, with "no consecutive effort." The story was first published in 1933. "If it has any continuity it is marvelous," Steinbeck wrote. "I can't think of any possible medium which would include it." He would eventually discover that medium, but not before concluding that his original scheme in the story had been incomplete.

In "The Gift" a pony is given and dies; in "The Great Mountains" a dying man returns to the place of his birth. The two-part story ends with these words: "A longing caressed him, and it was so sharp that he wanted to cry to get it out of his breast. He lay down in the green grass near the round tub at the brush line. He covered his eyes with his crossed arms and lay there a long time, and he was full of a nameless sorrow." Jody's desire for experience has been aroused, but his faith in its power to satisfy has not been requited. Death has come into his world without the promise of deliverance. His story is like our first fall before the promise of new life; knowledge is the bitter consolation for loss.

Steinbeck declares his dissatisfaction with this scheme in "The Promise." The third part of "The Red Pony" was written near the end of 1936 and first published in 1937. In it Steinbeck returns to his original material in order to conceive a story in which initiation delivers the possibility of hope. In so doing, he completes "the medium" – the story sequence called *The Long Valley* – that can include his original story.

A sentence in "The Gift" had alluded to Jody's sense of "uncertainty in the air, a feeling of change and of loss and of the gain of new and unfamiliar things." *Gain* only balances out *loss* in Steinbeck's second try, which becomes a story about a second chance. A new pony is born. Jody's is the story in which a disastrous initiation can take on, through the logic of later events, the character of a fortunate fall.

"The Red Pony" actually consists, in its final version, of four parts. Steinbeck added also a section called "The Leader of the People," in which Jody's grandfather struggles to maintain his life by telling stories about the movement west. The parts of this fourfold structure fall into two related pairs. In sections 1 and 3, Jody receives and tries to be worthy of a gift; in sections 2 and 4, old men attempt to die on their own terms. The two sets of stories balance and answer each other; if the first set deals with the pain of human beginnings, the second affirms the persistent significance of those beginnings, now transformed into an imaginative preserve, in the way we shape our ends. Structural as well as thematic parallels within these paired sections suggest that Steinbeck returned to his material in a conscious act of retelling.

"The Gift" and "The Promise" each begin with a son alert to the terms in which he must honor gifts from the father. Jody lives in a world in which "Punishment would be prompt." Obedience is the issue from the start. "The triangle picked him up out of sleep. It didn't occur to him to disobey the harsh note." Curiosity is a trait that must be muffled. Jody wants to ask about the day's doings, but refrains: "His father was a disciplinarian. Jody obeyed him in everything without questions of any kind." (Billy Buck is a mediator who answers questions, as when he initiates Jody's sex education by pointing to the spot of blood in the egg: "That's only a sign the rooster leaves.") Jody's one rebellion in this kindly regimented garden is to point a gun at his house. It is unloaded. "Two years was enough to wait for cartridges. Nearly all of his father's presents were given with reservations which hampered their value somewhat. It was good discipline." With his internalized conscience fully established, Jody seems prepared to accept and honor the father's imminent gift. But the story turns on negligence and bad luck, not disobedience, and as the pony's frustrating sickness takes hold, Jody endures a loss for which he bears no responsibility.

In "The Promise," Steinbeck makes the Adamic situation explicit. There is the same indirect and portentous announcement of a gift: Carl Tifflin's "I'm going to need you in the morning" becomes, in "The Promise," his wife's "your father wants to see you." The son's response is conditioned and immediate: "Do you – is it something I did?" Jody lives in the shadow of a guilt-inducing father, and his young mischief is continually checked by the knowledge that in this garden "it was impossible to know what might later be construed as a crime." In "The Gift," Jody commits no crime but is punished anyway; in "The Promise" he participates in what Yeats calls "the crime of death and birth" and is delivered, by his willingness to bless and forgive the process, into a hard-earned sense of life's painful sweetness.

"To start right at the start": this is what Carl Tifflin wants, in Billy Buck's words, for his son. Whereas in "The Gift," Jody receives a gift that he loses without fully comprehending, in "The Promise" he engages from the start in generating the very nature of the gift. Jody is again offered a pony, but one he must help to "raise . . . up." He walks Nellie to the ridge ranch and insists on watching her be bred. Sexuality here incarnates itself as a crazed stallion, and any lingering questions over what the rooster leaves are laid to rest. Then Jody must wait. In talking with Billy during the gestation, Jody faces squarely the possibility that the colt may be lost, and learns that birth sometimes forces a choice between lives. "My ma died when I was born," Billy Buck tells him. It is having bungled the first gift that haunts Billy, and he determines that Jody will not again suffer from the fallibility of the fathers, even if something dear to him must be sacrificed. So, instead of offering Jody a *gift* that he is unprepared to defend, Billy makes him a *promise* that carries with it the awareness of how hard it may be to keep.

The promise, when it is fulfilled, is a hard and bitter agony:

> Billy dropped the knife. Both of his arms plunged into the terrible ragged hole and dragged out a big, white, dripping bundle. His teeth tore a hole in the covering. A little black head appeared through the tear, and little slick, wet ears. A gurgling breath was drawn, and then another. Billy shucked off the sac and found the knife and cut the string. For a moment he held the little black colt in his arms and looked at it. And then he walked slowly over and laid it in the straw at Jody's feet.

This is no less painful than the loss of the first pony; what differs is the quality of the pain. Jody is here a knowing participant, not an innocent bystander. In this ending he wrestles death (see the buzzard at the end of "The Gift") to a draw. New life comes out of loss, but, unlike Nick's initiation in Hemingway's "Indian Camp," there is no looking away. Jody has set himself to take the "black" along with the "white." He has already reconciled himself to imperfect love; restitution comes, as it always must, in the form of a substitute. Jody has in the process engaged the facts of life with greater courage and opportunity for insight than any of Steinbeck's more mature characters. If death is half the gift, something does survive to grow and be nurtured; not just a pony, but the possibility of Jody's full and passionate life.

The significance of Jody's story for *The Long Valley* and for Stein-beck's entire career is that in it he gives all of his characters a second chance by imagining a life which from "the start" confronts and accepts the terms within which mature ecstasy is possible.

As Jody falls into time, he falls out of a sense of belonging in place. His favorite retreat by the mossy tub becomes uncanny as the pony's illness deepens. "The place was familiar, but curiously changed. It wasn't itself any more, but a frame for things that were happening." Parts Two and Four of "The Red Pony" enlarge upon this emotion as the condition of old age. The grandfather's story repeats Gitano's; both are about the difficulty, as one nears death, of recovering the physical and emotional space of home. Both stories begin with old men walking toward a place where they are not welcome. "I have come back," Gitano says, but the hard lesson is that he returns only to a house now washed into the earth. Return is the theme, but the grandfather's story suggests that life is a movement out and away. "Once made, no step could ever be retraced": This is Jody's impression of his grandfather's physical gait, but it characterizes as well the man's lifelong fascination with the act of "westering." "It wasn't Indians that were important, nor adventures, nor even getting out here. It was a whole bunch of people made into one big crawling beast. And I was the head. It was westering and westering. Every man wanted something for himself, but the big beast that was all of them wanted only westering." For the grandfather this "movement" has become the condition of human life, and so when he comes "home" he returns less to a place than to a memory of a process with no destination. Grandfather at once em-bodies the origin and eventual fate of life in the Long Valley, which Steinbeck hoped, as he said, to make "the valley of the world." In a world of perpetual expulsion from Ede "westering" becomes a meta-phor of the potential and compensatory mobility of the spirit, a free-dom paradoxically bound up, as Jody's story suggests, with the actual cultivation of the hearth. Jody stands between his nostalgic but imagi-native grandfather (to whom he listens) and his rooted but unreflective father (whom he obeys) as a figure capable of extravagance and disci-pline, one who lives at once in a promised and an actual land.

At the garden's gate

Having established a working family in "The Red Pony," Steinbeck extends its structure in *The Grapes of Wrath* (1939). The Joads begin as family-bound provincials. They go on to re-form a jealously guarded intimacy into one where no man is a stranger. Warren French calls this process the "education of the heart"; J. P. Hunter has shown how the "widening of concern" culminates in Rose of Sharon's offer of her breast. The movement is outward toward larger and more inclusive structures, "from 'I' to 'we.' "

The Grapes of Wrath also marks the end of Steinbeck's conception of home as a place. The opening up of the family corresponds to a movement west in which the Joads discover the human power of indwelling. This is the power Tom invokes in his farewell speech, one he makes after finding that California will not provide his family a localized home. This promised land resists all attempts at entry, and so inspires, through its economic and geographical inaccessibility, a sublimation of the will to settle into citizenship in an immaterial domain of belonging.

Locating the first third of the action on the road is the book's major imaginative act. Steinbeck begins his book outside that "valley of the world" – California – that he had so carefully cultivated during the thirties as the site for his best work. We start east of Eden, and the book becomes a struggle to reenter a paradise from which we have become separated by space, if not divorced by the very nature of time. We begin with loss and move toward the possibility of gain. This is Steinbeck's first wholly postlapsarian book, one that focuses on the consequences of rather than the imminence of fall. Man is now stationed in the middle rather than at the beginning of history, and wandering is no longer a male but a human prerogative.

Peter Lisca argues that in *The Grapes of Wrath,* Steinbeck moralizes the necessity of motion. He reads the ongoing turtle as an embodiment of "the indomitable life force" that "drives the Joads." Life here does seem equipped and therefore perhaps intended for motion rather than fixity. It is "armed with an appliance of dispersal" and possessed of the "anlage of movement." The travel-readiness of the vegetable and animal worlds is met, however, by a reluctance to move in the human one ("They're just goddamn sick of goin' "), and the motion into which the Joads are propelled may be less a behavior affirmed than a condition to which they must adapt. When Steinbeck argues in Chapter 14 that the California migration is a "result," not a "cause," he defines that movement as a function of a state of dispossession, though one more primal than eviction from an Oklahoma farm.

For what *The Grapes of Wrath* imagines is a world without origins or ends, one in which archaeological thinking is no more appropriate than teleological thinking. Its characters believe that they have only temporarily given in to the road: "Folks out lonely on the road, folks with no lan', no home to go to. They got to have some kind of home." But the novel never delivers more than a momentary stay against the confusion of moving on. Man is the thing always on the way, and "way" becomes the word that here takes in the emerging sense of the finality of death and the uncertainty of life.

Casy begins as a man who wants to lead the people somewhere. Tom wonders why: "What the hell you want to lead 'em some place for? Jus' lead 'em." Steinbeck undercuts Tom's nonteleological thinking by having the narrative suddenly produce a goal-bound dog: "A thick-furred yellow shepherd dog came trotting down the road, head low, tongue lolling and dripping. . . . Joad whistled at it, but it only dropped its head an inch and trotted fast toward some definite destination. 'Goin' someplace,' Joad explained, a little piqued. 'Goin' for home maybe.' " The joke on Tom reminds us of the tenacity of those nostalgias the novel cannot requite. As the journey west unfolds, Casy reluctantly discards the hope for an end. "Seems to me we don't never come to nothin'. Always on the way." The experience of the way comes to dominate the imaginations of the major characters – Tom, Casy, and Ma. While they elaborate an understanding of the "way" out of their unique historical moment, this emerging vision universalizes itself into something akin to "the human condition." Like that other great book about westering toward California, George Stewart's *Ordeal by Hunger* (1936), *The Grapes of Wrath* becomes a study of human thrownness in which the act of moving through a landscape images an infinite and ever-receding supply. Steinbeck seems to have set himself the task of recovering the story of California's repulsion of the Donners in his own place and time. In both stories the human "way" has only one sure end, and our view of it remains obscured:

> "This here ol' man jus' lived a life and jus' died out of it. I don' know whether he was good or bad, but that don't matter much. He was alive, an' that's what matters. An' now he's dead, an' that don't matter. . . . He's awright. He got a job to do, but it's all laid out for 'im an' there's on'y one way to do it. But us, we got a job to do, an' they's a thousan' ways, an' we don' know which one to take."

Despite the certainty of death, the uncertainty of how to approach it converts life into an end-less or open-ended way. *The Grapes of Wrath* is not just a book about the difficult "way" to California; its subtle rhetoric generalizes the project into the problem of learning to live in existential time.

The very book in which Steinbeck fully establishes the claims and appeal of "home" is thus also the one in which he renders such places illusory or untenable. This is most strikingly demonstrated in his return to the fantasy of "Breakfast." Steinbeck incorporates the story into the middle of Chapter 22. Tom Joad has now become its protagonist. He wanders in and out of the story in a way that registers a dramatic shift in Steinbeck's attitude toward human destinations.

The core of the fantasy remains unchanged; we come upon the tent in the dawn, the promise of warmth, the nursing woman and her two men, the easy offer of a meal. But Tom here comes out of some-where – the moving and dwindling solidarity that the Joad family has become. When asked if he has eaten, the first thing Tom thinks of is the others: "Well, no, I ain't. But my folks is over there." And he comes with the intention to work. In "Breakfast" the wanderer's answer to the question "Picking cotton?" had been a simple "No." Tom's answer to the same question is "Aim to." When the men offer to "get" him "on," the wanderer says, "No. I got to go along." Tom says, "Well, that's mighty nice of you." The sudden generosity of the world sur-vives here, then, and fulfills itself in a purpose more abiding than the lovely pleasures of the moment. There is no walking "away down the country road." Instead, Tom returns to his tent, alerts Ruthie, and walks out to earn his bread with the sweat of his brow.

The pathos of this episode is that it refuses to become, for the Joads, more than a short story. The warmth and hope it offers are too tempo-rary to cast anything more than an ironic light on the surrounding text. We happen on an ecstasy no longer attractive or credible to Steinbeck; now he wants to earn such grace. But earning a home is precisely what this world will not allow, and our appetite is aroused only to have our hunger unappeased.

Instead of a local habitation with a name, *The Grapes of Wrath* offers a reformation of the lonely ecstasies in which his earlier characters stood imprisoned. Isolating self-consciousness is raised up, as Tom broods on a shared homelessness and a potential human solidarity, into an unvul-nerable realm of concern. We no longer try to occupy a spot, but survive, through love and imagination, in an "everywhere." Tom takes leave of his mother, but it is really impossible to say good-bye:

> "I'll be all aroun' in the dark. I'll be ever'where – wherever you look. Wherever they's a fight so hungry people can eat, I'll be there. Wherever they's a cop beatin' up a guy, I'll be there. If Casy knowed, why, I'll be in the way guys yell when they're mad an' – I'll be in the way kids laugh when they're hungry an' they know supper's ready. An' when our folks eat the stuff they raise an' live in the houses they build – why, I'll be there."

This speech marks the culmination of Steinbeck's major phase. He has learned the value of home while losing belief in the possibility of it. The strong books of the thirties have been moving toward Tom's qualified affirmation, one in which Steinbeck naturalizes the great myth of the West in *his* West. Tom appeals to the time-honored consolation for the loss of an earthly garden. As a departing Adam stands at the gates of Eden, Michael comforts him with the promise that if he adds love to faith, he will come to "possess / A paradise within thee, happier far." The beauty of the episode lies in the dreaming Eve's simultaneous incorporation of the promise, an act that enables her to voice, as she wakes to depart with her husband, the poem's radical insight about the relation of person to place. In a world where the wind is finally left to farm the dust, there is still left us the unlocalized garden of human love: "all places thou." Eve then takes Adam by the hand, and they begin walking. If they look back, they look back to see a flaming brand over paradise, the way an Oklahoma family would one day look back at a receding home to see "the windows reddening under the first color of the sun." Walking becomes their destination and their destiny, and the world in which they seek "Thir place of rest" resolves itself, not into a vale of privileged sites, but, in the last word of Milton's poem and the key word in Steinbeck's book, into a "way."

UNDER THE BIG PINE

Steinbeck abandoned California as a permanent home in 1941, two years after the publication of *The Grapes of Wrath*. The decision to depart may be attributable to the state's failure to right the wrongs exposed in the novel. (He was certainly no longer welcome in California; the undersheriff of Santa Clara County warned him not to go into a hotel room alone. "The boys got a rape case set up for you. You get alone in a hotel and a dame will come in, tear off her clothes, scratch her face and scream and you try to talk yourself out of that one. They won't touch your book but there's easier ways.") California remained what it had been since the breakup of the big ranchos, a state in which power on the land was concentrated in the hands of a small group of large landholders. Freeman Champney (writing in 1947) argued that "in its extremes of wealth and destitution, in the absence or impotence of any middle group representing the public interest, and in the domination of the organs of civil life by irresponsible private greed, it has been one of the few areas of American life that has closely approximated the Marxian predictions about capitalist society." If Steinbeck's reasons for moving focused on this persistent structure, he may have looked upon his proletarian novel as an insufficient sacrifice, a labor of anger and love that failed to redeem his native ground. He leaves a home he is unable to change.

Steinbeck's act of "eastering" consumed a decade before coming to an end in a "nice little house in New York" in 1950. In his letter writing during this time, personal concerns command his attention. It was his private failure to find ecstasy in his birthplace that most visibly troubled Steinbeck. What had been a dominant paradigm in the work now seemed to shape his interpretation of his life. The resolutions of the books of the thirties came to pose themselves as a desideratum for the man himself, and his inability to cultivate happiness with a woman in California ended, finally, in his moving away.

"It could have been ecstatic": This is Steinbeck summing up his first marriage, which ended in divorce from Carol Henning in 1943. They had separated in 1941, after a marriage of eleven years. Steinbeck had fallen in love with Carol while she typed his first manuscript in the confining winter of the Sierra Nevada. They had lived a mildly bohemian life until the income of the late thirties catapulted them into the middle class. With money and fame came the tensions of ownership, and as their marriage resolved into a dispute about how and where to live, husband and wife were driven apart.

In his resolutely unspeculative biography, Thomas Kiernan ventures one interpretation of Steinbeck's broken first marriage. Husband and wife came to grief over Carol's attachment to the ranch near Los Gatos:

> Where before she had been content to live under the plainest of conditions and in the simplest of surroundings, now she seemed to aspire more and more to all those middle-class values that he had long despised. . . . Upon settling in at the remote ranch, it was as if she had attained the pinnacle of her life's ambition. She was content to live the secure, quiet existence afforded by the ranch and to gather about her all the things that would provide them with comfortable self-sufficiency. In transforming herself in this way, she subtly demanded the same form of contentment and satisfaction from John.

Steinbeck had initially favored the Los Gatos venture as an "escape" from "the nasty fogs" of Pacific Grove. Four years after the move he could still say that "the ranch is wonderful now and I resent any time spent away from it. Cherries are just getting ripe and the vegetable garden is finally supplying food and we make our own butter and cheese and have lots of milk to drink." If when away Carol was "homesick for her garden," John was also capable of missing it. As his marriage deteriorated he would fasten, however, on her rootedness and possessiveness of place: "I'm very glad that you like the ranch. It is so beautiful that often I am embarrassed to be living here. I think it would be a better thing to visit than to own. But I haven't any sense of ownership about it anyway. If I think of owning, I consider it Carol's ranch and feel that I really am just visiting it." After moving out of the hills Steinbeck would speak of himself as having been deluded into the role of "gentleman farmer." If such feelings provided a rationalization for divorce, they also expressed an abiding ambivalence about the relation of person to place. Steinbeck's reluctance to put down roots had a long history and would have an even more complicated future. The major actors in this story were his first two wives, but an active part was played as well by a place rather than a person – the garden under the big pine.

The cottage in Pacific Grove had been the Steinbeck summer home since just after John's birth. Its cool fogs provided a retreat from the Salinas heat. At twenty-eight John had written Carl Wilhelmson about the enduring significance of the tree that shaded the garden:

> You know the big pine tree beside the house? I planted it when it and I were very little; I've watched it grow. It has always been known as "John's tree." Years ago, in mental playfulness I used to think of it as my brother and then later, still playfully, I thought of it as something rather closer, a kind of repository of my destiny. This was all an amusing fancy, mind you. Now the lower limbs should be cut off because they endanger the house. I must cut them soon, and I have a very powerful reluctance to do it, such a reluctance as I would have toward cutting live flesh.

At sixteen John discovered sex at the cottage with Maria, the Portuguese cleaning girl from Monterey. He brought Carol there after a few months of marriage spent in Eagle Rock. A year later he wrote that "My garden is so lovely that I shall hate ever to leave it." Six years after settling in the cottage the Steinbecks moved to Los Gatos and toward Carol's dream of the ranch.

Steinbeck would effect two important returns to Pacific Grove. In January 1941 he separated from Carol and moved into a newly purchased home near the cottage with Gwyndolyn Conger. They left for New York that summer. After Gwyn's request for a divorce in 1948 he made a second and last retreat to Pacific Grove, this time to the cottage itself. It was there that he restored his broken spirit and met Elaine Scott, who was to become, in December 1950, his third wife. Their move to New York in the fall of 1949 would mark the end of Steinbeck's life as a Californian, and the end of his need for the house under the big pine.

Marriage to Gwyn crystallized Steinbeck's attitudes toward happiness in a place. The affair he began with her in 1941 exiled him from the cottage. When he left Carol's Los Gatos ranch and took Gwyn to

Pacific Grove, it was not to the family seat but to a "little house" on
Eardley Street. While enjoying there a newfound sense of "hospitality,"
Steinbeck also began to amplify his sense of himself as unequipped for
ambitious settlement: "I was kidding myself thinking I was a gentleman
farmer. I'm not. I'm half bum and half voluptuary and half workman
and that makes me one and a half of something and that isn't enough."
He could think of himself and his new companion as two homeless
ones cast up together: "Do you know that the little time in the Grove is
the only time since she was a little girl that she ever had a home? And
oddly enough it is the only time I ever had one either." In view of the
almost immediate breakdown of this relationship, Steinbeck's astonish-
ment about falling into a "hospitable house" may strike the ear, like
many other statements he made about his second marriage, as the
sound of a man protesting too much. This "home" was in any case to
give way in two years to a move back to California. After the disastrous episode in Monterey ("Well there is no home coming nor any
welcome. What there is is jealousy and hatred and the knife in the
back.") the Steinbecks bounced back to New York. Before marrying
Gwyn, Steinbeck had detected and overlooked in her a drive toward
"security" greater than Carol's. What marriage to her would also reveal
was a self-admitted "restlessness" in both husband and wife that pre-
vented them from ever settling down.

Separation from Gwyn meant repossession of the cottage. (Steinbeck
wrote Bo Beskow in 1948 that "After four years of bitter unhappiness
Gwyn had decided that she wants a divorce.") His abiding resource was
the possibility of this place, a place he had not lived in continuously
since 1936. Just before leaving New York he wrote a friend that "I have
great sadness but no anger. In Pacific Grove I have the little cottage my
father built and I will live and work in it for a while." Steinbeck went
on to write about "how little I do need," and then returned to the fact
of the cottage. "My father built it before I was born. It has only three
rooms and a little garden. But it's a pleasant little house with big trees
and I think I will go back to it. Carol and I lived in it for years. I don't
for a moment think I will be unrestless there but I'll be restless and
lonely anywhere. But at least it will be a place for the transition time
and a place to work and I can always leave it." The collapse of his
second marriage was the crisis of Steinbeck's life. With unerring instinct
he effected a return that would at once complete an interrupted career
and initiate a new one.

The work he returned to was gardening alone.

This whole place is a mess but in two weeks you won't know it.
Garden will be cleaned and replanted and the house will be

painted inside and out. And during that time I do not intend to
touch a pen to manuscript. My hands are getting calluses already.
I don't know many people here any more and that is a good
thing. It will be more time for working and reading. Oddly
enough I do not feel lonely at all yet.

Few periods in Steinbeck's life betray such a sense of self-satisfaction; he
had found another use for the hands. Always a gardener, he took to the
work with a vengeance, and the anger not absorbed by the earth found
its way to another target:

> My little garden . . . is a thing to go out to look at every morn-
> ing. Some new god damned little leaf is there or a flower is
> curling. And the great war against snails and varmints, which are
> only less destructive and poisonous than us, goes on ceaselessly, I
> kill them and stomp on them – an enemy – and I admire them
> quite a lot too because they can't poison or stomp me and yet they
> keep ahead of me. These things I can love. And I think I could
> love a European woman or a negress or a Chinese but the breed of
> American woman – part man, part politician – they have the minds
> of whores and the vaginas of Presbyterians. They are trained by
> their mothers in a contempt for men and so they compete with
> men and when they don't win, they whimper and go to psycho-
> analysts. The American girl makes a servant of her husband and
> then finds him contemptible for being a servant.

This is the worst side of Steinbeck's work in Pacific Grove: gardening
as the misogynist's revenge. The cure he had sought out was to carry
him beyond such bitterness, although not without involving him in a
pattern of irony. For what Steinbeck became in those healing months of
1948 and 1949 was a character out of his own fiction, one who founded
his happiness in a garden upon the exclusion of a mate.

Steinbeck recommenced his life by recovering in it the circumstances
of our human beginnings. History stood abolished. He wrote from the
cottage that "sometimes it seems to me that nothing whatever has
happened. As though it was the time even before Carol." He spoke
again and again about the pleasure of "being alone." An Adam now
alone in a garden of his own cultivation, he prepared it unwittingly for
the eventual Eve. He met Elaine Scott on Memorial Day of 1949, ten
months after returning to Pacific Grove. With Elaine, Steinbeck tried,
in the words of *The Long Valley,* "to start right from the start." This
was not just one more try; throughout the next nineteen years, John
preserved a sense of his marriage to Elaine as unprecedented. She was a
repetition that delivered him from the need to repeat. A newspaper

The lady of the house is the author's third wife, the former Elaine Scott. They **were** married in 1950. Steinbeck **has two sons by second marriage.**

12. John and Elaine Steinbeck

photograph of John and Elaine years into their marriage bears the caption: "The lady of the house is the author's third wife, the former
Elaine Scott." In tribute to this original love, the man of the house has
scrawled on the margin: "She's really the *first* wife."

Marriage to Elaine was also founded on the growing conviction, as
Steinbeck put it, that "living is people, not places." Steinbeck had

voiced this sentiment in the third year of his marriage to Gwyn, but it was only after repossessing his California garden that he was able to live up to it. Elaine spent time at Pacific Grove, and they were happy there. She spoke of it as John's home, but he was quick in answering her to redefine the term: "I think I have no 'place' home. Home is people and where you work well." Over the years of this last and fulfilled marriage, he would return to this theme. "I have always been a mobile unit in wish if not in actuality. . . . I even go through the form of establishing a home. But it's only a place to go away from and to come back to. I am fortunate in that Elaine has my same restlessness. She will move at the stir of a suitcase." Their shared love of motion was certainly a powerful bond; restlessness became, in what was also the most settled of Steinbeck's marriages, a condition accepted, even embraced. Just as crucial to the success of the marriage, perhaps, was John's having outgrown the sense that a man's love for a woman depends on the possibility of a "retreat." No longer would John's tree, and the shadowy garden underneath it, be the "repository" of his destiny. It was in 1930 that he had first written about the need to cut the lower limbs. Eighteen years later he returned to the garden and began pruning the pine. It was a task that could no longer be put off; it was time, as he said, to let in the light.

Chapter 7

Chandler, marriage, and
"the Great Wrong Place"

Landscape south of Tehachapi resolves into a subdivision of the mind. Joshua Tree, San Gorgonio, the Channel Islands – these outposts of wilderness make little impress on the whole. It has been like this from the start in Southern California. Actual development came late (Los Angeles expanded from 12,000 in 1884 to 50,000 in 1887), but the Anglo-American experience of the Los Angeles basin nevertheless began as one in which the extension of a mental grid over physical space ruled out unmediated natural encounter. The vast ranchos marked out by nothing more than a skull on a post staked their claims with a fiction of ownership as thoroughgoing as the miner's forty square feet of pay dirt. In theory there was little free space. And the land booms that tried to lure the first large populations confronted the immigrant with whole towns laid out in comforting right angles, lots that were to become nothing more than homes for tumbleweeds. "In Los Angeles County in the two principal boom years," Franklin Walker tells us, "there appeared sixty mushroom towns with more than 500,000 lots and less than 2,500 people in all of them put together." T. S. Van Dyke's novel about the boom, *Millionaires of a Day* (1890), initiates the tradition of life in the basin as a fantasy of development gone wrong. His Virgilian hopes for a country of small landholders lost in a "maze of green" contracts into the fact of real estate, "a sufficient acreage chopped up fine enough." Oppression of space by the human casually reverses itself, for Joan Didion, into oppression of the human by space. Life in California is an ironic victimization of scale in which some abiding natural fact – the lack of water, the Santa Ana winds – chastens any extension of the will. In her recent collaboration with her husband on the screenplay of his novel *True Confessions* (1977), she scripts a morality play in which developed space enacts its revenge; fantasies of domination over the City of Angels end in "exile" in the desert, burial in "the middle of all that goddam sand."

13. Agoraphobia: Robert DeNiro and Robert Duvall approach their grave plot in *True Confessions*

Landscape and the will: These are the antagonists in the best work about Southern California, and the victories are not, as in Didion, always Pyrrhic ones. The region even claims its simple celebrants. Margaret Collier Graham hymns the pastoral quietude of its ranches in *Stories of the Foot-Hills* (1895). In *Life in the Open* (1906), Charles Frederick Holder urges the region upon his fellow sportsmen as the world's most abundant larder. Peter Viertel's *The Canyon* (1940) is a luminous evocation of boyhood in Santa Monica's canyons. These books deal with what nature offers, not with what man has done, and it is with this problem, finally, that the strong imaginations of the region have had to grapple. This is just what Reyner Banham has done in the most persuasive book about adaptive life in the golden land. "Whatever man has done . . . to the climate and environment of Southern California," he argues, "it remains one of the ecological wonders of the habitable world. Given water to pour on its light and otherwise almost desert soil, it can be made to produce a reasonable facsimile of Eden." In *Los Angeles: The Architecture of Four Ecologies* (1971), Banham trains his architect's eye on the essential regions into which the region is quartered: Surfurbia (the beaches), the Foothills, the Plains of Id (the flats), the Autopia (the freeways). This is a sociologist's vision, one that accepts and measures the "built form" that gives Los Angeles its unique fluidity. Los Angeles emerges as the first American city to have made natural space fully responsive to the perpetual "sense of having room to manoeuvre." The tension, for Banham, is not between freedom and form; in Los Angeles, freedom *is* the form.

Although a tradition of description and even celebration of landscape in Southern California does survive, the most powerful work about the region deals with the human incorporation of space. No writer has been more sensitive to this process than the creator of Philip Marlowe.

Raymond Chandler (1888–1959) thrusts his imagination into a place claustrophobically formed. His Los Angeles may seem at first the disposable wasteland of West, Waugh, and Pynchon. Compared to their jeremiads there is something in Chandler's abiding obsession with the city, however, that takes on the nature of a lover's quarrel. Chandler belongs to the tradition of those who came not to visit. but to stay. He had to find a way to rationalize the fact of his fidelity to the place. He took pride in having been, in his words, "the first writer to write about Southern California at all realistically." The motto for his work could be borrowed from the state's most ambivalent nineteenth-century booster, Hinton Rowland Helper, who boasted in *The Land of Gold: Reality Versus Fiction* (1855) that "California can and does furnish the best bad things that are obtainable in America." How the best can become the bad, how the wrong lies buried within the right: This is the mystery of Chandler's career, and one he raised up and dignified into a serious theme. Thus, W. H. Auden, in his essay on detective fiction, can set Chandler apart as engaged in a project uniquely his own: "I think Mr. Chandler is interested in writing, not detective stories, but serious studies of a criminal milieu, the Great Wrong Place, and his powerful but extremely depressing books should be read and judged, not as escape literature, but as works of art."

One site in Chandler's novels sums up his sense of the wrongness of the present place and the implied rightness of the past. It is also the first major enclosure imagined in his first novel, the greenhouse in *The Big Sleep*:

> The path took us along to the side of the greenhouse and the butler opened a door for me and stood aside. It opened into a sort of vestibule that was about as warm as a slow oven. He came in after me, shut the outer door, opened an inner door and we went through that. Then it was really hot. The air was thick, wet, steamy and larded with the cloying smell of tropical orchids in bloom. The glass walls and roof were heavily misted and big drops of moisture splashed down on the plants. The light had an unreal greenish color, like light filtered through an aquarium tank. The plants filled the place, a forest of them, with nasty meaty leaves and stalks like the newly washed fingers of dead men. They smelled as overpowering as boiling alcohol under a blanket.

Through successive acts of penetration (the voice notates doors, walls, roof, and tank) Marlowe approaches Chandler's heart of darkness. Here flowers are confused with flesh. The secret Chandler's novels have to tell is revealed at the outset, and it is of a voraciousness that swallows up the natural world. What has been lost here is the whole realm of the "outside." The hero finds himself submerged in a totally humanized space. Marlowe's Southern California is *made* space: not just one that man enters, but one for which he alone – so extravagant has been the extension of his will – is responsible.

Chandler is a failed pastoralist, and his work can be read as an elegy for the "Good Green Place" he had known and lost. His early years were English years, and absent England was destined to haunt his vision of present Los Angeles. Born in Chicago in 1888, Chandler summered in Nebraska until his parents' divorce. At seven he sailed with his mother to England to take up residence with a grandmother and an aunt. In 1900 the household moved from South London to the 1,500-acre Dulwich Valley, where they lived across the playing fields from Dulwich College preparatory school. Chandler graduated from Dulwich at seventeen, prepared for the civil service in Paris and Munich, and entered the Admiralty as a clerk of Naval Stores. He quit after six months and struggled along as a journalist until, at twenty-three, he set sail for America. On the steamer he met the Warren Lloyds, a cultured family from Los Angeles who would eventually introduce him to his future wife. It was his acceptance of their invitation to visit that brought him, some months later, to California.

When Chandler settled in Los Angeles in 1912, he brought with him more than the principles and inhibitions of the public school code. His life would be marked by an abiding nostalgia for England, by a sense of "exile from a world he thought he loved." A poem written in 1932 shows that twenty years had only sharpened his taste for the lost site of culture, respite, and hierarchy:

> There are no countries as beautiful
> As the England I picture in the night hours
> Of this bright and dismal land
> Of my exile and dismay.

The poem reads like the subtext of his incipient career; Chandler wrote it in the year he decided to become an author.

If the values Chandler associated with England can best be described as "pastoral," it is because his vision of the city exposes the ways in which nature and culture collide. The pastoral conceives a world of continuous and cooperative dialogue between the given and the created, a nature in which man is set free to be more fully himself. Marlowe moves through the landscape of monologue in which the human has absorbed the natural and now tries to create the illusion of it. It is the omission of undomesticated landscape from Chandler's Los Angeles that gives his books their special mood of encroachment. Natural space where noted is assimilated to the geometry of development – "the flawless lines of the orange trees wheeling away like endless spokes into the night" – or imminent doom: "There was loneliness and the smell of kelp and the smell of wild sage from the hills. A yellow window hung here and there, all by itself, like the last orange. Cars passed, spraying the pavement with cold white light, then growled off into the darkness again. Wisps of fog chased the stars down the sky." It was not only England, it was prewar Los Angeles that had been lost, as Marlowe muses in *The Little Sister*:

> A long time ago. There were trees along Wilshire Boulevard. Beverly Hills was a country town. Westwood was bare hills and lots offering at eleven hundred dollars and no takers. Hollywood was a bunch of frame houses on the interurban line. Los Angeles was just a big sunny place with ugly homes and no style, but

goodhearted and peaceful. It had the climate they just yap about now. People used to sleep out on porches. Little groups who thought they were intellectual used to call it the Athens of America. It wasn't that, but it wasn't a neon-lighted slum either.

If Chandler's novels appropriate the universal theme of the ruins of time, they also register an impassioned protest against meretricious progress. Instead of simply recurring to a lost plaisance, Chandler writes a "complex pastoral" in which the longing for a garden poises itself against the determination to confront the world of the machine.

Why did Chandler proceed to unite his angry pastoral with the novel of detection? If England stood behind his vision of place, an experience equally profound sent up Chandler's sense of plot. "The story is this man's adventure in search of a hidden truth." In "The Simple Art of Murder" Chandler applies this formula to Philip Marlowe, but, in looking at the life, we can apply it as well to Chandler himself. His story is of a man in search of a hidden truth, and the search that was to become the plot of his novels has a significant source in his mysterious and wonderful marriage.

One fact dominates Chandler's adult life: His wife was seventeen years his senior. Chandler had known Julian and Cissy Pascal in Los Angeles before the war, and when he returned from the trenches in 1919 (he was the sole survivor of a German artillery attack on his unit), he and Cissy quickly fell in love. She was forty-eight; he was thirty-one. Frank McShane remarks that "In 1919 Cissy had strawberry blonde hair and a marvelous figure and complexion. She was lively and original and liked to be naked when she did housework. She was also an excellent cook of the old-fashioned kind. . . . Here was a woman with sexual maturity who also had the brains to be an intellectual companion as well." Cissy divorced Julian within six months of Chandler's return, but, as a considerate son, Chandler postponed the wedding for more than four years until after his mother's death. For the ceremony in 1924, Cissy listed her age as forty-three. McShane comments: "This was a deliberate deception. She was in fact fifty-three."

The first phase of Chandler's marriage appears to have been haunted by the gradual revelation of this "hidden truth." He would work eight more years for the Dabney Oil Syndicate and rise to vice-president before being fired for absenteeism and drinking. Why a man making a thousand dollars a month would put himself in a position to lose his job in the depths of the Great Depression has puzzled many, and McShane speculates that Chandler was driven to drink and other women by a growing awareness that he had allowed himself to be deceived. Within

five years of the wedding the "discrepancy" in ages had become evident. From the start of the marriage Chandler had often gone out
alone – tennis was his major social activity – and as the twenties waned
he began to drink heavily in public. "In the company of the young
wives of his friends and associates, he realized that he was missing the
quality of youthful love they were enjoying." In affairs with office girls
he tried to shake off "a wild feeling of despair." He often threatened
suicide. By the early thirties Chandler was sometimes absent from
work for weeks at a time. So serious became his drinking that in 1931
he and Cissy were forced to separate. In 1932 he was fired, at the age of
forty-four.

The Chandlers put their furniture in storage and began a nomadic life
in rented rooms. Silver Lake, Big Bear, Cathedral City, Pacific Palisades,
Riverside: The places sound a litany out of a Chandler novel. In 1946,
after fourteen years of life "constantly on the move," the Chandlers
settled in La Jolla. Cissy was seventy-six. The forty-thousand-dollar
house by the sea was a "reward" for the hard years. And the years had
been hard; there are few spectacles more moving than the loser in love
and work, turning back, in middle age, toward the lifelong desire to
write. Chandler had begun reading the pulps during the slack months
after losing his job, and he produced, between 1933 and 1939, twenty
stories based on their rigid formulas. In 1938, a good year, he made only
$1,275. The Chandlers had, during this time, almost no joint social life
and few friends. "I never slept in the park," he was later to say, "but I
came damn close to it." *The Big Sleep* came in 1939, and the break into
big money in 1943, when Billy Wilder asked Chandler to collaborate on
the script of *Double Indemnity*. James M. Cain was to speak of the Chandlers as "Hollywood's happiest couple," but on the night Chandler's first
movie premiered he invited his secretary to accompany him. He had
forgotten that it was also his wedding anniversary. By the time Chandler
fell into Hollywood, he had written his first four and most characteristic
novels. From 1943 until his death, his story becomes one not of trying to
overcome failure, but of staving off the distractions of success.

It is nearly impossible to imagine the life Cissy managed to live
during these years, shuttled about as she was from flat to flat, without
friends, or money, or work of her own, or children. She has no voice
that has survived. She collected editions of her husband's work. Above
all, she stayed. Dilys Powell, who knew the Chandlers in London, saw
her as a "smiling, propitiary figure whom he guarded and defended."
Her "fading eyes" contained "the look . . . of appeal." Certainly Raymond's awareness of Cissy's advancing age, as well as their almost total
isolation together for a decade, transformed the marriage into an intense
discipline of caring. McShane sees the hard years as a time of growing

solidarity between husband and wife. "Her willingness to endure hard-
ships spurred him on as a writer. In Chandler, the artist developed
through his own strength and through the knowledge that his wife
believed in him. There was a passion that encompassed the thing itself
and the artist who created it, working with the help of his wife. The
stories and novels that were to follow were, in a sense, their children."
If the novels were a product of the marriage, they grew out of its
darkness and secrets as well as its love. Love and marriage become, in
Chandler's novels, the site of secrecy itself, and the recognition that the
woman Chandler was to call "the light of my life" had lied in order to
keep him must, at some point, have shaped his sense of human story.
The mystery in the life is not when did he first discover Cissy's secret,
but how he came, as he apparently did, to accept it.

Chandler's seven novels trace a history of despair over and final
accommodation to the deceptiveness of surfaces. The ur-crime hides
itself behind a pattern of results, resemblances, and repetitions that
Marlowe must eliminate as peripheral and belated. Character exists to
confound plot; like Degarmo, other people set themselves against Marlowe's attempt to "let the whole story come out." The climax comes as
a moment of exposition in which Marlowe reorders details of the plot
into a sequence that locates the primal event at the beginning of the
story. The event is a betrayal that recurs. Plot in Chandler originates in
the "jealous rage" of disappointed love.

In Chandler's career the novels form an inverted parabola that bottoms out in *The Little Sister*. The downward arc of the first five novels
is offset in the last two by a quality we might call, to use Chandler's
word, "redemption":

	Places
The Big Sleep (1939):	haunting; discovery of the subtext
Farewell, My Lovely (1940):	transport; the trip; paranoia
The High Window (1942):	remembering and forgetting
The Lady in the Lake (1943):	dispersion of guilt; loss of shelter
The Little Sister (1949):	despair; loss of habitat
	People
The Long Goodbye (1953):	friendship and sympathy
Playback (1958):	marriage

In a fictional universe dedicated to the preservation of secrets, Chandler's attitudes toward place and person converge on the question of
trust: How much can we extend to a world not what it seems? Over the
course of twenty years Marlowe's growing disillusionment with place
is offset by his increasing reliance on people. The novels can, in fact, be

read as a deferred epithalamium in which an author searches for a woman with whom true marriage is possible. Very simply, the novels tell the story of a man who discovers that loyalty can undo a lie.

The Big Sleep. On page 1, the "knight in dark armor" that decorates the Sternwood entrance doors announces Marlowe's assumption of the quest. Marlowe is *like* the knight; Chandler opens a novel of similes with a simile that announces as well Marlowe's fall into the figurative. Things are at best not what they seem; at worst, wholly unlike what they seem. The dawning recognition that there is a level of significance beyond the literal makes detection necessary, and the casual assertion of resemblance ("I sure did run the similes into the ground," Chandler later admitted) betrays Marlowe's need to bridge the gap between a revealed vehicle and a hidden tenor. The Sternwoods refuse to see that in Los Angeles "Everything is like something else." In the plasticity of its surfaces under the pressure of human greed, the city itself becomes one vast simile. The meaning of the Sternwood story lies in the gap between their fenced-in mansion and the oil fields that finance it. Both sites still open upon each other: "The Sternwoods, having moved up the hill, could no longer smell the stale sump water or the oil, but they could still look out of their front windows and see what had made them rich." Carmen's love lies buried in the sump; the site of the family's success is also the grave of its crimes. Marlowe learns from the Sternwoods that an obsession with surface signifies the suppression of depth, and as he walks out of their world he has lost faith that anything can ever seem just like itself again: "Outside, the bright gardens had a haunted look, as though small wild eyes were watching me from behind the bushes, as though the sunshine itself had a mysterious something in its light." Marlowe moves henceforth through a world haunted by its repressed history.

Farewell, My Lovely. In this most liminal of Chandler's novels, Marlowe crosses the line to the surreal with terrifying ease. Detection has become a drug (he must kick morphine) that carries Marlowe over forbidden thresholds. "I walked along to the double doors and stood in front of them. They were motionless now. It wasn't any of my business. So I pushed them open and looked in." This is the most gratuitous of Marlowe's cases; he assigns it to himself out of some uncomprehended affection for Moose Malloy. He is literally carried away; simple journeys become "trips"; movement means not only a change in location but a sea change, *transport*. The book has the temporal structure of a dream (simultaneity prevails over successiveness), and even reflects on that structure: "Time passes very slowly when you are actually

14. Claustrophobia: Humphrey Bogart and Colonel Sternwood in the greenhouse of *The Big Sleep*

doing something. I mean, you can go through a lot of movements in a very few minutes. Is that what I mean? What the hell do I care what I mean? Okay, better men than me have meant less." Marlowe repeatedly finds himself out of his head. "I stopped thinking. Lights moved behind my closed lids. I was lost in space. I was a gilt-edged sap come back from a vain adventure. I was a hundred dollar package of dynamite that went off with a noise like a pawnbroker looking at a dollar watch. I was a pink-headed bug crawling up the side of the City Hall." The offshore world of Bay City threatens to engulf the only apparently more anchored life on land. Anne Riordan's place provides the first and last "Sanctuary" until Marlowe's house on Yucca Avenue, but it is too incredibly pacific to be integrated into the extremity of the main plot. Having opened up the realm of the figurative in his first novel, Chandler quickly moves to the limits of the credible. The challenge is no longer to discern hidden likeness but to resist a paranoia that connects all things. It is a paranoia that rules out love; Marlowe insults the receptive Anne into taking him home. "I unlocked the door of my apartment and went in and sniffed the smell of it, just standing there, against the door for a little while before I put the light on. A homely smell, a smell of dust and tobacco smoke, the smell of a world where men live, and keep on living."

The High Window. After the expansion into phantasmagoria, Chandler contracts his energies into his most conservative and causal plot. "I believe," he said in 1949, that "*Farewell, My Lovely* would be called the best of my books, *The High Window*, the worst." The linear logic of his third novel suggests that Chandler had reacted against the expansiveness of *Farewell, My Lovely*, but his later comment indicates that the reaction upset him even more. For *The High Window* is the most reductive of Chandler's novels and the most Oedipal, the one in which all can be traced back to the effect of a primal scene. The exposed chain of consequences repudiates the implication in *Farewell, My Lovely* that sequence is a narrative fiction, and that extension in time is required largely to prolong the delivery of the clues. Because action flows here from Merle's repression of a memory, the work of the novel is to investigate the human will to forget. (Chandler's plots tend to get a second wind at the point where Marlowe, now acting on his own, refuses to "forget the whole mess.") The dominant trope here is synecdoche (Merle is all "hair," "eyebrows," "nostrils," "chin," and "eyes"); people are encountered as pieces because they insist on remembering only parts of their lives. Only the doubloon has a determinable "history." So Marlowe must become the surrogate patient, the paid rememberer of the past.

"Look," I said slowly, "did something happen to you when you were a little girl?"

She nodded, very quickly.

"A man scared you or something like that?"

She nodded again. She took her lower lip between her little white teeth.

"And you've been like this ever since?"

In *The High Window*, Chandler understands that his books are less concerned with justice in the present than in accurate remembering of the past. In each of the first three, Marlowe lets a killer go. His interest is in bringing character to the bar of its own memories. Forgetting is the real crime, and the expiation is remembering, seeing the past as it was. Carmen reenacts Regan's murder; Malloy sees that Velma set him up; Merle discovers her role in Horace Bright's fall. *The High Window*, like *Dora*, exposes the compulsion to arrest one's development over traumas that are only fantasies. Merle's forgetting is really an act of willful misremembering: "It's true I never remembered very well." The cure is a return home, to Kansas, and an agreement to forget all around: "I had a funny feeling as I saw the house disappear, as though I had written a poem and it was very good and I had lost it and would never remember it again." *The High Window* is finally a book about its own genre, about refusing to put the pieces together, about remembering well, about the strain of being in a detective story.

The Lady in the Lake. The poem Marlowe will never remember again is the dream of shelter. Chandler's fourth novel closes off more than the first phase of the career; it generalizes its vision of Los Angeles as "waste land" to all of Southern California. Cannibalized from the short story "No Crime in the Mountains," *The Lady in the Lake* refines the irony of that title. Driving east out of the city only arouses the elements: "We reached the long slope south of San Dimas that goes up to a ridge and drops down into Pomona. This is the ultimate end of the fog-belt, and the beginning of that semi-desert region where the sun is as light and dry as old sherry in the morning, as hot as a blast furnace at noon, and drops like an angry brick at nightfall." The San Bernardino mountains may feel "like paradise," but they, too, have succumbed to the compulsion to detect. "Tall yellow pines probed at the clear blue sky." "A scarlet-topped woodpecker stopped probing in the dark long enough to look at me with one beady eye and then dodge behind the tree trunk to look at me with the other one." Deadness floats beneath the surface of calm; the "peaceful" air is shattered by "a voice that growled like mountain thunder," and Marlowe starts probing too:

The depths cleared again. Something moved in them that was not a board. It rose slowly, with an infinitely careless languor, a long dark twisted something that rolled lazily in the water as it rose. It broke surface casually, lightly, without haste. I saw wool, sodden and black, a leather jerkin blacker than ink, a pair of slacks. I saw shoes and something that bulged nastily between the shoes and the cuffs of the slacks. I saw a wave of dark blonde hair straighten out in the water and hold still for a brief instant as if with a calculated effect, and then swirl into a tangle again.

This is the most brilliant delayed revelation in Chandler, and reminds us of how often the problem of knowledge reduces, for Marlowe, to a matter of focus. Here the repeated "It's" and "I saw's" keep refocusing attention on the word "something." Crystal's body prefigures Degarmo's – "Something that had been a man." People become "somethings" in this novel; the theme is the disfigurations of love, and the guilt goes everywhere, even into makeshift graves.

The Little Sister. Chandler went to work for Hollywood in 1943 and moved, with his sudden wealth, to La Jolla in 1946. Restless internment in the Golden Graveyard was followed by what Philip Durham calls "The Remove." Chandler had made a habit of complaining about his locale, but from the safety of La Jolla he felt free to annihilate it. He admitted that his fifth novel "was written in a bad mood." And from the vantage point of his new home he went even further: "I know now what is the matter with my writing or not writing. I've lost any affinity for my background. Los Angeles is no longer my city, and La Jolla is nothing but a climate and a lot of meaningless chi-chi." This self-contempt spills over into Marlowe ("I was the page from yesterday's calendar crumpled at the bottom of the waste basket"), suffuses his environment, and even evicts him from what had been his most comforting interior space, his office: "I opened the inner door and inside it was the same dead air, the same dust along the veneer, the same broken promise of a life of ease." Chandler's vision of human life has become one with the cops'. "Civilization had no meaning for them. All they saw of it was the failures, the dirt, the dregs, the aberrations and the disgust." California now offers "The most of everything and the best of nothing." There is no place left in which to dwell or hide, but relationship has not yet become, as it will in the last novels, an alternative haven. Chandler's despair over love and place is complete. In its "scathing hatred of the human race," *The Little Sister* finds comfort only in apocalypse. The limited loss of local shelter in *The Lady in the Lake* ramifies, in David Smith's words, into the utter loss of "geographical refuge." The earth, as Marlowe says, has become a "frozen star."

The Long Goodbye. Chandler's sixth novel is the first to start with a person rather than a place. (The first five begin with an act of penetration, a movement from outside to inside, from lawns and streets to rooms.) Marlowe borrows the plot of *The Great Gatsby* and embarks on the labor of interpreting, with generosity, a crooked friend's life. He volunteers for the job, and the willingness to give more than one is asked or paid to give proves infectious. The book is full of moments of uncanny understanding, gratuitous extensions of sympathy. A taxi driver refuses extra money. A reporter divines a jailed Marlowe's altruism. "A hoodlum with sentiment" mourns the rejection of his help. An alcoholic writer offers Marlowe sudden love. Sympathy prevails over suspicion; above all, Marlowe does not want to know the truth. "I can't be told about it." A friend now rather than a detective, he puts his trust in trust. What finally matters is the tenacity of Marlowe's faith, not the worthiness of its objects. He has gone beyond any concern with the deceptiveness of surfaces; a man literally changes his face – his looks are a lie – and Marlowe still cares. If this seems like despair over reciprocal fidelity, it is also an honest admission that a man's feelings are the only feelings over which he has any control, and that if loyalty can redeem a deceiving partner, only luck can provide a true one. Marlowe's parting lecture to Terry on character (the book is full of lectures; it is a symptom of the need to move from complaint to understanding) in no way revokes the trust given. We are stuck, the novel seems to say, with the people we have happened to love.

So, as Cissy Chandler slowly died, her husband wrote a story about a dead friend who is really alive. The fantasy is of bringing someone back to life, of giving, through imagination, someone life. It was to his wife that Chandler was making a last and long good-bye. After kissing her for the last time, in December 1954, Chandler wrote:

> Of course in a sense I had said goodbye to her long ago. In fact, many times during the past two years in the middle of the night I had realized that it was only a question of time until I lost her. But that is not the same thing as having it happen. Saying goodbye to your loved one in your mind is not the same thing as closing her eyes and knowing they will never open again.

Chandler would even explain why the novel lacked his normal "gusto": "You could not know the bitter struggle I have had the past year even to achieve enough cheerfulness to live on, much less to put in a book. So let's face it: I didn't get it into the book. I didn't have it to give."

Whatever the disappointments and deceptions, they had been caught up into the drama of the end. "I was a loving and faithful husband for almost thirty-one years, and I watched my wife die by half-inches and I wrote my best book in the agony of that knowledge, and yet I wrote it." Chandler here lays claim to a faithfulness that had not been his. What he had kept faith with was an emerging fiction about human trust with which he merged his last judgment on his marriage. *The Long Goodbye* was the best book, he felt, because in it the story in his book and the story of his life converged with a shock that required of him the "intensity of artistic performance" that was the only thing to which he was willing to give the name "literature." He did not break up his lines to weep: "It was the supreme time of my life."

Playback. Chandler's career leads up to the birth of Marlowe's marriage and the death of his own. The author sometimes confuses himself with the character. Caught between memory and hope, the Marlowe of *Playback* acts as much like a widow as a prospective groom. Love has gone, but will it come again? "I had a dream here once, a year and a half ago. There's still a shred of it left. I'd like it to stay in charge." A man talks as if a relationship were over when in fact it is about to begin. Marlowe moves through a novel in which his is the story that asks to be "solved." From the beginning he unwittingly practices to receive Linda Loring's call. Arriving at Esmeralda, he impersonates a bereft husband. He allies himself with happy couples. Fred Pope cries when he thinks of his "old woman," and the motel keeper's wife "glows every time" she looks at him. Plot has ceased to matter; Marlowe spends his time waiting rather than detecting, and the mystery is solved when Betty Mayfield's persecutor simply decides to turn up. What Marlowe waits for is love, and it descends like grace, through a wire in the sky. "I've been faithful to you." Linda's unsolicited fidelity opens up, at the end, an unlooked-for range of trust. Philip and Linda have been "true" to a contract never formalized, and so protect their love from compromise in the realm of appearance. For all the hard years Chandler here offers Marlowe an austere and purified reward, love without the pretension or even the expression of love. In his last novel Chandler adds luck to loyalty, and so surprises "the hard inner heart that asked for nothing from anyone" with a satisfaction for which it has continually and quietly asked.

Read as a sequence, Chandler's novels tell the story of a man in search of an outright fiction. The discipline of detection leads beyond the need to suspect, and what opens up, as Chandler withdraws from the "dismal land" of his exile, is a provisional belief in a place called "marriage." In a literal act of dis*place*ment, Chandler substitutes relationship for location as the proper sphere of human dwelling. At the end he falls back on the old Romantic logic; gain in an inner world compensates for loss in an outer one.

The last novels have been called sentimental, and they are, but the fiction they project is meant to offset what Chandler took to be an earlier and more serious failure of feeling. Such compensations are unstable; romance was to offer no more secure a haven than irony. "I left Marlowe in a situation where he could be married – but it was not certain. I hope I picked the right woman." A hope alive as late as February 1958, it was one Chandler revoked in the month before his death: The "idea that he should be married, even to a very nice girl, is quite out of character. I see him always in a lonely street, in lonely rooms, puzzled but never quite defeated." Even had Chandler not thought better of marrying off his hero, he had pretty well undermined such a fantasy in advance by having written off any sustaining earthly locale. His despair over a locatable happiness issued in the last irony of proposing to settle a married Marlowe in the supreme California never-never land, a place resolutely out of this world – Palm Springs.

Chapter 8

Jeffers, Snyder, and the ended world

In the middle of a difficult war, a poet recently married surveys a California hillside and dreams of building a house. The act once begun produces, in his wife's words, "a kind of awakening." Peripatetic in mind and body, the poet now confirms the pleasures of manual labor and enjoys the disciplines of settlement. He begins to lead a new life and to write in a new measure. The poet feels that he has come to his "inevitable place."

Robinson Jeffers in 1916; Gary Snyder in 1968. The two poets who have had the most to say about California landscape both ground their vision in the building of a house. Jeffers's Tor House became the work of many years; Snyder's Kitkitdizze still grows. One poet chose the wind and cold light of the Carmel headlands; the other, the hot, pine-studded foothills of the Sierra Nevada. Jeffers built a tower for his Una, won in 1913 after a six-year quest; Snyder built a sauna with his Masa, brought from Japan after a wedding on the lip of an active volcano. To each couple two sons were born. Both men chose unlevel ground where little would easily grow. Both chose granite, though Snyder's is mostly decomposed.

Locality: This is the dimension that binds. What divides these men – and this will be my argument – is their stance toward their moment in time. Snyder chooses his place with a commitment to his historical moment that Jeffers made in his life but avoided in his work. As an imagined place, Jeffers's California points beyond itself toward a network of timeless and even apocalyptic significance. Snyder, caught in a more sensual music, increasingly refrains from commending either his life or his poems to an artifice of eternity. If his commitments seem more perilous and adaptive, it is because they are made to a world that is and may be, not to one that is ending and ended. Elegy tempts both poets away from the task of living in time and place, and it is a temptation to which Jeffers finally succumbs. If Snyder survives the temptation and writes instead a poetry about "How we go on," creating work in which an actual present invokes a possible future, he does so in part on the strength of his forerunner's lonely and chastening counterexample.

Robinson Jeffers (1887–1962) discovered Carmel a month after World War I began, in one of the most terrible years of his life. His first child, Maeve, had been born in May 1914, and had lived only a day. His father would die in December, leaving him a legacy of two thousand dollars a year to support his incipient career. The war itself had defeated the Jeffers's plans to live in England, and so, as Una Jeffers wrote, the newly married couple left Pasadena and headed north: "The August news turned us to this village of Carmel instead; and when the stage-coach topped the hill from Monterey, and we looked down through pines and sea-fogs on Carmel Bay, it was evident that we had come without knowing it to our inevitable place." Robinson felt as well the sense of sudden election, as he wrote in *Californians* (1916):

> You know how our hearts were moved at looking down
> From the high peninsula yoke; the breath of the morning
> Hung in the pines; and this, we felt, was our home;
> This, the narrow bay; the promontories;
> The islands, each one rock; the capes beyond,
> To the left, of Lobos, and yonder of Pescadero.
> We were glad: we had found our place. . . .

Both husband and wife write of this vision in the first-person plural. The world that here lies all before them they enter hand in hand. The tone of uncanny assurance – there is no hint here of surprise – makes the discovery seem like a recovery. It is as though at Carmel they enter something they already know and deserve, and the life they were to lead there was to establish, but for the "bad dreams" that issued as Robinson's poems, a kind of second paradise.

Few men have so dedicated themselves to confirming their sense of home through the building of a house. California preserves many strange and wonderful houses; certainly the abiding dream of the state is of a place where one can own a house of one's own. (Los Angeles still contains more private homes per capita than any other large city on earth.) It is a state in which designing selves have been altogether free – too free, West grumbles in *The Day of the Locust* – to protect themselves through domestic containers unconstrained by any architectural tradition, let alone a building code. Remarkable eccentricities have been the result: Charles Lummis's hacienda of stream boulders, complete with doors copied straight out of Velázquez' *Las Meninas*; the Greene and Greene brothers' great wooden bungalows, like outrigger canoes plowed into the earth; Simon Rhodia's Watts Towers, not a dwelling but a fantasy of a total dwelling, a one-man city of glued tidbits inching slowly upward. All have one thing in common: They are built by hand. Houses usually are, but these make special reference in the quality of their detail to the part played by the hand that carved, lifted, planed. Houses built by such men seem to grow rather than to end; they become a lifework. "Life-style" – the incessant tinkering to find just the right balance between creature comforts and objects of status – is the parody of what these self-built environments reflect. For those who miss the point, the instruction manual is not *Walden* but *Sunset* magazine.

For Jeffers, handiwork was lifework. He wrote and worked in stone, and he did both as long as he was able to lift the weight. Tor House was built in 1919, after the Jefferses had purchased a piece of land on the sea at Mission Point. Legend has it that Jeffers built the house himself, but in fact he was at the start little more than a hod carrier. Murphy the contractor and Pierson the stonemason directed the work. Boulders were lifted by chute up to the crowning knoll. Progress was slow, and the Jefferses convinced Murphy to hire Robinson to keep an eye on the men. He worked for four dollars a day, mixing and carrying mortar. Begun in the spring, the house was finished in early August. "It was thus," Una wrote, "he learned to handle stone."

Patterned after a Tudor barn Una had fancied in England, Tor House had no telephone, electricity, or heat except that provided by fireplaces and a Franklin stove. Light was provided by kerosene lamps. The first floor contained a living room, guest bedroom, bath, and kitchen. The windows on the west overlooked the sea. Above this lay the heart of the house, one large gabled room surrounding the chimney. In each of the four corners stood a bed, one each for the husband, the wife, and the two boys. Jeffers worked upstairs at a desk overlooking the courtyard, within hearing of the surf. Rumor had it that he loved the fog and hated the sun. He spent the mornings writing, and turned in the afternoon to his work in stone. Una kept the visitors at bay. Life was lonely and good there; besides, Jeffers wrote a friend in 1927, "I'm set here like a stone in cement." He would live in Carmel fourteen years before traveling further away than Pasadena.

Building Tor House was an act of withdrawal and embowerment; building the Hawk Tower was one of gratuitous aspiration. After completing the house Jeffers had gone on to finish the garage alone. Una then once again suggested a project: a tower with a room for herself, a "dungeon" for the twins, and a turret for gazing seaward. It was to be modeled after the round medieval towers of Ireland. The work took five years. Jeffers worked alone, becoming to his neighbors a fixture of "slow unchangeability." Ella Winter wrote of "the same figure . . .

15. Tor House and the Tower

watched by indifferent and then increasingly curious neighbors . . . as
it hauled great granite boulders from the beach and rolled them up an
inclined plane, higher and higher in the course of the five or six years
that Robinson Jeffers took to build his Hawk Tower. Early Carmelites
recall how in those days they first wondered, and then ceased to
wonder. . . . You cannot wonder all of six years." So Jeffers labored on
at his wife's commission, a Sisyphus in the service of his love.

Jeffers wrote a few short poems about his home in Carmel. He even
wrote one on the ceiling above Una's bed:

> I will build a stone house for young life and rock walls for the
>   seedlings of love,
> Ribs of rock around a hot soft heart, crannies in granite for the
>   roots of flowers;
> Waves wrestling below, winds ranging above,
> Braggarts, go by, the old earth is our friend, touch nothing of
>   ours.

Remarkable here is the way in which the poet of the nonhuman world
domesticates some of its forces as allies while warding off others as
threats. It is a positioning of himself within a stable human space and
against the mutability of an outer one, a position Jeffers rarely occupies.
The poet nestles in, as the Indians once "nestled by" the rock that has
become the cornerstone of his house. The house is a body enclosing a
"hot soft heart." In comparison with the famous longer poems about
other people's houses, Jeffers's poems to his house skirt sentimentality.
They pull back from a vision of process and address instead the imminence of personal loss. That's why he builds the house – as a lie against
time. Or so he admits in "To the Stone-Cutters":

> Stone-cutters fighting time with marble, you foredefeated
> Challengers of oblivion
> Eat cynical earnings, knowing rock splits, records fall down,
> The square-limbed Roman letters
> Scale in the thaws, wear in the rain. The poet as well
> Builds his monument mockingly;
> For man will be blotted out, the blithe earth die, the brave sun
> Die blind and blacken to the heart:
> Yet stones have stood for a thousand years, and pained thoughts
>   found
> The honey of peace in old poems.

The poem turns upon the "Yet," and in so doing turns away from the
hard facts into a fiction that counters not only the poem's rhythm but
its emotional momentum. Jeffers rarely allows a poem to end in sur-

mise, especially one that takes comfort in the works of man. That this was an admitted favorite is tantalizing, and that this was a mode that Jeffers so sparingly allowed himself is the mystery of his career.

The mystery is more like an irony, since it is clear from even a passing knowledge of the life that Jeffers chose to write not out of his actual and settled happiness, but out of imagined pain. It was precisely against his tranquil domestic routine that his poetry went to war. The man who as much as any other found a way to live in California as a home chose instead to write about it as an end.

Among American poets only Whitman and Crane have been as willing as Jeffers to plot their location on a continental scale. These lines are from *The Women at Point Sur* (1927):

> From here the great shed of the mountain shot in bronze folds,
> Seemed humming like bells under the strokes of the sun; in the
>   creases the winter stream-beds,
> Haired with low oak, but higher between deep ridges spiring to
>   redwood, netted the edge of the continent
> With many-branching black threads; the wall steepened below
>   and went down
> To a sea like blue steel breakless to Asia, except the triangle-shaped
>   sand-flat as low as the ocean.
> The lighthouse rock apexed, and the lesser morro
> Flanked on the south; these two alone breaking the level
> Opposite the straight sea-wall of the ended world.

These lines seem to describe California simply as the place where the land stops. It is "the ended world." The concern here is with extension in space, with "up" and "down" as well as "out" and "across." Ridges spire, walls steepen, rocks apex, the morro flanks. The land dips and rises as it is crushed up against the "straight sea-wall." As in Norris, the vertical is a condition of grace and tension sustained against an inexorable horizontality. It is the resistance of this land to its fate – it will crumble into the sea – that moves Jeffers. But it is the fact that it all ends that arrests and compels him.

From this recognition Jeffers made a key and determining leap: His poems envision California not just as an end but as a place where endings occur. History converges with geography here in a metaphor of doom in which it is impossible to distinguish tenor from vehicle. The End of the West proves also the Fall of an Age, and one of the sadnesses of Jeffers's career is that the sequence of world events through which he was to live – especially the two world wars – dramatically confirmed his early forebodings.

For early Jeffers, what had ended is the movement Steinbeck calls

"westering." In the "Invocation" to *Californians,* a poem George Sterling thought the book's best, Jeffers imagines the power of the evening
star to draw his ancestors westward, as "free wanderers":

> They would look for thee
> At fire-lighting each night; but when thy face
> Was hidden, there they halted, eagerly
>
> Awaiting thy new birth, and in that place
> Built huts, and plowed the field. Thy light renewed,
> They rose, and tracked westward the wilderness.
>
> Now I, the latest, in this solitude
> Invoke thee from the verge extreme, and shoal
> Of sands that ends the west. O long-pursued,
>
> Where wilt thou lead us now? What greater goal
> Gleams for our longing down the abysm of time?
> What weariness of body and worn soul?
> What farther west? What wanderings more sublime?

The questions posed here were to take negative answers. Jeffers's California becomes in the twenties and thirties a place where human desire
redounds back on itself as repression and revenge, where families at
odds with the deepest taboos come to mirror in their fate the death
struggle of civilizations. These poems end with the fall of a house, the
end of a line. We come to expect these predictable disasters, and we are
asked to turn, in consolation, to the surrounding splendor of place, to
"the beauty of things, not men." Yet the unyielding finality of the land
itself ("The old ocean at the land's foot, the vast / Gray extension beyond the long white violence") has become so premonitory of human
loss that it proves difficult to take comfort in its difficult beauty.

Any investment in history depends much more on a myth of progress than we may like to believe; as a story we are telling about our
collective way, it necessarily moves in our minds from and toward a
point. Even a myth of decline is preferable to a cyclical theory of time,
because it at least provides the minimal consolations of narrative. For
those who hope that the human story has a shape, Spengler consoles
more than Heraclitus. Lawrence Clark Powell speaks of Jeffers as "an
example of Spengler's western man," but Jeffers's myth of decline is
too caught up into a vision of repetition to warrant the association.
Powell's description of the Jeffers imagination assumes as much: "Its
progress is from the immediate to the distant: from the poet's personal-
ity, his house and children and trees and poems, to the significance of
the Pacific coast in the westward migration, then to the fall of our

civilization, end of the earth, death of the solar system, on and on into space." This is scarcely a "progress" at all; it is the *Cosmos* vision in which man is star-stuff, Carl Sagan's "billions and billions of stars." Powell then quotes "The Cycle," the one short Jeffers poem that best captures his sense that the motion of history is not only over but has never effectively begun.

High on a cliff above the Pacific, the speaker watches the sea birds wheel in "windy spirals." Like Yeats watching his swans at the turn of the same age, he counts the birds and anticipates the future in which they will survive him:

> the clapping blackness of the wings of pointed cormorants, the
>   great sails
> Of autumn pelicans, the gray sea-going gulls,
> Alone will streak the enormous opal, the earth have peace like
>   the broad water, our blood's
> Unrest have doubled to Asia and be peopling
> Europe again, or dropping colonies at the morning star: what
>   moody traveler
> Wanders back here, watches the sea-fowl circle
> The old sea-granite and cemented granite with one regard, and
>   greets my ghost,
> One temper with the granite, bulking about here?

In a vision this repetitious, one's location in space or time scarcely matters. The poem embodies its subject in its structure; the line with which I began repeats the poem's opening one. The circling of the birds at the beginning is initially contrasted against the "westering lights of heaven," and against the men who through history have followed them. In the act of watching a star one enjoys, after all, the illusion of a linear procession across the sky. But in a swift and savage analogy Jeffers goes on in the lines quoted to imagine that "our blood," having now reached the end of that motion, will simply double on to Asia and people Europe again. An endless circumnavigation of the globe is no less cyclical than the stars dropping over the horizon or the birds wheeling in the air; through this brilliant superimposition of natural onto human motions, Jeffers argues that history has and reaches no point.

Given this continual motion through and around, Jeffers advances here a poem about the indifference of all places. This is the ideological core of his attitude toward place. On the other hand, Jeffers often betrays an untoward emotional response to his California that runs contrary to his insistent argument. In "The Cycle," after all, Jeffers stubbornly persists in haunting the California coast, in "bulking about

here." He loved California in spite of himself; it may even be fair to say
that he worshipped it. When Milton warned Adam that "God attributes
to place / No sanctity," he meant to prevent him from locating his sense
of God in any of his material works. Jeffers acts as if he set out to defy
this injunction; his plots demand the literal return of blood to the
ground. His coast is a demanding altar, and the persistent claiming of
the life lived on it reveals Jeffers as an idolator of place.

   In each of the long poems, emphasis falls on where the hero dies. It is
as if a wandering pain sought out the most appropriate background for
its end, a background that finally supplants the human foreground. In
the most cinematic of these endings, a dying Reave Thurso is brought
at last to his fateful "sea-brow." His arrival there at the edge of the
world is a result of his uncanny will: "only the cripple's insane invinci-
ble stubbornness had brought them to it." The end of a life seeks the
end of the land, and the suffering of the hero is balanced by the pitiless
termination of space, a finality that implies a judgment:

> The platform is like a rough plank theatre-stage
> Built on the brow of the promontory: as if our blood had
>   labored all around the earth from Asia
> To play its mystery before strict judges at last, the final ocean
>   and sky, to prove our nature
> More shining that that of the other animals. It is rather ignoble
>   in its quiet times, mean in its pleasures,
> Slavish in the mass: but at stricken moments it can shine terribly
>   against the dark magnificence of things.

Jeffers stages here a play about what is left to man in the last days: He
can shed his blood to cast light back upon the world's beauty. We are
all Isaacs being shepherded to the appointed altar by the father who
hears a voice in the wind crying, "God is here."

   But Abraham had his Sarah, and their love is the undersong that sends
up Jeffers's tragic music. Robinson first met Una at the University of
Southern California in 1905. She had been married for three years to
Theodore Kuster, and the friendship between the married woman and
the minister's son at first grew slowly. Although the two fought the
growing attraction, by 1908 they were deeply in love. In 1910, Jeffers
took a leave from both love and medical school and enrolled in forestry
at the University of Washington. The sabbatical did not help. On returning to Los Angeles a year later, Jeffers was to stop at a busy inter-
section only to have a roadster pull up at the corner with Una at the
wheel. The two again succumbed to their attraction, and Una soon
confessed the whole to her husband. He insisted that she absent herself to
Europe. Four months later he secured an interlocutory decree, and

Una returned from abroad to settle her affairs. She was divorced on August 1, 1912, and married Robinson the next day. "So without the wish of either of us," she was to write, "our life was one of those fatal attractions that happen unplanned and undesired."

Jeffers had few if any mature friends, and marriage with Una provided him with the one essential emotional bond of his adult life. But for a tiff in Santa Fe when a jealous Una shot herself (the bullet grazed the stomach) over her husband's purported dalliance, there is no record of tension between them. Una was the keeper of the keys, the muse who had the power to usher others into the Jeffers's private space, and she narrowly defined the elect. Jeffers's closest friends appear to have been none other than Una's first husband and his third wife, Theodore and Ruth Kuster. Once Tor House was finished, Kuster bought the adjoining property, built a stone house, and settled permanently in Carmel. Years later Mabel Luhan would write of "Kuster's undying devotion to Una." Ruth would go on to write Una's biography.

Jeffers founded his life in California on his marriage, but he did not found his poetry on it. Although he was to say that Una "co-authored" his poems, their life as husband and wife together never becomes – until after Una dies – the occasion for a major poem. Una died in 1950. Elegy subsequently became the dominant mode in a career that previously had looked on suffering with a cold eye. In "Hungerfield" the grieving husband's project stands revealed as a displaced love poem:

> Una has died, and I
> Am left waiting for death, like a leafless tree
> Waiting for the roots to rot and the trunk to fall.

All that had been done was done for her; hence the death of the surviving poet's will to live. In "The Deer Lay Down Their Bones," one of the most moving poems Jeffers ever wrote and also one of the last, he portrays the work of his final decade as the search for a fit place to die. He finds a small clearing and a pool in the midst of oak and laurel. He thinks about the gift of life: "Mine's empty since my love died." He wonders whether he should live ten more years before

> I crawl out on a ledge of rock and die snapping, like a wolf
> Who has lost his mate? – I am bound by my own thirty-year-old
>   decision: who drinks the wine
> Should take the dregs; even in the bitter lees and sediment
> New discovery may lie. The deer in that beautiful place lay
>   down their bones: I must wear mine.

So the poet resolves to go on. His reluctance to do so registers his dependency on the presence that had inspired all of his work. It is not a

presence admitted directly into the poems, but one that twisted them
rather into their unique and troubled shape.

The recurring bad dream in Jeffers's plots is of a woman undoing a
man. Love is incest in Jeffers; the prototypic sexual encounter is between brothers and sisters or fathers and daughters. When he confines
the choice of love object to the natural family, Jeffers equates desire
and doom. William Everson has written eloquently about the way in
which every house in Jeffers becomes the House of Atreus, full of
strong, betraying Clytemnestras and wailing Cassandras. The core of
this myth is a fear of women and of the dangerous magnetism of our
first source: The obvious misanthropy in Jeffers's work would appear
to mask a more fundamental misogyny. But if Jeffers's fantasies of
attraction and betrayal express an uncomprehended obsession, they
also issue from a consciously adopted defensive strategy. This is, at
least, the argument he advances in "Apology for Bad Dreams," perhaps the most self-revealing poem in the canon. In it he questions
why he has chosen to sacrifice himself and his characters to the fatal
demands of place:

> This coast crying out for tragedy like all beautiful places: and
>   like the passionate spirit of humanity
> Pain for its bread: God's, many victims', the painful deaths, the
>   horrible transfigurations: I said in my heart,
> "Better invent than suffer: imagine victims
> Lest your own flesh be chosen the agonist, or you
> Martyr some creature to the beauty of the place."

There are in our literature few more frank admissions of the defensive
purposes of poetry. For all that we know, Jeffers suffered nothing
extraordinary in his chosen place. Instead, as he admits in "Apology,"
he made awful poems to serve as "phantoms" that he could throw as
sacrifices to the "wolves" of pain, and terror, and desire. "I imagined
victims for those wolves, / I made them phantoms to follow, / They
have hunted the phantoms and missed the house." The act of writing
poetry here is seen as an act of warding off. It is something one does for
the protection of one's house.

The "Apology" argues, then, that Jeffers projected onto landscape his
fear of doom and then created female characters who would provoke
and male characters who would suffer it. He had, after all, taken away
another man's wife after a six-year struggle; marriage had been born
out of an act of betrayal. The man who had been left behind even came
to live next door. The task became to prevent repetition of the event in
the life by continually reenacting versions of it in the work. Jeffers
imagined a place that required repeated sacrifice and fall as a charm
against his rooted and cherished life. Read in this way, the excess and

the pain become a measure of his love for his wife and for the islanded life they made together on a rocky beach in California.

Jeffers is the California Milton: difficult, epic, distracted by original sin. His stance overshadows all subsequent projects, yet few poets from his region display any outright signs of influence. Four California poets invite particular comparison with Jeffers, and the variety of their achievement measures the power of his own.

The first is Kenneth Rexroth, younger contemporary and announced competitor. When it comes to places, Rexroth often lodges his thought in those that lie beyond locality, worlds revealed by the microscope and the telescope. He writes beautifully of compounds and constellations. But he also displays a resistance to a poetry devoted, as Jeffers's often seems to be, to "the closed world of things." Early on, Rexroth scorned Jeffers's "laboring of the pathetic fallacy," his confounding of the human foreground with the natural background, and so he turned from landscape to eros. In his strong poems he becomes the California Marvell, singing about love as the lie against time. These poems typically occur in an outdoor space, but one fully in human scale, the world of mountain and waterfall. Though mutability is here the theme, "it is nevertheless always the Californian earth and sky and sea that form the vital imagery infusing his verse with its power."

These words were written by William Everson, Jeffers's one announced heir. Everson began his career while growing grapes in the Central Valley, spent twenty years as a lay brother in a Dominican order, left the monastery in his late fifties to marry and pursue a life of writing and teaching. In *Fragments of an Older Fury*, he identifies himself explicitly with Jeffers, including the Family Romance in which each poet, the son of a father twenty years older than the mother, "transposed the maternal *imago* to unspoliated nature." Whereas Jeffers persists in this act of projection, Everson sees through it and proceeds to substitute a revealed for a natural religion. From his vineyards he harvests not grapes but "souls." And so he becomes the devilish disciple, the Blake who embraces and inverts the master's message. Everson also writes of violence and the West, but the stages in his three-part career aspire to a level of self-fashioning – of soul-making – quite foreign to Jeffers's distrust of the *me*. Although he has called his work "a California odyssey," the net effect is of a psychomachia more cosmic than localized.

Raised in Southern California, Yvor Winters spent all but a few years of his adult life on the peninsula south of San Francisco. He joined the English department at Stanford in 1928 and retired in 1966. In the year he began teaching he also "abandoned free verse and returned to traditional meters." Winters subsequently became a critic in defense of reason, the scourge of poetry that failed to display a logical structure.

During these years he used his formidable poetic gifts to memorialize a California trying not to vanish. In the lives of John Muir ("I might have been this man") and John Sutter he tried to find precedents for living in concord with "the shining land." In his masterpiece, "On a View of Pasadena from the Hills," he brought all his discipline to bear on the current prospect from his childhood home, now a lost Arcadia in which "man-made stone outgrows the living tree." If we extend our comparison to other literary histories, Winters assumes the role of the California Sidney, the critic whose best defense of poetry is his actual practice of it on behalf of a loved place.

And then there is Gary Snyder (1930–   ). Snyder is the California Wordsworth, the poet of landscape and memory and the longing to break through to a present he can fully inhabit. Snyder read Jeffers and knows Everson. He hiked with Rexroth in the Sierra and has emulated his eclectic, Eastern-leaning learning. Yet he has set himself, however consciously, to complete and revalue Jeffers's unfinished project, and any argument for continuity in the poetry of their region rests on an understanding of how Snyder has found a way to begin again in a place where Jeffers saw hope as temporary and terminal.

Snyder's career has been expressed through two motions that are at once unique and complementary: turning and returning. The first is a motion out and away; the second, a going back. Turning emphasizes all that is unique, passing, lost; returning, all that is collective, located, able to be held. Turning and returning are in Snyder's world motions basic to the nature of things, the actions of persons, and the strategies of poems. Snyder has spent his career trying to find ways in which a poetry committed to these motions can display the resonance between the physical, the ethical, and the aesthetic. His discernible movement away from the habit of turning and toward a vision of return also reveals the changing commitments in his work and his life.

The strongest poem in Snyder's latest book, *Axe Handles* (1983), beautifully captures the tensions that have informed his best work. It is called "True Night." As the poem begins the sleeping poet is suddenly awakened by the clatter of raccoons in the kitchen. He chases them outdoors only to find himself caught by the temptation of permanent escape:

> As I stay there then silent
> The chill of the air on my nakedness
> Starts off the skin
> I am all alive to the night.
> Bare foot shaping on gravel
> Stick in the hand, forever.

Stripping away history like clothes, the early Snyder had often sought
for a moment such as this in which the self, lost to all others, commits
to a moment of pure vision or sensation. The poet stands a long moment, listening to crickets "Faint in cold coves in the dark." But he has
long since accepted the pull of a contrary motion:

> I turn and walk slow
> Back the path to the beds
> With goosebumps and loose waving hair
> In the night of milk-moonlit thin cloud glow
> And black rustling pines
> I feel like a dandelion head
> Gone to seed
> About to be blown all away
> Or a sea anemone open and waving in
> Cool pearly water.

Dispersal into space and of self: These remain the attractively threatening possibilities that haunt even this conservative turning back. Time
has conspired, however, to transform the poet's life into a series of
repetitions he ruefully and quietly accepts:

> Fifty years old.
> I still spend my time
> Screwing nuts down on bolts.

It is the choices made in time that now continually pull him back.
When he mentions what lies within the shadowed house, it is as if poet
and reader agree to remember what they have temporarily agreed to
forget:

> At the shadow pool,
> Children are sleeping,
> And a lover I've lived with for years,
> True night.
> One cannot stay too long awake
> In this dark
> Dusty feet, hair tangling,
> I stoop and slip back to the
> Sheath, for the sleep I still need,
> For the waking that comes
> Every day
>
> With the dawn.

Snyder's *Axe Handles* returns to love and work. How he achieves this
utter and yet gently reluctant resolve is the story of his career.

Published when he was twenty-nine, Snyder's first book empties the mind of the "damned memories" that clog it in an ascesis that marks the beginning of his quest. In *Riprap* (1959) he turns from America toward the East and begins the motion out and away that will preoccupy him for fifteen years. *Myths & Texts* (1960) promotes Snyder's emerging vision of process in a dialectical structure that resolves that all form is a momentary stay, "stresses that come into being each instant." In a world where "It's all falling or burning" the experience of place is only a fiction, and there can be therefore nothing to return to. *Mountains and Rivers Without End* (1965–) will contain twenty-five sections and is as yet unfinished. This may prove the major work of Snyder's career, although, as in Pound's *Cantos,* the poet can seem more committed to the theory than the poetry of this poem. The theory holds, in Snyder's words, that "every poem in *Mountains and Rivers* takes a different form and has a different strategy." A poem built on the impulse of turning away from its own realized structures, *Mountains and Rivers* would seem a work about journeys, about "Passing / through." Its fascination, however, with what Snyder has called the "focal image" and with a realm above the Blue Sky also reaches toward timelessness. These growing tensions as well as the poem's quality as a running rumination on all that Snyder holds dear place it at this point beyond any developmental model of Snyder's career.

The *Back Country* (1968) is in this argument the pivotal book, the one most openly engaged with Snyder's own history of turning. What begins as a reprise of *Riprap* – in "Far West" Snyder amasses his reasons for moving and forgetting – proceeds by discovering an opposing impulse to return and remember. *Regarding Wave* (1970) shores up the position gained in *The Back Country* by valorizing a new and conserving pattern – the wave – capable of storing and releasing the energy Snyder had earlier discovered in the stream. A book about "What's Meant by Here," *Turtle Island* (1974) registers Snyder's emerging commitment to a structure that stays in place. Homesteading replaces hitchhiking as the privileged human activity as Snyder's act of settlement in California expands into a sense of stewardship over the entire planet. In *Axe Handles,* Snyder begins with work around the house and ends with journeys. Travel is now seen as the venturing out from a hearth, and thus the controlling metaphors ("Loops" and "Nets") are of structures that return upon themselves or are intentionally pulled back. The grounding act here is the dedication of the book – to San Juan Ridge, the place where Snyder lives.

The momentum of these changes confers no special authority on the more recent work. Snyder's earlier poems may in fact be stronger and more original. As Thomas Parkinson has noted, Snyder's poetry since *The*

Back Country displays a tendency toward orthodoxy and toward a commitment to a way of life – "a complex of being" – in which the poetry plays only a part. We can honor Snyder for his choice, and for his recognition that his recent desideratum – to "get a sense of workable territory" – requires a principled distribution away from poetry of the poet's time. His art may have carried him beyond a pure commitment to art; where it has carried him is a question that needs to be worked out poem by poem.

TURNING

Snyder's first book opens with a stillness in which no decision is necessary. *Riprap* and the career begin with the brief clearing away in "Mid-August at Sourdough Mountain Lookout":

> Down valley a smoke haze
> Three days heat, after five days rain
> Pitch glows on the fir-cones
> Across rocks and meadows
> Swarms of new flies.
> I cannot remember things I once read
> A few friends, but they are in cities.
> Drinking cold snow-water from a tin cup
> Looking down for miles
> Through high still air.

Captured here is a state in which, in the words of "Piute Creek," "All the junk that goes with being human / Drops away." A mind emptied of memories and hope experiences no pressure to proceed or retreat. The line-breaks here are strong, and the independence of the lines allows the reader to proceed without suspense or the need for recoil. The speaker observes an external motion while he simply drinks, or looks, or reads. Speaker and reader are confronted with a spectacle before which nothing at all needs to be done.

But *Riprap* goes on to become a book about fateful early turns and choices. The poems increasingly imagine a pivoting, as of someone caught in a tight spot. In the second poem in the volume the speaker has fallen into a world of work and unemployment in which his wish to escape to Mount Baker is checked:

> I must turn and go back:
>> caught on a snowpeak
>> between heaven and earth
> And stand in lines in Seattle
> Looking for work.

Snyder here obliquely sounds the theme of his volume, the search for vocation. It turns out that his is a world in which a man is twisted by the need to have something "to do," and, by the time he writes "Nooksack Valley," the lookout, ranger, and hay bucker no longer has any place left to turn. Snyder has been cornered in and by America, and the poem captures as well as any he has written the felt pressure that sent him to the East:

Nooksack Valley

February 1956

At the far end of a trip north
In a berry-pickers cabin
At the edge of a wide muddy field
Stretching to the woods and cloudy mountains,
Feeding the stove all afternoon with cedar,
Watching the dark sky darken, a heron flap by,
A huge setter pup nap on the dusty cot.
High rotten stumps in the second-growth woods
Flat scattered farms in the bends of the Nooksack
River. Steelhead run now
    a week and I go back
Down 99, through towns, to San Francisco
      and Japan.
All America south and east,
Twenty-five years in it brought to a trip-stop
Mind-point, where I turn
Caught more on this land – rock tree and man,
Awake, than ever before, yet ready to leave.
    damned memories,
Whole wasted theories, failures and worse success,
Schools, girls, deals, try to get in
To make this poem a froth, a pity,
A dead fiddle for lost good jobs.
    the cedar walls
Smell of our farm-house, half built in '35.
Clouds sink down the hills
Coffee is hot again. The dog
Turns and turns about, stops and sleeps.

Nooksack Valley is located in the Cascade Range north and east of Seattle, in the very corner of the country. Snyder here returns to a place he has often visited. He is a latecomer here, a young man in an overused country of "second-growth woods," woods the result perhaps of logging with his father as a boy. Having helped to exhaust the margin of a continent and a forest, Snyder judges it time to leave, and, like the migrating trout, he runs, or turns, away.

Remarkable here is how quickly Snyder carries us into this place and then out of it. In three lines we move from Washington through California to the eastern Pacific:

> . . . Steelhead run now
> a week and I go back
> Down 99, through towns, to San Francisco
> and Japan.

No act of choosing is relayed here; the poet arrives and leaves, as if departure were reaction rather than decision. He and we suddenly come upon the "I" doing this; the pronoun enters the poem as an offhand surprise, and leaving is an event that seems merely to have befallen it. Snyder is concerned to register not the process of choice but the conditions that make for sudden turnings in the way.

The real action in the poem is, then, a turn that occurs before it is understood. The last five sentences (beginning with "All America") recapitulate the reasons for moving, and they are written in the present tense. The moment of turning is thus given a kind of second life in the poem as we watch the speaker caught between the now and the then, the immediate and the far away. The poet stands at once at a "trip-stop" and a "mind-point"; the symmetry between physical and mental turnings, departures and forgettings, is clear. And then the key line-break:

> . . . where I turn
> Caught more on this land – rock tree and man,
> Awake, than ever before, yet ready to leave.

The poem pivots on the verb "turn." What we might expect is a turn *away,* toward the new life across the sea. What we get is a turn *back,* toward all the things on which and ways in which Snyder is still "caught." It is as if the land, like a lover, reaches out one last hand to stay him in a coercion that makes the farewell more sweet. It is through this final and surprising sensation of being held back, in which both speaker and reader participate, that Snyder registers the necessity of its being time to go.

It is because he is caught that he has to go: The poem's profound and tacit assumption seems to be that the proper response to the love of a thing is to let it go. Leave places; release lovers; forget pasts; abandon elegies – these are not so much desiderata as inevitabilities, given the ethic and the metaphysic that Snyder is in the process of structuring. His refusal to grasp after experience simply acknowledges his belief, fully expressed in "Lookout's Journal" and *Myths & Texts,* that it can't be grasped, and that the return yielded our attention to the things of this world is a vision of their transitoriness. The poem can and should no longer be an elegy, a "pity" or a "dead fiddle" for what has been lost. Such holding on, the poem seems to say, is not only pathetic but gratuitous. "Nooksack Valley" is honest enough, however, to show that memory keeps pulling him back; the farmhouse, after all, smells of home. But then that life was also one of unfinished projects, of "half built" houses from which attention eventually turns away. Present pleasure in any case reasserts itself: "Coffee is hot again." As we subside back into the forgetfulness that is now, the dog does his little dance, and so performs an exemplum of the entire poem. His turning and turning about has the form but not the meaning of Snyder's motion, although, in that the turning is circular, it may be Snyder's cautiously reassuring prediction of a return.

Snyder left America for Japan in May 1956. He was twenty-six. He spent most of the next thirteen years there, traveling and studying at its Zen monasteries. Married in 1967, he and his third wife, Masa Uehara, returned to live permanently in California in December 1968. He had by then found a place to settle, but what he had also found was something to do. The sequence of poems in *Riprap* enacts this process of discovery, as Snyder wanders through Japan, departs on a tanker bound for Suez, and finally arrives at the vocation always halfway in mind. The destination was poetry, as the last poem in *Riprap* makes plain:

Riprap

> Lay down these words
> Before your mind like rocks.
>   placed solid, by hands
> In choice of place, set
> Before the body of the mind
>   in space and time:
> Solidity of bark, leaf, or wall
>   riprap of things:
> Cobble of milky way,
>   straying planets,
> These poems, people,
>   lost ponies with
> Dragging saddles –
>   and rocky sure-foot trails.

> The worlds like an endless
>   four-dimensional
> Game of *Go.*
>   ant and pebbles
> In the thin loam, each rock a word
>   a creek-washed stone
> Granite: ingrained
>   with torment of fire and weight
> Crystal and sediment linked hot
>   all change, in thoughts,
> As well as things.

Snyder's characteristic abundance of monosyllables here presents words as integrated, undivided things. The lines also contain more strong beats than the abbreviated number of syllables would normally allow, and so acquire a gravity in excess of their apparent weight. By enjambing so few lines with verbs and prepositions (he uses only "set" and "with"), Snyder deters the lines from reaching forward and allows instead that they complete themselves in an independent unit of sense. All but six of these lines end in a noun. Snyder intermixes abstract and concrete nouns (word–rocks / hands–mind). The effect, as is usual in such juxtapositions, is to ground the abstract, to demonstrate that "thoughts" as well as "things" can be handled, kept by the poet manageably in place. The opening imperative casts over the ensuing poem an atmosphere of sureness and control. The gathering effect is of a rhetoric that is discrete, palpable, grave.

To notice all this is to notice also that these strategies are marshaled to ward off or pacify the poem's subject, which is that poetry, with all its temporal rhythms and concretions, spans an uncertain surface. A riprap is a trail of stone laid across slopes of polished, slippery granite. The willed concreteness of the laid corridor of rock is nearly an impertinence on the larger current of stone, a hardness that seems to flow. It is an insubstantial world in which mountains must be paved by rock. The world imagined here is, after all, one in which planets stray and ponies are riderless. "Poetry" here provides, in the words of *Myths & Texts,* "a riprap on the slick rock of metaphysics." So, in the end, the poem's syntax may be subverted by its imagery and argument. The weight of each line and word in "Riprap" becomes a measure of the streaming forces it momentarily stays.

Snyder's early metaphysic holds that experience is a flow subject to the temporary obstructions of form. He clings only loosely to things that stay rather than change. *Myths & Texts* advances this vision in an untroubled mood:

Human tenderness scuttles
Down dry endless cycles
Forms within forms falling
                clinging
Loosely, what's gone away?
              −love

Clung to while being released here is Western man's persistent belief that he lives in a universe of care. What goes away in a universe of cycles is the potential permanence of love, a permanence never to be expected in mortal life but one granted rather, or so the fiction has it, by the faith that the world has been made by a mind that cares for man and carries him toward a benevolent end. For Christianity, the descent of spirit into matter is a measure of God's love, and once the Incarnation has been achieved matter and history can never again be scorned. In Snyder's early Mahayana Buddhism, "the boundless compassion / Of diatoms, lava, and chipmunks"−the compassion of the created world−is only an illusory mercy, one consigned to the final fact of change. "Nature" is but "a vast set of conventions, totally arbitrary, patterns and stresses that come into being each instant; could disappear totally anytime; and continues only as a form of play."

In "Lookout's Journal," written in 1952−53 and a major source for *Myths & Texts,* Snyder records his most explicit jottings about a world that just turns:

> Almost had it last night: *no identity.* One thinks, "I emerged from some general, non-differentiated thing, I return to it." One has in reality never left it; there is no return.
>   my language fades. Images of erosion.

"There is no return." This is a vision immune to loss, because it imagines all creation and experience as a leaving that is also a staying. Life can know no desire because it knows no distance from its source. Given such a view, one need not−indeed, one cannot−invest in a person or a place. Perhaps the most serious limitation of such a vision from a writer's point of view is that before it, "language fades." All that the poet is left to announce is that all is one.

Although Snyder never renounces this metaphysic, the emphasis shifts in his later work away from the illusoriness and toward the usefulness of forms. As Snyder gets older he starts to experience the emotion of regret, and the mounting instances of this very simple emotion begin to suggest to him that there are real distances he has traveled, and things he has truly lost. The eternal return of his early vision gives way to a poetry of unique and historical return as the poet chooses to commit himself to the people and places he will love.

RETURNING

"And I was obsessed with a plan": This is Snyder's most succinct self-judgment, one voiced in "December at Yase" in *The Back Country*. The poem broods on the way solitary self-cultivation during the fifties and sixties has led to the loss of love. This is a mood that pervades *The Back Country*: The book is one in which Snyder comes across the possibility of regret. "I must make it alone," his young self had sworn, and now, as his thirties wane, the poet confidently sums up what he has become. He also reckons the cost.

The poems in the first section of the book, "Far West," show Snyder in his favorite American landscapes performing his habitual motions. The things of this world are there to be consumed, gotten around, or cleared away; the recurring actions are trail-building, hiking, and eating. The poems are instruction manuals that fill the being before the mind can think.

It is therefore noteworthy that "Far West" ends with a poem of memory:

For the Boy Who Was Dodger Point Lookout Fifteen Years Ago

[On a backpacking trip with my first wife in the Olympic mountains, having crossed over from the Dosewallips drainage, descended to and forded the Elwha and the Goldie, and climbed again to the high country. Hiking alone down the Elwha from Queets basin, these years later, brings it back.]

> The thin blue smoke of our campfire
> down in the grassy, flowery,
> heather meadow
> two miles from your perch.
> The snowmelt pond, and Alison,
> half-stoopt bathing like
> Swan Maiden, lovely naked,
> ringed with Alpine fir and
> gleaming snowy peaks. We
> had come miles without trails,
> you had been long alone.
> We talked for half an hour up
> there above the foaming creeks
> and forest valleys, in our
> world of snow and flowers.
>
> I don't know where she is now;
> I never asked your name.

> In this burning, muddy, lying,
> blood-drenched world
> that quiet meeting in the mountains
> cool and gentle as the muzzles of
> three elk, helps keep me sane.

The occasion for the poem is a return that brings back the memory of happiness in a beloved place; this is as close as Snyder will get to "Tintern Abbey." Up until this poem, Snyder has steadily refused to make his work a "dead fiddle" for anything lost, and he often relies, as Ekbert Faas has shown, on the tenselessness of a gerund to create a sense of presentness and concreteness in poems that are unavoidably located in the past. He has tried to live at a kind of spiritual noon. The last admission he would want to make is one everywhere made by Wordsworth, one framed by Coleridge: "Nothing affects me much at the moment it happens."

Early Snyder disdains Wordsworth's poems as devoted to a spurious present, relying as they do on the inability to penetrate duration expressed as a hope that the present is a moment that can someday be remembered. "Here I stand, not only with the sense / Of present pleasure, but with pleasing thoughts / That in this moment there is life and food / For future years." What Wordsworth is really present to, Snyder might have argued, is his own capacity for storing the moment away. The advantage of Wordsworth's method is that you can always someday have what today you certainly will miss; his is the poetry of the second chance, of lost immediacy as the fortunate fall. The past is the Eden we never had but to which we can recur. In "Milton by Firelight," Snyder discards this mode of experience – "No paradise, no fall" – and with it the myth that the Romantics raised up into a universal psychology: That history, whether individual or collective, is some kind of falling away from a state of undivided attention that demands the perpetual consolation of memory.

We remember the feeling that a thing evoked because the thing is no longer present; there is no need to remember what we still have. Up until *The Back Country,* Snyder had been successful in banishing memory from his poems by paying careful attention to what comes next; life had been a matter of turning toward and turning away. The path may be crooked, but the motion is resolutely forward:

> *Switchback*
> turn, turn,
> and again,   hard-
> scrabble
> steep travel a-
> head.

Now, in "Dodger Point," he finds himself not only turning back – remembering – but sustained by the very process he had sought to avoid.

The basic act in the poem is the premature departure from a friend; the hikers leave before they ask the lookout's name. The act is repeated with "my first wife." Snyder married Alison Gass in 1950 and divorced her in 1952. "I don't know where she is now." This is a familiar pattern: I let go of things, Snyder often admits; I don't keep track. We can even hear a faint reprise of *Myths & Texts*: "this burning . . . lying . . . world" echoes "It's all falling or burning." The churning participles here conjure up, however, no calm vision of process. Instead they convert the familiar universe of benign turning into a world of loss and deceit. The only stays we have in such a world are not apparently stable surfaces or openly changeable essences but the arresting power of the returning mind. Snyder's dependency on a faculty he had hoped to repress can be measured by his turning back to the most basic of the tropes of poetry: the simile. The poem ends with a flat-footed and unapologetic comparison:

> that quiet meeting in the mountains
> cool and gentle as the muzzles of
> three elk, helps keep me sane.

What the poem shares with Wordsworth beyond the structure of elegy (a present recalls a past that contains an imagined future) is the intention to communicate not a memory but the *feeling* that memory evokes. Wordsworth's announced project had been to capture the soul "Remembering how she felt, but what she felt / Remembering not." His attention to the sensation rather than the object of memory allowed his work to retain "an obscure sense / Of possible sublimity." In "Dodger Point" Snyder celebrates a sanity founded on the remembered similitudes of poetry. The simile conveys the "how" but not the "what"; a feeling is what the simile is meant to conjure up, not a concrete scene. *I felt like this.* Wordsworth knew that feelings are what can truly be kept, and that a life bereft of them, a life without a poetry competent to call them up, would be insane. Snyder here recognizes this. Henceforth, his poetry will display as one index of its imaginative health the felt remembrance of spots of time.

The structure of *The Back Country* is circular. Divided into four sections, the book begins with "Far West," arcs through "Far East" (Japan) and "Kali" (India), and then recurs to the American West in the last section, "Back." The poems continually imitate the pattern of this unfolding plot; the larger story of return is acted out through many figures of regret. The poet discovers that what he has turned away from he still carries with him:

> I always miss you—
> last fall, back from the mountains
> you'd left San Francisco
> now I'm going north again
>   as you go south.
> I sit by the fire at the ocean.
> How many times I've
> hitchhiked away;
>   the same pack on my back.

The figure of the hitchhiker/backpacker is Snyder's most powerful
early self-character. Up through *The Back Country* life is *kinhin*, a
walking meditation, and the hero is one who can carry his whole life
on his back. Snyder even gives him a bounding outline in "The Blue
Sky," where he prints the figure of the petroglyph that stands as a
composite of Amerindian and Chinese wandering poet/planters. Here,
in "Robin," Snyder questions hitchhiking's perpetual promise of new-
ness, and suggests that within the chance for discovery it also conceals
the impulse of flight. And flight proves illusory anyway; he carries
everywhere the same pack on his back. These poems of memory,
then, bring increasing weight to bear on what lies behind rather than
ahead of the moment of turning.

In "Across Lamarck Col," Snyder considers whether his reasons for
turning have not amounted to the avoidance of love:

Across Lamarck Col

> Descending hillsides in
>   half morning light, step over
>   small down pine,
> I see myself as stony granite face.
> All that we did was human,
>   stupid, easily forgiven,
> Not quite right.
>
> A giving stream you give another
>   should have been mine
> had I been not me
>   —to whom not given—
> Who most needed waited,
> Stoppt off, my me,—my fault
>   your black block mine—our—ours—
> Myself as stony granite face—
> You giving him because an other

> I also now become another.
> > what I
> Had not from you, for you,
> > > with a new lover,
> > Give, and give, and give, and
> > > > take.

Throughout this book runs the figure of a woman from whom Snyder has taken a premature or incomplete farewell. In this, the last of the poems on this theme, Snyder at once fully admits and casts out any regret. The book initiates and completes a process of mourning for lost options, and here, in a brilliant transvaluation of its central trope, refigures turning away as new giving:

> > what I
> Had not from you, for you,
> > > with a new lover,
> > Give, and give, and give, and
> > > > take.

It is a practical recognition – and also a moral one – that the way to honor past loves is to turn with energy toward future love. A pattern of behavior that Snyder has been reviewing as careless or evasive is here seen as potentially generative. The history of the poet's loves is a "giving stream" in which the abiding force of what he is losing nevertheless sends up, like a wave, the possibility of a future giving and taking.

In *Regarding Wave,* Snyder celebrates the sustaining recurrences he now enjoys in living with his wife. "What my hand follows on your body / Is the line," he had written in *The Back Country,* and here, as his "vision idly dallies on the hills" of that body, Snyder discerns new shapes and meanings in the landscape of love. "Wife" means "wave," we are told in *Earth House Hold* (1969), and as he cultivates his marriage with Masa, Snyder reflects on the ways in which life seems increasingly informed by the "laws of waves." Waves "bend and regain"; they create and conserve energy by redounding back upon themselves. Just as his marriage is sustained by his love for the lines of his wife's body and the vow to return, so experience itself stands revealed less as a stream in which all flows away and more as a series of waves that rise and fall in place. Water still runs, yet the will of things to stay can be remarked even in water in motion, as Snyder had noticed many years ago in "Lookout's Journal":

> Water in motion is precise and sharp, clearly formed,
> holding specific postures for infinitely small frozen moments.

The poem that best captures this felt pattern of recurrence and that completes a period of physical and emotional journeying is in *Turtle Island:*

On San Gabriel Ridges

I dream of —
soft, white, washable country
clothes.
woven zones.
scats
up here on the rocks;
seeds, stickers, twigs, bits of grass
on my belly, pressing designs —

O loves of long ago
       hello again.
all of us together
with all our other loves and children
twining and knotting
through each other —
intricate, chaotic, done.
I dive with you all
and it curls back, freezes;
the laws of waves.
as clear as a canyon wall
as sweet,
as long ago.

woven
into the dark.
squirrel hairs,
squirrel bones crunched,
tight and dry in scats of
fox.

Here all the metaphors come home to rest. Life had been a stream and the poem used words like rocks to resist the flow. Now what interests Snyder is the form of that motion, the will of the water itself to resist the flow. It, and the life it images, casts back upon itself, in Frost's words, "As if regret were in it and were sacred." Snyder certainly has moved beyond regret here, but it is probably because he has already moved through it, and admitted memory and loss, that he is so convincingly able to release it all here: "intricate, chaotic, done." Words and lines are accordingly set more casually in place; few are the strong

16. Gary Snyder walking with his wife, Masa Uehara

line-breaks and initial trochees that gave "Riprap" its subverted rhythm of reluctance. Lines twine together in a more continuous rhythm that suggests the dependency of each on what has gone before. A poetry of forgetting has become a poetry of remembering, and the substance of the past is seen not as junk to be discarded but as humus into which the poet can "dive" for fertilization. To love something means not that one must leave it but that one can use it again.

This process is not elevated but humbled through the bracketing images of animal scats. What has been consumed is reprocessed and dropped somewhere along the way; memory's as basic as shit. There is no waste in this new vision of process but instead a continual turning under and a continual harvest. In a talk given in 1978, Snyder elaborated this metaphor of recycling and suggested that the best possibility for transcendence in our current "climax situation" lies downward, toward the ground. In such a moment "a high percentage of the energy is derived not from grazing off the annual production of biomass, but from recycling dead biomass, the duff on the forest floor, the trees that have fallen, the bodies of dead animals":

When we deepen or enrich ourselves, looking within, understanding ourselves, we come closer to being like a climax system. Turning away from grazing on the "immediate biomass" of perception,
sensation, and thrill; and re-viewing memory, internalized perception, blocks of inner energies, dreams, the leaf-fall of day-to-day
consciousness, liberates the energy of our own sense-detritus. Art
is an assimilator of unfelt experience, perception, sensation, and
memory for the whole society. When all that compost of feeling
and thinking comes back to us then, it comes not as a flower, but –
to complete the metaphor – as a mushroom: the fruiting body of the
buried thread of mycelia that run widely through the soil, and are
intricately married to the root hairs of all the trees.

Snyder chose California ground: The years surrounding his fortieth
birthday were those in which he settled in his own woven zone. His
first son, Kai, was born in 1968, before his return to California later
that year. Gen was born in the next year, and in 1971 he built his home
near Nevada City in the foothills of the Sierra. Since that time Snyder
has devoted himself to understanding this act of settlement and return.
    In settling at Kitkitdizze, Snyder has set himself against all myths of
the fall. The prevailing myth of our culture is that the earth is a place
into which we fell. Since Eden, nature has trapped spirit in a body that
thwarts the final finding of our desire. Snyder has argued from the start
against the hegemony of this view in the West. "At the root of the
problem where our civilization goes wrong is the mistaken belief that
nature is something less than authentic, that nature is not as alive as
man is, or as intelligent, that in a sense it is dead." It is on this ground
that Snyder and Jeffers come together. Both act as spokesmen for
nonhuman nature, and both see it as persisting with a dignity that
deserves respect. But whereas Jeffers can only praise nature by damning
man, Snyder imagines a coexistence between them reminiscent of the
early Wordsworth. The extremity of Jeffers's position he openly considered early on, in "Lookout's Journal":

> – If one wished to write poetry of nature, where an audience?
> Must come from the very conflict of an attempt to articulate the
> vision   of poetry nature in our time.
>
>> (reject the human; but the tension of human
>> events, brutal and tragic, against a non-
>> human background? like Jeffers?)

The answer was to be no. Snyder chose eventually not to reject but
to immerse himself in the human, to lose himself in his life. This is also
part of the Romantic tradition, although one much neglected by critics

who value the extremity of the vision over the accommodations to which it may be asked to yield. It is worth reminding ourselves that the most unequivocal statement in "Tintern Abbey" has nothing to do with a sublimity beyond sense but rather with the anonymous discipline of our daily round. What Wordsworth prizes as the "best portion of a good man's life" is something Snyder has come to as well: "His little, nameless, unremembered, acts / Of kindness and love." It may be true that Wordsworth and Snyder produced their best work before they were forty and that their marriages and ensuing domestication rendered poetry increasingly peripheral to their needs. If so, what we need is a criticism that can at least acknowledge if not actually evaluate what they went on to do, which was to lead happy and generative lives.

This is perhaps the most a poet can do for a place – show us how to live in it. Jeffers certainly domesticated a California place, although he seems to have taken small comfort in his success. Held fast by his myth of decline, he was unable to take his own life as the model for a countervailing myth. Perhaps his actions will finally speak as powerfully as his words. Snyder has devoted his words to rationalizing his actions as an exemplary way. He is closest to Muir in that he refuses to accept a California that is ended or ending. Although he believes with Muir that nature's vanishment must be caught up in the preserve of a text, he also knows with Muir that its loss can be stayed through action. His has been an effort to close the gap between a writing (and typically elegiac) self and a doing (and typically place- and time-bound) self. For the perfection, as Yeats had it, of divorce between the life and the work, Snyder substitutes an imperfect marriage.

So where does Snyder live, and what does he do? Here is his description of the place, from "What's Meant by 'Here' ":

Crackly grass and Blue oak, the special smells of pungent sticky flowers, give way, climbing, through Digger pine and into Black oak and Ponderosa pine; sweet birch, manzanita, kitkitdizze. This is our home country. We dig wells and wonder where the water table comes from.

We wonder where the deer go in the summer heat, and where they come from in the fall. How far east into the high Sierra. In thirty steady climbing miles the ridge contacts the crest, eight thousand feet. Pure granite; little lakes.

This is a portrait of his immediate watershed, and the area above the ridge where Snyder has built his home. "My sense of place," Snyder would add, "is the whole West Coast. No, not the whole West Coast, Northern California, Oregon, and Washington are where I feel most at home." This is the region within which Snyder has concentrated his imaginative range. The consequence of this choice is that he lives along the lines laid down by the most ancient culture of the area – a life like that of an American Indian.

In Snyder's accounts of Indian life, two themes predominate: no waste and little wandering. The typical California Indian rarely strayed more than thirty miles from where he was born, and the consequence was that he could not afford to foul his own nest. Snyder, in fact, works his land in summer, travels for poetry readings in the spring and fall, and stays in the house in winter to write. He acknowledges his citizenship and need to know about a nation that pays for his work, but he refuses to extend much attention to the media culture and sees it as projecting an illusory urgency that distracts us from tasks more ready to hand. Four or five types of activities now fill his time: scavenging and gathering, recycling, playing, conjuring the spirit (writing and performing), making camp. From a casual survey of *Turtle Island* and *Axe Handles,* one sees days and seasons taken up with making trails, picking up deer hit by cars, laying up firewood, gathering mushrooms, drying apples, writing, drying berries, painting the local school, shooting arrows at a bale of straw. Snyder built his house with his own hands and says that "I *love* getting together with a bunch of people and wailing away, building an earth dam, or peeling poles, or trucking gravel." He says that knowing a place means, above all, knowing its plants. He does his share of "the tiresome but tangible work of . . . local politics," reading his work at fire stations and schools, appearing before the county supervisors. He washes with his wife and two boys in the sauna he built and has given us one of the most frankly erotic family encounters in English, "The Bath."

Snyder has successfully centered his life by forsaking an interest in being central. "It is a commitment to place, and to your neighbors, that – with no loss of quality – accomplishes the decentralization of poetry. The decentralization of 'culture' is as important to our long-range ecological and social health as the decentralization of agriculture, production, energy, and government." Snyder has accordingly relaxed any quest for fame. Certainly he may already be secure enough, his work long since canonized by the imprimatur of New Directions. But his pattern of publication, especially since *Turtle Island,* has been that of a career rendering itself increasingly anonymous. Snyder no longer aggressively seeks a national forum. He often brings out his work in small presses and regional journals, and his time is given over to readings and the evanescence of voice. In this principled act of self-dispersal, Snyder scatters himself throughout the West to fertilize rather than to overshadow the ground. His has been a journey of turning and returning in which an initial motion out and away discovered within itself a contrary impulse to go back. As the poet gazes back over his career he takes pleasure in simply having closed a circle, although the old wanderlust abides. It is, Snyder might say with surprise, a story that rhymes:

> I certainly feel good and strong about being in a place that I intend to live in for the rest of my life. I think that this is a basic human need. Which is not to say that a certain amount of traveling and wandering isn't also a need. But my earliest poems start here in America on the Pacific Coast, with travels in India and Japan in between. So it does complete a circle. Starting with Douglas fir and Ponderosa pine and ending with Douglas fir and Ponderosa pine.

Epilogue: Fictions of space

Innocent of history and unsure of its culture, America turned to its landscapes as a unique possession to which its response could give meaning and value. For Milton, nature had been a *book* written by someone else (God), and the "sensuous poverty" of his Edenic landscapes expressed his conviction that any natural prospect serves ordained purposes in a stable spiritual allegory. The proper response to landscape was awe, and worship. For Emerson, nature has become a *text,* and the proper response to landscape is curiosity, and interpretation. Emerson founds his declaration of independence on the indeterminacy of the natural world: *Nature* declares that meaning has passed over to the discretion of the eye. To this day strong imaginations in America have remained geographers, engaged, in Carl Sauer's phrase, in "a reading the face of the earth."

Through their encounters with natural space, writers on the continent developed new ways of knowing. Unsponsored imaginations found in unfallen landscape a stage on which to reenact Milton's story: We have heard enough about American Eves and Adams. For those who eschewed archetypes, landscape could solicit the self into unexplored dimensions of autobiographical expression. In its responsiveness to projection, landscape evolved into a palimpsest on which Americans could revise Old-World ideas about friendship and marriage, work and play, sanity and the sublime. And in agreeing to read the face of the continent as a measure of its destiny, the young country proposed to the world that the images of a nation could be grounded in natural as well as in political, cultural, and military history.

California acts as the site for such discoveries because her landscapes, beautiful, looming, and austere, remain a dominant fact in the experience of her culture. It is the perception as well as the fact of landscape of which I speak, the regional belief, deeply held, that one acts always in concert, for better or for worse, with natural fact. In this California intensifies the national myth that America has been set apart from the beginning by its freedom to test itself against the unmediated. If landscape has meant one thing to Americans, it has meant innocence, and the ways in which we make use of it – the ways we fall into it or make it fall – constitute a telling record of the price we are willing to pay for experience.

The story of each of these California careers is a story of loss. Hetch Hetchy becomes a sullen lake; Austin's Inyo reverts to sand; Steinbeck prunes his childhood garden and leaves it forever. This is not an original story; the old archetype is hard to shake. Robert Hass, a contemporary California poet, ruefully admits to the way human scripts repeat themselves, even amid guarantees of oblivion on the edge of the world:

> All the new thinking is about loss.
> In this it resembles all the old thinking.

Hass is a poet who has chosen to stay home (he lives in Berkeley and was born and raised in the Bay Area) in order to testify to the inescapability of the old thinking, even in California. The site of his poetry is a landscape for which there are already too many field guides, a landscape that still demands original praise. His is the recurring discovery that he has stumbled into a time-worn garden, a place in which "names" have already been given to "things."

I have been no more successful at escaping the old thinking. When I started this book, it did not occur to me that each of my chapters would trace a fall *out* of Eden. A book conceived as an act of praise gradually became an elegy for the belief that happiness can be founded in natural space. The challenge became, as I wrote on, to find the gain in the loss, the "recompense" of which Wordsworth spoke when he stood in a once-loved place and felt how far experience had carried him from ever again returning to it as a unique and sustaining home.

Recompense came, if it did, through the economy of paradox. Landscape as a category of experience and value kept calling up, in each of these careers, some implied opposite. The most simple and obvious dialectic was between places and people. "Life is an affair of people not of places," says Wallace Stevens, "but for me life is an affair of places and that is the trouble." This rueful self-judgment is one most of these writers implicitly voice, and the affair is one some of them try to break off. Certainly as I wrote this book the matter of other people came to haunt my thinking about our affairs with place. In the English-language tradition, the old thinking insisted on reminding me, the pursuit of happiness (a New World ideal) merges with the allegory of love (an Old World ideal), and any fantasies about escape into the "territory" usually come up against the felt need to colonize the country of marriage.

Jack London's two Sonoma novels turn on the moment when his hero and heroine reenter the gates of paradise: "They were like two persons, after far wandering, who had merely come home again. There was less of the unexpected in their dealings with nature, while theirs was all the delight of reminiscence." Burning Daylight and his bride are here choosing Glen Ellen as a home. Escape from the city to the country – the novel's ostensible subject – is here forwarded and superseded by a more profound act of embowerment in which husband and wife recover a sense of belonging through the mediation of a human bond. Marriage or something like it – a deep and abiding human tie – tantalizes Steinbeck, Chandler, and Snyder as the "space" in which we become most fully human. Lawrence's complaint about a national failure of nerve is not lost on them: "Absolutely the safest thing to get your emotional reactions over is NATURE." The more self-conscious of these writers finally seek out an "other" less willing to accept their projections. The freedom to conduct a dialogue is, they concur, a more rewarding activity than the freedom to remain (landscape can't answer back) the hero of a monologue. Adam didn't occupy the garden long before he thought to ask for Eve.

My book was overtaken by a second paradox: Careers that began as celebrations of an outer world often ended by affirming the reality of an inner one. It was Satan who declared most powerfully the potential independence of the mind from place, and the young Francis Parkman anticipates many westering imaginations when he ends his manuscript account of his venture into America's unplotted spaces by quoting Milton:

> The mind is its own place, and in itself
> Can make a heaven of hell, a hell of heaven.

Milton tried to redeem this solipsistic declaration through the promise of "a paradise within," a consolation I have frequently invoked. In the wake of our exile, the internal Eden provides a sanctuary in which to dwell. We know this sanctuary, after Blake and Wordsworth, Frye and Bloom, by the name of Romantic Imagination. The consequences of this sublimation for the Anglo-American imagination have been disturbing and profound. For it is the tendency of Romantic Imagination – in what might be called the Heresy of Internalization – to collapse into a demonic parody of itself. In most careers dependent on this consolation, the dialectic between what we "half-create / And what perceive" breaks down, and the mind finds itself divorced from the natural world it had hoped to marry. For Dana, Frémont, Austin, and King, writing becomes a way of preserving a private ecstasy within once-loved spaces that allow no further extension of the will.

The final paradox was one in which space seemed to call up and valorize the supremacy of time. We live, according to Sauer, at the behest of two sets of facts: "The facts of geography are place facts; their association gives rise to the concept of landscape. Similarly, the facts of history are time facts; their association gives rise to the concept of period." Sauer here speaks of these two concepts as if they were independent functions, although throughout his work the facts of geography emerge as a fiction – a momentary stay against confusion – dependent for its stability on a suspension of historical perspective. Place (the "morphology of landscape") is the stopped frame in the continuous film of change. In his scholarly and unassuming way, California's most eminent geographer joins that company of imaginers who brood on the dimensions in which we live. The recent history of the imagination shows time and space as threatening to collapse into or become confounded with one another. Lessing, Bergson, Pater, Pound, Lewis, and Warren have all speculated on the ways in which one of these dimensions is contained in or rendered irrelevant by its opposite. "Modernism" can in fact be read as the triumph of the fiction of space: Certainly its major adepts project a vision of the world and strive for a form that denies or ignores the pressure of ongoing and irreversible time.

Charles Olson has celebrated the American tendency to evade the burden of history through an affair with space. "I take SPACE to be the central fact to man born in America, from Folsom cave to now." I don't want to join here in the debate over "spatial form" or the American anxiety over temporal identity. What I would like to point to is the recurring pattern in the careers read here, in which a vision dedicated to the facts of geography is overridden by the facts of history. Despite the power and beauty of California space, each of these writers becomes increasingly compelled by the shape of his or her motion through it. If we are *in* anything, these careers seem to say, we are in a story, a sequence with a beginning, a middle, and an unforeseeable but inevitable end. Landscape itself is subject to change, and the notion of specific location may be a function of the brevity of our perspective. More importantly, time is the medium of memory and desire, of gain and loss, and hence the very guarantor of the possibility of *value*. The more radical of these careers finally suggest that our anxiety over time is, in Frost's phrase, "most us," and that that which extends around us is a wonderful abstraction from and defense against meaning generated by a life that is passing. Hass captures the human wish to spatialize the time-bound in a beautiful pun:

> Longing, we say, because desire is full
> of endless distances.

Out of our need and out of our love, we tell ourselves that the obstacle to happiness is distance, not duration. In the most ambitious book yet written about California landscape, Norris maintains that Bergson was right: Space is the generous and enabling lie told by time.

So the conclusion is this: Writing about landscape carries us beyond the need for landscape. It is not a sufficient partner (one cannot marry or befriend it); it is not created but given (one cannot "make" or imagine it); it is not the dimension in which we live (space is a fiction of a time-ridden mind). The space we call "landscape" is, from the fully human standpoint, an illusion of the given world on which we depend, but an illusion in which we cannot finally dwell. In its apparent stability and concreteness, landscape is the most widely available donor of the experience we call "presence," and its peculiar fate is therefore to arouse our longing for all in human life that is or can be absent and lost. It was given to John Muir to embody rather than to know this, and I would nominate him as the writer most responsive to the tension between landscape and imagination in California. His career is dedicated to a celebration of landscape as the mercy of the earth, and to a loving suppression of the knowledge, disclosed by and hidden within his beloved glaciers, that its face is as poor a passing fact as our own.

Notes

═══════

The initial phrases of each note indicate the beginning and end of the passage in the text to which the note pertains. Those works listed in the Bibliography are referred to in the Notes by author and title only. For quotations of well-known authors, such as Milton and Yeats, I have made brief notes but have not included full bibliographical data.

PROLOGUE: THE MYTHOLOGY OF THE REGION

["rank weeds"] William Brewer, *Up and Down California*, 106.

["a dead . . . holy water"] Ibid., 107.

["I find . . . and decay"] Ibid., 58.

["a mythology . . . its region"] Wallace Stevens, *The Palm at the End of the Mind* (New York: Random House, 1972), 398.

["dissolving views"] Bayard Taylor, *El Dorado,* 44.

["The classic . . . a place"] William Carlos Williams, "Kenneth Burke," in *Imaginations,* ed. Webster Schott (New York: New Directions, 1970), 356.

["very close . . . Terrestrial Paradise"] Garcí Ordóñez de Montalvo, *Las Sergas de Esplandián,* Seville, 1510.

SPECTATORSHIP AND ABANDONMENT: DANA, LEONARD, AND FRÉMONT

["Deer scarce"] John Bakeless, ed., *The Journals of Lewis and Clark,* 60.

["Proceeded on"] Ibid., 79.

["in future . . . *for myself*"] Ibid., 246.

["weakness of the eyes"] Richard Henry Dana, *Two Years Before the Mast* (1840 edition; rpt. Penguin), 40.

["to do . . . been right"] Zenas Leonard, *Narrative of the Adventures of Zenas Leonard*, 100.

["stripped of . . . and dissipation"] *Two Years* (1840 edition), 133.

["Miles out . . . thousand inhabitants"] Ibid., 499.

["The first . . . tallow-bags"] Ibid., 118–19.

["solitude . . . spectacle"] Ibid., 498.

["hated coast"] Ibid., 362.

["The land . . . not conceive"] Ibid., 146.

["I was . . . have disappeared"] Ibid., 506.

["The old spots"] Ibid., 519.

["the climate has altered"] Ibid., 509.

["When I . . . not realized"] Ibid., 500.

["obstinate questionings . . . outward things"] William Wordsworth, "Ode: Intimations of Immortality from Recollections of Early Childhood," lines 141–2.

["I was . . . a passenger"] *Two Years* (1840 edition), 510.

["softening"] Ibid., 511.

["I alone . . . I here"] Ibid., 514.

["A man . . . his loss"] Ibid., 77.

["There is . . . at sea"] Richard Henry Dana, *Two Years Before the Mast* (1869 edition; rpt. Dutton), 8.

["There is . . . can give"] *Two Years* (1840 edition), 47.

["When once . . . water meet"] Ibid., 362.

["stillness . . . solitude"] Ibid., 497.

["Day after . . . their sunlight"] Ibid., 261.

["The only . . . in California"] Ibid., 196.

["a small . . . hundred feet"] Ibid., 197.

["Compared with . . . had led"] Ibid., 197.

["It was . . . like poetry"] Ibid., 158.

["broken bricks . . . of mortar"] Ibid., 514.

["The past . . . unnatural, repellant"] Ibid., 514.

["To rally . . . *sub Jove*"] Ibid., 515.

["He professed . . . but mine"] Ibid., 503.

["to steer . . . the Pacific"] Leonard, *Adventures,* 104.

["restore our lost fortunes"] Ibid., 103.

["a large mountain"] Ibid., 119.

["Our horses . . . of rabbits"] Ibid., 121.

["unbroken level . . . awfully sublime"] Ibid., 124.

["stupid and stiff"] Ibid., 125.

["this inhospitable region"] Ibid., 128–9.

["more distressing every hour"] Ibid., 128.

["Here we . . . our horses"] Ibid., 129.

["ridge between . . . these chasms."] Ibid., 130.

["superior to . . . ever eat"] Ibid., 131.

["brink of the mountain"] Ibid., 132.

["In looking . . . to sight"] Ibid., 132.

["In the . . . the ground"] Ibid., 136.

["having spent . . . crossing over"] Ibid., 136.

["It is . . . remarkably plenty"] Ibid., 136.

["the fattest . . . to eat"] Ibid., 140.

["the most . . . water course"] Ibid., 138.

["two long . . . of ammunition"] Ibid., 100.

["I sometimes . . . some profit"] Ibid., 105.

["remarkable"] Ibid., 110.

["gazing . . . curiosities"] Ibid., 110.

["We spent . . . nature's handy-work"] Ibid., 129.

["Here was . . . had traversed"] Ibid., 148.

["About noon . . . a ship"] Ibid., 150.

["This night . . . had discovered"] Ibid., 139.

["The idea . . . great west"] Ibid., 146.

["as there . . . the year"] Ibid., 170.

["no floor . . . bare walls"] Ibid., 166.

["she should . . . as possible"] Ibid., 155.

["Of a . . . wicked nature"] Ibid., 186.

["as if . . . were dogs"] Ibid., 191.

["stupid Spanish"] Ibid., 195.

["bent upon . . . this region"] Ibid., 196.

["California mountain"] Ibid., 197.

["Soon after . . . them together"] Ibid., 146.

["perishing for . . . extensive desert"] Ibid., 205.

["felt as . . . to California"] *Two Years* (1840 edition), 360.

["Travelling along . . . homeward direction"] *Adventures*, 205.

["That unless . . . we read"] William Carlos Williams, *In the American Grain*, 109.

["descent . . . the ground"] Ibid., 213.

["The English . . . was able"] Ibid., 108.

["Nearly all . . . into flower"] Ibid., 157.

["The emptiness . . . look further"] Ibid., 63–4.

["whole weight . . . wild continent"] Ibid., 68.

["With thinking . . . friends sometimes"] Henry David Thoreau, *Walden* (New York: Norton Critical Edition, 1966), 90–1.

["What was . . . being alone"] Ibid., 212.

["It was . . . of civilization"] John Charles Frémont, *The Expeditions of John Charles Frémont*, 1:270.

["the course . . . the narrative"] Ibid., 575.

["in at . . . large book"] Ibid., 270.

["I never . . . last forever"] William H. Goetzmann, *Army Exploration in the American West*, 84.

["You are . . . romantically truthful"] Allan Nevins, *Frémont: Pathmarker of the West*, 303.

["I fancy . . . geniune fame"] Josiah Royce, *California*, 35.

["from that . . . little cost"] Nevins, 197.

["to give . . . our continent"] *The Expeditions*, 1:426.

["to open California"] Nevins, 338.

["repress this . . . *must look*"] Bernard DeVoto, *The Year of Decision: 1846*, 196.

["In all . . . the country"] *The Expeditions*, 1:8.

["reckless"] Ibid., 57.

["royal hunt"] Ibid., 17.

["object . . . existing uncertainty"] Ibid., 57.

["There is . . . reached certainty"] Ibid., 57.

["feels a . . . of grandeur"] Ibid., 185.

["the chase . . . nothing else"] Ibid., 187.

["We entered . . . the dust"] Ibid., 187.

["A thick . . . and clear"] Ibid., 187–8.

["We, therefore . . . the scene"] Ibid., 199.

["the buffalo . . . real life"] Ibid., 200.

["overcoming space"] William H. Emory, *Notes of a Military Reconnaissance*, 28.

["Uncertain as . . . of surveying"] Stephen Fender, *Plotting the Golden West*, 48.

["There is . . . the West"] Ibid., 44.

["loaded wagons . . . serious interruption"] Lansford Hastings, *The Emigrant's Guide*, 71.

["flesh of . . . undergoing putrefaction"] Ibid., 85.

["very easy"] Ibid., 71.

["unfurled the . . . waved before"] *The Expeditions*, 1:270.

["We reached . . . something sublime"] Ibid., 501.

["great river . . . San Francisco"] Ibid., 574.

["No river . . . Sierra Nevada"] Ibid., 669.

["abandoned all . . . its existence"] Ibid., 662.

["The course . . . the narrative"] Ibid., 575.

["It was . . . the Sacramento"] Ibid., 611.

["The latest . . . follow it"] Charles Preuss, *Exploring with Frémont*, 94.

["there was . . . entering California"] Nevins, 151.

["We here . . . the deviation"] *The Expeditions*, 1:668–9.

["It was . . . had climbed"] Thomas Hart Benton, *Thirty Years' View*, 2:581.

["It required . . . been before"] *The Expeditions*, 1:654.

["I reminded . . . the Sacramento"] Ibid., 626.

["on the . . . dividing ridge"] Ibid., 638.

["Having only . . . *not* facile"] Ibid., 638.

["But, after . . . us disappointment"] Ibid., 639–40.

["again the . . . our minds"] Ibid., 640.

["My plans . . . that December"] *The Expeditions,* 2:106.

["I felt . . . frontier travel"] Ibid., 107.

["How fate . . . horses' feet"] Ibid., 107.

["The information . . . take California"] Ibid., 110.

["And I . . . all planned"] Ibid., 106.

["I hope . . . they find"] Ibid., 106.

["to move . . . Sacramento valley"] Ibid., 111.

["This decision . . . of California"] Ibid., 111.

["For the . . . left them"] Ibid., 113.

["By heaven . . . rough work"] Ibid., 119.

["no more . . . the West"] DeVoto, *The Year of Decision,* 466.

["guided only . . . Frémont's *Travels*"] Goetzmann, 108.

["humane tenderheartedness"] Royce, *California,* 26.

["bloodless playfulness"] Ibid., 26.

["Civilized warfare . . . badly hurt"] Ibid., 25.

["the degradation . . . our own"] Ibid., 88.

["Frémont and . . . California history"] Kevin Starr, *Americans and the California Dream,* 159.

MUIR AND THE POSSESSION OF LANDSCAPE

["to look . . . denser portions"] John Muir, *The Yosemite,* 40–1.

["to creep . . . be removed"] Ibid., 41.

["Down came . . . thundering bath"] Ibid., 41.

["Would the . . . be swayed"] Ibid., 42.

["moved gently . . . idle wind"] Ibid., 42.

["steadiness of the light"] Ibid., 42

["sound and . . . mid-night bath"] Ibid., 42.

["In the . . . of God"] Ralph Waldo Emerson, *Nature.*

["Sharp at . . . sweet fern"] Ernest Hemingway, *In Our Time* (1925 and 1930; rpt. New York: Scribners, 1970), 137.

["The river was there"] Ibid., 133.

["To engage . . . a geometry"] William Carlos Williams, *Spring and All* in *Imaginations*, 108.

["The raw . . . the mountain"] *The Yosemite*, 27.

["mistress and his wife"] William Faulkner, *Go Down, Moses* (1942; rpt. New York: Random House, 1973), 326.

["sudden disenchantment"] *The Yosemite*, 41.

["Prior to . . . Red Mountains"] John Muir, *The Mountains of California*, 28.

["weird under-world . . . the crevasse"] Ibid., 33.

["tender"] Ibid., 16.

["strange thrilling . . . learn something"] *The Yosemite*, 78.

["indweller"] Thoreau, *Walden*, Norton Critical Edition, 31.

["The tried . . . more complete"] *The Mountains of California*, 64–5.

["I recognise thy glory"] William Wordsworth, *The Prelude* (1850), 6:559.

["No pain . . . a crystal"] *The Yosemite*, 131.

["the transparence . . . He is"] Wallace Stevens, *The Palm at the End of the Mind*, 187.

["I never turn back"] *The Mountains of California*, 92.

["more plainly visible"] Ibid., 265.

["it would . . . wider outlook"] Ibid., 251.

["Never before . . . a reed"] Ibid., 252.

["the heart . . . wild rush"] Ibid., 263.

["trampling near . . . cañon head"] *The Yosemite*, 66.

["When the . . . ever experienced"] Ibid., 67.

["huge coarse mouth"] Ibid., 50.

["one homogeneous buzz"] *The Mountains of California*, 288.

["ever vigorous . . . your company"] Ibid., 276.

["He *must* . . . heavens fall"] Ibid., 282.

["cheap adjectives"] Linnie Marsh Wolfe, *Son of the Wilderness: The Life of John Muir*, 128.

["grandiloquent"] Starr, *Americans and the California Dream*, 187.

["no wavering . . . and joy"] *The Mountains of California*, 279.

["unmodulated"] Ibid., 288.

["multitude of . . . antagonistic impressions"] Ibid., 265.

["ascend . . . united and harmonious"] Ibid., 265.

["It is . . . the others"] John Muir, *My First Summer in the Sierra Nevada*, 175–6.

["similitude in dissimilitude"] William Wordsworth, *Preface to Lyrical Ballads* (1800).

["summit-peaks . . . and featureless"] *The Mountains of California*, 3.

["one vast . . . of stone"] Ibid., 16.

["when we . . . the universe"] *My First Summer*, 211.

["how curiously . . . repeated herself"] Josiah Whitney, *The Yosemite Guide-Book*, 98–9.

["is bent . . . like Yosemite"] John Muir, "Rambles of a Botanist Among the Plants and Climates of California," 35.

["vast perpendicular . . . El Capitan"] Ibid., 35.

["The first . . . of Yosemite"] Ibid., 35.

["a position . . . Yosemite Fall"] Ibid., 35.

["correspond with . . . Yosemite wall"] Ibid., 35.

["Anyhow I'll . . . killing me"] Wolfe, *Son of the Wilderness*, 340.

["The first . . . likewise despoiled"] *The Yosemite*, 257.

["one of . . . the nation"] Everson, *Archetype West*, 53.

["California forests . . . the world"] *The Mountains of California*, 251.

["inviting openness"] Ibid., 140.

["monotonous uniformity"] Ibid., 140.

["long, curving bands"] Ibid., 144.

["never so . . . their individuality"] Ibid., 101.

["the sugar . . . to year"] Ibid., 100.

["here are . . . all alike"] Ibid., 52.

["Going to . . . them before"] Ibid., 60.

["majestic domed pavilion"] *My First Summer*, 80.

["mountain hollow . . . sweet home"] Ibid., 85.

["influences . . . quiet room"] Ibid., 65.

["fond of . . . flesh fly"] Ibid., 184–5.

["one well-defined . . . called supernatural"] Ibid., 242.

["He seemed . . . my face"] Ibid., 241.

["lost in the brush"] Ibid., 247.

["half-happy"] John Muir, *The Story of My Boyhood and Youth*, 132.

["Father was . . . as possible"] Ibid., 11.

["Play as . . . and disobey"] Ibid., 36–7.

["carefully hidden . . . father's eye"] Ibid., 192.

["John, he . . . am doing"] Ibid., 202–3.

["I really . . . of rest"] Wolfe, *Son of the Wilderness*, 90.

["I was . . . yet completed"] *Story of My Boyhood*, 228.

["constant and . . . impulse"] Wolfe, *Son of the Wilderness*, 110.

["the wonder . . . unexpected supply"] Robert Frost, "The Figure a Poem Makes."

["The University . . . the Wilderness"] *Story of My Boyhood*, 228.

["the gobble . . . of economics"] Wolfe, *Son of the Wilderness*, 102.

["early-rising machine"] *Story of My Boyhood*, 203.

["Loafer's Chair"] Wolfe, *Son of the Wilderness*, 65.

["rather weak . . . and gristmill"] *My First Summer*, 103.

["the stomach . . . its own"] Ibid., 102.

["Bread without . . . of nourishment"] Ibid., 103.

["the bread . . . to wanderers"] Ibid., 4.

KING AND CATASTROPHE

["impassable gulfs"] Clarence King, *Mountaineering in the Sierra Nevada* (1872), 256. All references unless otherwise specified are to the 1872 edition.

["a lately . . . deep grave"] Ibid., 256–7.

["right side . . . of coffee"] Thurman Wilkins, *Clarence King: A Biography*, 109.

["I always . . . these climbs"] *Mountaineering*, 245.

["I have . . . and myself"] Wilkins, 21.

["duty"] Ibid., 131.

["the most . . . our time"] Ibid., vii.

["One good Turner deserves another"] Ibid., 295.

["Scheherazade"] Ibid., 198.

["geological Micawber"] *Mountaineering,* 158.

["willful misapplication"] Wilkins, 339.

["evaded into space"] Ibid., 348.

["the present . . . the past"] Ibid., 208.

["modified"] Ibid., 209.

["extirpated all . . . earliest introduction"] Clarence King, "Catastrophism and the Evolution of Environment," 9.

["the west . . . dynamic sense"] Ibid., 16.

["Muir, John . . . glacial blunders"] Clarence King, *Systematic Geology,* 792.

["those terrible . . . rending asunder"] *Mountaineering,* 33.

["*plasticity* became . . . of salvation"] "Catastrophism," 34.

["terrible and . . . telluric energy"] Ibid., 5.

["impending crises"] Ibid., 7.

["novelty"] J. C. Levenson, "Henry Adams and the Art of Politics," 57.

["abruption"] Robert Frost, *The Poetry of Robert Frost.* ed. Edward Connery Lathem (New York: Holt, Rinehart & Winston, 1969), 510.

["intake of fire"] Ibid., 266.

["He who . . . into being"] "Catastrophism," 37.

["mirage"] *Mountaineering,* 17.

["geology itself . . . constructive imagination"] Harry Herbert Crosby, "So. Deep a Trail: A Biography of Clarence King," 110.

["Indeed, I . . . and difficulty"] *Mountaineering,* 235.

["upon a . . . the sky"] Ibid., 237.

["Afar in . . . thousand feet"] Ibid., 239.

["We must . . . social *régime*"] Ibid., 291.

["Out of . . . noble race"] Ibid., 292.

["the grand . . . this trip"] Brewer, *Up and Down California,* 309.

["I looked . . . his life"] *Mountaineering,* 54.

["campaign for . . . of California"] Ibid., 51.

["getting his ears frostbitten"] Brewer, 465.

["the greatest muscular endurance"] Ibid., 525.

["the one . . . death with"] *Mountaineering*, 51.

["a sort . . . and me"] Ibid., 58.

["A single . . . softened perceptibly"] Ibid., 60.

["forty feet . . . smooth granite"] Ibid., 89.

["Don't be . . . I know"] Ibid., 90–1.

["I will . . . myself gone"] Clarence King Papers, Notebook D-4 in the Huntington Library, 45.

["We reached . . . without accident"] Ibid., 37.

["Dick climbed . . . almost nothing"] Ibid., 45.

["cleanly cut . . . of granite"] *Mountaineering*, 76.

["rocky tower . . . Mount Tyndall"] Ibid., 278.

["Distinctness terrible"] Ibid., 167.

["shut in . . . nothing recognized"] Ibid., 92.

["desert of death"] Ibid., 80.

["tumult of . . . of space"] Ibid., 80.

["the serene . . . hollow space"] Ibid., 78.

["I have . . . present order"] Ibid., 79.

["Above us . . . our feet"] Ibid., 277.

["I saw . . . had climbed"] Ibid., 278.

["feeling quite . . . our direction"] Ibid., 279.

["to carefully . . . of topography"] Ibid., 280.

["*this peak . . . Mount Whitney*"] Francis P. Farquhar, *History of the Sierra Nevada*, 173.

["All honor . . . before me"] Wilkins, 146.

["*that we . . . the Alps*"] William Wordsworth, *The Prelude* (1850), 6:591.

["break through"] Ibid., 6:597.

["Our being's . . . invisible world"] Ibid., 6:602–4.

["At intervals . . . other circumstances"] Thomas De Quincey, *Literary Reminiscences* (1861), 1:314–15.

["a gentle . . . mild surprise"] Wordsworth, *The Prelude* (1850), 5:382.

["One's own . . . the soul"] Clarence King, *Mountaineering in the Sierra Nevada* (1874), ed. Francis P. Farquhar, 302.

["vacant solitudes . . . sheltering nearness"] Ibid., 303–4.

["That fearful . . . and wall"] Ibid., 303.

["a strange . . . and air"] Ibid., 303.

["highest bliss"] Wordsworth, *The Prelude* (1850), 14:113.

["awful Power"] Ibid., 6:594.

["the consciousness/Of Whom"] Ibid., 14:115.

["on the . . . of myth-making"] *Mountaineering* (1874), 305.

["It is . . . with consciousness"] Ibid., 304.

["the hard . . . Mount Whitney"] Ibid., 306.

["I saw . . . geological empire"] Ibid., 306.

["inanimate forms . . . gone forever"] *Mountaineering,* 78.

["the eloquence of death"] Ibid., 78.

["flat upon . . . the fire"] Ibid., 96.

["acres of tranquil pork"] Ibid., 100.

["spread so"] Ibid., 96.

["riding, her . . . immovable seat"] Ibid., 108.

["determined . . . probe Susan"] Ibid., 109.

["Thet–thet . . . *the hogs!*"] Ibid., 110.

["*Venus de* Copples"] Ibid., 218.

["a fear . . . my ear"] Ibid., 220.

["vast potatoes . . . massive pears"] Ibid., 220.

["mules . . . their spell"] Ibid., 246.

["a cañon . . . beyond portrayal"] Ibid., 179.

["it seemed . . . from sight"] Ibid., 179.

["in the . . . was discovered"] Ibid., 179.

["All this . . . should be"] Ibid., 180.

["Down the . . . of nature"] Ibid., 180.

["at that . . . his career"] Henry Adams, *The Education of Henry Adams,* 312.

["He had . . . at all"] Ibid., 312.

["Much that . . . Clarence King"] Ibid., 346.

["King's education . . . fitness unrivalled"] Ibid., 346.

["California instincts . . . of change"] Ibid., 313.

["grave faults"] Gertrude Atherton, *California: An Intimate History*, 262.

["mobile desiring fantasy"] Leo Bersani, *Baudelaire and Freud*, 110–11.

MARY AUSTIN: NATURE AND NURTURANCE

["Mary went . . . at supper"] Mary Austin, *Earth Horizon*, 247.

["pattern"] Ibid., vii.

["hostages of . . . and affection"] Ibid., vii.

["engaged against . . . of fulfillment"] Ibid., vii.

["that the . . . the Wilderness"] Ibid., 174.

["the sacred . . . are equidistant"] Ibid., 274.

["freely to . . . proper arc"] Ibid., 274.

["God happened . . . walnut tree"] Ibid., 51.

["was the . . . the child"] Ibid., 244.

["the most . . . in America"] Edward T. James, ed., *Notable American Women: A Biographical Dictionary* (Cambridge, Mass.: Harvard University Press, 1971), 68.

["mother-wit"] *Earth Horizon*, 14.

["result achieved . . . effect produced"] Ibid., 15.

["a year . . . his marriage"] Ibid., 34.

["Mary Patchen . . . gold hair"] Ibid., 35.

["note from . . . an end"] Ibid., 36.

["It remained . . . of heart"] Ibid., 38.

["I didn't . . . the child"] Ibid., 316.

["We talked . . . these things"] Ibid., 317.

["It was . . . ever known"] Ibid., 317.

["never homesick . . . own house"] Mary Austin, "Tejon Notebook," 6.

["I can't . . . be taken"] Rae Galbraith Ballard, "Mary Austin's *Earth Horizon:* The Imperfect Circle," 495–6.

["I remember . . . of widowhood"] *Earth Horizon*, 86.

["It came . . . *at all*"] Mary Austin, *A Woman of Genius*, 21.

["my mother . . . me away"] *Earth Horizon*, 86.

["You forgot . . . Mary-by-herself"] Ibid., 47.

["I have . . . care of"] Ibid., 351.

["Take care of Mary"] Ibid., 273.

["one voluntary . . . to remember"] Ibid., 238.

["During all . . . vital connection"] Ibid., 255.

["I can't . . . knew myself"] *A Woman of Genius*, 126.

["I know . . . the child"] *Earth Horizon*, 244.

["There was . . . my child"] Ibid., 256.

["There was . . . the child"] Ibid., 268.

["There was . . . be known"] Ibid., 294-5.

["There were . . . Family Pride"] Letter in Huntington Library, from Mary Austin to Charles Lummis, December 28, 1918, Box 1.

["vacuity of . . . lovely vessel"] Helen MacKnight Doyle, *Mary Austin: Woman of Genius*, 180.

["I never . . . my child"] Donald P. Ringler, "Mary Austin: Kern County Days, 1888-1892," 53.

["called away . . . of things"] Doyle, 157.

["well organized . . . the schools"] "If I Had a Gifted Daughter," unpublished manuscript in Huntington Library, Box 25, 4.

["neighbors told . . . too nerve-wracking"] Doyle, 206-7.

["opening movement . . . my baby"] *A Woman of Genius*, 140.

["needless blight and pain"] *Earth Horizon*, 295.

["The first . . . from Kearsarge"] Ibid., 296.

["to get . . . few years"] Letter in Huntington Library, First National Bank of Monterey to Mary Austin, May 20, 1929, Box 24a.

["You have . . . Mr. Shrader"] Letter in Huntington Library, Mary Hunter to Mary Austin, undated, Box 24a.

["I am . . . and care"] Letter in Huntington Library, Mary Austin to S. E. Vermilyea, February 24, 1919, Box 24a.

"Finding that . . . to Carmel"] *Earth Horizon*, 338.

["shown marked . . . creative ability"] Ibid., 355.

["stupid and base"] Letter in Huntington Library, Mary Austin to George Hunter, January 15, 1927, Box 24a.

["being forced . . . entirely normal"] Letter in Huntington Library, Mary Austin to George Hunter, April 15, 1927, Box 24a.

["disfiguring skin disease"] Letter in Huntington Library, Mary Austin to George Hunter, January 15, 1927, Box 24a.

["Over on . . . a child"] "Tejon Notebook," 21.

["wish for . . . personal encounter"] Mary Austin, *Lost Borders,* 198.

["She came . . . with talk"] Ibid., 196.

["own account"] Ibid., 199.

["the contradiction . . . of her"] Ibid., 198.

["The best . . . a child"] Ibid., 201.

["three things . . . the rest"] Ibid., 201.

["The flock . . . flock together"] Ibid., 202.

["I stayed . . . in October"] Ibid., 207.

["And whenever . . . well covered"] Ibid., 208.

["To work . . . small cry"] Ibid., 207.

["fullest understanding"] Ibid., 207.

["the look . . . the eyes"] Ibid., 206.

["I do . . . touched me"] Ibid., 206.

["in some . . . for *me*"] Ibid., 206.

["as to . . . and young"] Ibid., 198.

["Far down . . . and white"] Ibid., 209.

["incipient symptoms . . . that inheritance"] *Earth Horizon,* 32.

["At least . . . more importance"] *Lost Borders,* 209.

["She had . . . take it"] Ibid., 208.

["It was . . . or feeling"] Ibid., 201.

["little in . . . to love"] Mary Austin, *The Land of Little Rain,* 5.

["This is . . . at last"] Ibid., 3–5.

["this long . . . the affections"] Ibid., 11.

["Squeezed up . . . of chaos"] Ibid., 3.

["water privileges"] Thoreau, *Walden,* Norton Critical Edition, 175.

["the virtue . . . of men"] Mary Austin, *The Lands of the Sun,* 32.

["aloof but solicitous care"] Ibid., 42.

["She has . . . the Rains"] Ibid., 51.

["the heavy . . . the flock"] *The Land of Little Rain,* 49–50.

["If the . . . the snow"] Ibid., 50.

["Think of . . . Pocket Hunter!"] Ibid., 50.

["untroubled by . . . dramatic sense"] Ibid., 75.

["emptiness . . . the land"] Ibid., 77.

["Here you . . . its perquisites"] Ibid., 78.

["three days' babe nozzling"] Ibid., 73.

["this piece of luck"] Ibid., 73.

["Bret Harte . . . own breath"] Ibid., 73.

["I am . . . the words"] "Tejon Notebook," 22.

["If the . . . for perpetuity"] *The Land of Little Rain,* xv.

["intimacy"] Ibid., xvi.

["So by . . . surer title"] Ibid., xvi.

["locked ranks . . . windy dome"] Ibid., 118.

["They troop . . . for rain"] Ibid., 118.

["Seyavi made . . . of desire"] Ibid., 107.

["she danced . . . her hair"] Ibid., 107.

["sits by . . . spirit's need"] Ibid., 111.

["sufficiency of mother wit"] Ibid., 103.

["Years of . . . decaying hide"] Mary Austin, *The Flock,* 21–2.

["soft, shuddering . . . accustomed bleat"] Ibid., 24.

["the return . . . immeasurable law"] Ibid., 24.

["Every now . . . her young"] Ibid., 24.

["going and coming"] Ibid., 72.

["The great . . . its snows"] Ibid., 72–3.

["One finds . . . rainless land"] Ibid., 221.

["But one . . . the sheep"] Ibid., 239.

["I suppose . . . with it"] Ibid., 11.

["home fold"] Ibid., 25.

["Iliad of adventure"] Ibid., 249.

["the parting . . . the flocks"] Ibid., 28.

["Love weaves . . . of story"] *Lost Borders,* 110.

["deep-breasted . . . desiring her"] Ibid., 10–11.

["It is . . . the land"] Ibid., 10.

["the vast . . . of desertness"] Ibid., 41.

["the souls . . . the edges"] Ibid., 3.

["meticulously strict . . . before ladies"] *Earth Horizon,* 10.

["Things that . . . of Mothers"] Ibid., 5.

["in a . . . have passed!"] Ibid., 5.

["It was . . . before Mary"] Ibid., 5.

["A man's . . . them out"] *Lost Borders,* 93.

["All this . . . be stroked"] Ibid., 108.

["If it . . . children's sake"] Ibid., 108.

["Death Valley . . . final word"] Ibid., 94.

["the middle . . . or ended"] Ibid., 95.

["There was . . . in it"] Ibid., 97.

["one of . . . Mine!"] Ibid., 98.

["For her . . . man, Whitmark"] Ibid., 100.

["I sat . . . have it!"] Ibid., 103.

["The crux . . . of time"] Ibid., 101.

["I have . . . you *so*"] Ibid., 106.

["Vera good . . . mucha like"] Ibid., 92.

["Tiawa . . . Great One!"] Ibid., 50.

["Mine!"] Ibid., 37.

["You ought . . . a story"] Ibid., 6.

["I will . . . a story"] Ibid., 7.

["The earth . . . every comer"] *The Land of Little Rain,* xvi.

["sphinx"] *Lost Borders,* 11.

["All reports . . . Southern California"] *Earth Horizon,* 307–8.

["Her trouble . . . of observation"] Ibid., 194–5.

["malnutrition"] Ibid., 193.

["something grubbed . . . the woods"] Ibid., 195.

["overwhelming scale . . . sensuous faculties"] Mary Austin, *The Land of Journey's Ending*, 42.

["confused restoration . . . vanishing culture"] Vernon Young, "Mary Austin and the Earth Performance," 161.

["the secret . . . life triumphant"] *The Land of Journey's Ending*, 56.

["The landscape . . . most beautiful"] John C. Van Dyke, *The Desert*, 56.

["The light . . . fading out"] Ibid., 232.

["have we . . . the–desert"] Ibid., 230–1.

["sand and rock"] Ibid., 231.

["For death . . . its development"] Ibid., 231.

["false perspective"] Ibid., 113.

["Within the . . . of dying"] Mary Austin, "The Lost Garden," unpublished manuscript in Huntington Library, Box 41, second and revised version, 17–18.

NORRIS AND THE VERTICAL

["I think . . . thoroughly American"] Franklin Walker, *Frank Norris: A Biography*, 237.

["a figure . . . dried apricots"] Frank Norris, *The Octopus*, 2:357.

["His finished . . . with burrs"] Frank Norris, *Vandover and the Brute*, 54.

["pull up . . . thing four-footed"] Ibid., 268.

["feeling for . . . desolate landscapes"] Ibid., 21.

["an absolutely . . . of country"] Frank Norris, *The Third Circle*, 240.

["The desert . . . and sand"] Ibid., 236.

["last stand"] Ibid., 240.

["Even the . . . the spirit"] Ibid., 240–1.

["Forever and . . . earth again"] Ibid., 281–2.

["carriage"] Frank Norris, *Blix*, 25.

["Huge, blonde, big-boned"] Frank Norris, *Moran of the Lady Letty*, 251.

["Twice Grettir . . . their mass"] *The Third Circle*, 145.

["For a . . . He fell"] Ibid., 146.

["on his knees"] *Vandover*, 311.

["some weakness . . . inopportune moments"] *The Third Circle*, 22.

["I must . . . down me"] Ibid., 117.

["he was . . . shooting-match"] Ibid., 264.

["bolts"] Ibid., 44.

["Such he . . . he fell"] Ibid., 44.

["inherited tendencies"] Ibid., 45.

["reaching the . . . his wife"] Walker, *Frank Norris,* 95.

["McTeague goes . . . from help"] Frank Norris, *McTeague,* ed., Donald Pizer, 295.

["In McTeague . . . and destruction"] Donald Pizer, *The Novels of Frank Norris,* 72.

["Oh, Mac! . . . the stairs"] *McTeague,* 6.

["relative positions"] Ibid., 28.

["By and . . . to sleep"] Ibid., 1.

["Bull-like . . . the street"] Ibid., 3.

["a point of vantage"] Ibid., 5.

["Day after . . . unroll itself"] Ibid., 18.

["leaps . . . Down, down"] Ibid., 18.

["In spite . . . first met"] Ibid., 28.

["down her . . . enormous strength"] Ibid., 50.

["Mac, I'll . . . between you"] Ibid., 32.

["He can't . . . of *me*"] Ibid., 83.

["I'll not . . . with um"] Ibid., 89.

["He swung . . . of clothes"] Ibid., 133.

["At first . . . old habits"] Ibid., 161.

["The McTeague's . . . and lower"] Ibid., 188.

["down on . . . and knees"] Ibid., 208.

["A tremendous . . . to man"] Ibid., 212–13.

["He recognized . . . at once"] Ibid., 214.

["returning prodigal"] Ibid., 217.

["There was . . . his own"] Ibid., 239.

["the dentist . . . the desert"] Ibid., 220.

["a flat, dazzling surface"] Ibid., 241.

["Hands up . . . was Marcus"] Ibid., 241.

["Well, let's . . . stopping here"] Ibid., 247.

["up again"] Ibid., 248.

["As McTeague . . . gilt prison"] Ibid., 248–9.

["the empty . . . vacant space"] Wallace Stevens, *The Palm at the End of the Mind,* 114.

["in space . . . in time"] G. E. Lessing, *Laocoön,* Chapter 16.

["It was . . . all directions"] *The Octopus,* 1:21.

["turn through the country"] Ibid., 21.

["All about . . . the ground"] Ibid., 11.

["landmark"] Ibid., 2.

["a gigantic scroll"] Ibid., 27.

["reach . . . heat-ridden"] Ibid., 27.

["prone upon the ground"] Ibid., 41.

["As from . . . entire country"] Ibid., 42.

["campanile . . . long windbreak"] Ibid., 43.

["the eye . . . the mind"] Ibid., 44.

["the great . . . of landscape"] Ibid., 43.

["A sudden . . . mere immensity"] Ibid., 44.

["His brain . . . moving scroll"] Ibid., 37.

["in a hurry"] Ibid., 8.

["Just after . . . to refuse"] Ibid., 1.

["the insistent . . . inevitable, prolonged"] Ibid., 135.

["marking the time"] Ibid., 3.

["*Atropos* . . . turns aside"] Thoreau, *Walden,* Norton Critical Edition, 79.

["plan"] *The Octopus,* 1:1.

["to get . . . as possible"] Ibid., 13.

["contracted horizon"] Ibid., 10.

["But evidently . . . that day"] Ibid., 14.

["Presley turned sharply aside"] Ibid., 29.

["On the . . . shepherd stood"] Ibid., 29.

["Here was . . . its development"] Ibid., 32.

["beard had . . . an inch"] Ibid., 40.

["the same"] Ibid., 32.

["Then one . . . an explosion"] Ibid., 35.

["found the . . . overspiring trees"] Ibid., 35.

["a track of terror"] Ibid., 36.

["thread . . . been snapped"] Ibid., 36.

["impenetrable mystery"] Ibid., 36.

["Vanamee's strange . . . Long Trail"] Ibid., 45.

["shut from sight"] Ibid., 45.

["the component . . . the West"] Ibid., 45.

["epic"] Ibid., 38.

["But suddenly . . . an interruption"] Ibid., 46.

["to grasp . . . its entity"] Ibid., 46.

["Abruptly Presley remembered"] Ibid., 46.

["Abruptly"] Ibid., 47.

["abruptly"] Ibid., 47.

["to drop down"] *The Octopus*, 1:40.

["without warning"] Ibid., 31.

["away"] Ibid., 47.

["accuracy of . . . and objectivism"] William B. Dillingham, *Frank Norris: Instinct and Art*, 19–20.

["Like many . . . wide brush"] Richard Chase in *McTeague*, ed. Pizer, 341–2.

["scenes are . . . theoretical devices"] Ibid., 342.

["Expectation in . . . to surprise"] S. T. Coleridge, *The Literary Remains of Samuel Taylor Coleridge*, 2: Henry Nelson Coleridge, ed. (London: W. Pickering, 1836–9), 77.

["preparations of effect"] Frank Norris, *The Responsibilities of the Novelist*, 116.

["that abrupt . . . a thunderclap"] *The Octopus*, 1:254.

["Abruptly Vanamee rose"] Ibid., 129.

["The fall . . . long one"] *The Octopus*, 2:351.

["Annixter stood suddenly upright"] Ibid., 81.

["At ten . . . Hooven fell"] Ibid., 318.

["bent earthwards"] *The Octopus,* 1:94.

["rigidly upright"] Ibid., 172.

["I'd quit . . . right down"] *The Octopus,* 2:46.

["down"] Ibid., 197.

["stood nearly free"] Ibid., 198.

["Let's stand . . . *one* fight"] *The Octopus,* 1:183.

["in passing"] Ibid., 7.

["Hope, after . . . seen reversed"] Ibid., 137.

["she came . . . him again"] Ibid., 150.

["series of . . . a kinetoscope"] Ibid., 202.

["Long after . . . of smoke"] Ibid., 252–3.

["prepared for . . . initial chapter"] *The Responsibilities of the Novelist,* 116.

["No one . . . its speed"] Ibid., 113.

["the sudden . . . must decline"] Ibid., 114.

["Now the . . . its presentation"] Ibid., 115.

["With the . . . your feet"] Walker, *Frank Norris,* 266.

["little things"] *The Octopus,* 2:344.

["material world . . . Vision"] Ibid., 94–5.

["Reality dwindled . . . a point"] Ibid., 94.

["a simple . . . her lover"] Ibid., 347.

["devil of a driver"] *The Octopus,* 1:23.

["waste his time"] Ibid., 25.

["cross-grained"] Ibid., 72.

["hardness"] *The Octopus,* 2:209.

["I'm tired . . . besides myself"] Ibid., 80.

["measureless distances"] Ibid., 80.

["Annixter stood suddenly upright"] Ibid., 81.

["A realization . . . aggression"] Ibid., 209.

["The little . . . to light"] Ibid., 82.

["The morning . . . inviolable pledge"] Ibid., 83.

["For a . . . the stars"] Ibid., 94.

["upon the . . . sombre land"] Ibid., 94.

["something"] Ibid., 101.

["It was . . . to himself"] Ibid., 102.

["Answer of the night"] Ibid., 96.

["Such phenomena . . . external reality"] C. J. Jung, *Memories, Dreams, Reflections* (1961; rpt. New York: Random House, 1973), 231.

["round-topped . . . protuberant"] *The Octopus*, 1:63.

["more interested . . . inspired it"] *The Octopus*, 11:86.

["frenzy"] Ibid., 86.

["He had . . . the People"] Ibid., 86.

["*impersonal*"] Ibid., 86.

["a character . . . a type"] *The Octopus*, 1:6.

["dealing with . . . with men"] *The Octopus*, 2:285.

["And with . . . inquire whither"] *The Octopus*, 1:232.

["who had . . . knew whither"] *The Octopus*, 2:377.

["Instantly the . . . then stillness"] Ibid., 233.

["Delaney, shot . . . his face"] Ibid., 233.

STEINBECK'S LOST GARDENS

["This was . . . his life"] Elaine Steinbeck and Robert Wallsten, eds., *Steinbeck: A Life in Letters*, 27.

["the thing . . . seems good"] Ibid., 329.

["repository of my destiny"] Ibid., 31.

["storytelling imagination"] Thomas Kiernan, *The Intricate Music: A Biography of John Steinbeck*, viii.

["fictional . . . empirical"] Robert Murray Davis, ed., *Steinbeck: A Collection of Critical Essays*, 9.

["warring qualities"] John Steinbeck, *The Long Valley*, 33.

["the long structure"] *A Life in Letters*, 542.

["inevitable stream"] Ibid., 543.

["A man . . . isn't new"] Ibid., 474–5.

["Maybe the . . . the cold"] John Steinbeck, *Cup of Gold*, 9.

["be coming . . . blood's sake"] Ibid., 10.

["This woman . . . my questing"] Ibid., 128.

["There was . . . risen star"] Ibid., 16.

["direct rebellion . . . our house"] *A Life in Letters,* 90.

["And some . . . have seen"] Alfred, Lord Tennyson, "The Holy Grail," in *Idylls of the King,* lines 899–915.

["slow sullen movement"] *A Life in Letters,* 98–9.

["Evening of . . . green pool"] John Steinbeck, *Of Mice and Men,* 9–10.

["trouble"] Ibid., 34.

["I think . . . do her"] Ibid., 90.

["Nobody never . . . their head"] Ibid., 72.

["Carol is . . . done it"] *A Life in Letters,* 201–2.

["It would . . . were too"] John Steinbeck, *The Log from the Sea of Cortez,* 27.

["rough wooden cross"] Ibid., 71.

["A man . . . the place"] Ibid., 71–2.

["a slow . . . makes it"] Ibid., 72.

["deep and . . . going home"] Ibid., LI.

["Tropism . . . a stimulus"] Ibid., 276.

["The Palace . . . a home"] John Steinbeck, *Cannery Row,* 138.

["monstrous"] John Steinbeck, *East of Eden,* 82.

["I mean . . . driven out"] Ibid., 194.

["tendencies"] Ibid., 82.

["sexuality"] Ibid., 86.

["Garden of . . . and Abel"] Ibid., 306.

["father"] Ibid., 308.

["original sin"] Ibid., 305.

["plotted . . . of green"] John Steinbeck, *The Pastures of Heaven,* 239.

["holy"] John Steinbeck, *To a God Unknown,* 30.

["huge and light"] Ibid., 179.

["Nothing was . . . my imagination"] Ibid., 101.

["there was . . . and twigs"] Ibid., 4.

["Everything's food"] Ibid., 10.

["a trail . . . innumerable meanings"] Ibid., 5.

["The mountain . . . snarling whisper"] Ibid., 51.

["Here is . . . of pregnancy"] Ibid., 52.

["I'll have . . . other side"] Ibid., 53.

["It's a . . . other side"] Ibid., 53.

["The bitterness . . . an ecstasy"] Ibid., 53.

["recent . . . first half"] *A Life in Letters*, 52.

["valley was . . . sprang up"] Ibid., 42–3.

["protected valley"] *The Pastures of Heaven*, 86.

["damned serpent"] Ibid., 8.

["grow somehow . . . mountain pool"] T. K. Whipple, *Study Out the Land* (Berkeley: University of California Press, 1943), 105.

["One day . . . few minutes"] *The Pastures of Heaven*, 8.

["He kept . . . for her"] Ibid., 7.

["This farm . . . ever came"] Ibid., 7.

["Vermont house"] Ibid., 190.

["I shall . . . to move"] Ibid., 205.

["big, luxurious house"] Ibid., 206.

["accidents of blood"] Ibid., 207.

["female troubles"] *The Long Valley*, 136.

["longing"] Ibid., 179.

["He reads . . . nor how"] *A Life in Letters*, 91.

["crying weakly"] *The Long Valley*, 12.

["The high . . . closed pot"] Ibid., 1.

["On the . . . should come"] Ibid., 1.

["The chrysanthemum . . . her energy"] Ibid., 2.

["Her figure . . . corduroy apron"] Ibid., 1.

["strong fingers"] Ibid., 2.

["protected"] Ibid., 2.

["You've got . . . with things"] Ibid., 3.

["Good for you"] Ibid., 3.

["It will . . . good dinner"] Ibid., 12.

["prairie schooner"] Ibid., 4.

["When they get started"] Ibid., 5.

["That's a . . . a fight"] Ibid., 4.

["Looks like . . . colored smoke"] Ibid., 6.

["I know . . . a piece"] Ibid., 6.

["like unwatered flowers"] Ibid., 4.

["planting hands . . . passionately"] Ibid., 8.

["The man's . . . and lovely"] Ibid., 8.

["It's nice . . . it ain't"] Ibid., 8.

["In the . . . her back"] Ibid., 10.

["That's a . . . glowing there"] Ibid., 10.

["is designed . . . reader's knowledge"] *A Life in Letters*, 91.

["Mary Teller . . . that is"] *The Long Valley*, 13.

["Would the . . . a man?"] Ibid., 13.

["the garden . . . like him"] Ibid., 13.

["I like . . . the garden"] Ibid., 15.

["You're kind . . . move around"] Ibid., 16.

["enemy"] Ibid., 17.

["answer to . . . decisive answer"] Ibid., 20.

["She went . . . Mary whispered"] Ibid., 18.

["There were . . . see myself"] Ibid., 18.

["How I . . . like this"] *The Long Valley*, 22–3.

["Oh, Lord . . . so lonely!"] Ibid., 25.

["I am . . . now, Mama"] Ibid., 31.

["A desire . . . in him"] Ibid., 50.

["This thing . . . with pleasure"] Ibid., 59.

["I was . . . us, then"] Ibid., 59.

["And I . . . country road"] Ibid., 61.

["I don't . . . warm pleasure"] Ibid., 58.

["no consecutive effort"] *A Life in Letters*, 78.

["If it . . . include it"] Ibid., 78.

["A longing . . . nameless sorrow"] *The Long Valley*, 179.

["uncertainty in . . . unfamiliar things"] Ibid., 139.

["Punishment would be prompt"] Ibid., 153.

["The triangle . . . harsh note"] Ibid., 137.

["His father . . . any kind"] Ibid., 138.

["That's only . . . rooster leaves"] Ibid., 138.

["Two years . . . good discipline"] Ibid., 141.

["I'm going . . . the morning"] Ibid., 141.

["your father . . . see you"] Ibid., 181.

["Do you . . . I did"] Ibid., 181.

["it was . . . a crime"] Ibid., 181.

["the crime . . . and birth"] W. B. Yeats, "A Dialogue of Self and Soul."

["To start . . . the start"] *The Long Valley*, 192.

["raise . . . up"] Ibid., 185.

["My ma . . . was born"] Ibid., 193.

["Billy dropped . . . Jody's feet"] Ibid., 197.

["The place . . . were happening"] Ibid., 162.

["I have come back"] Ibid., 169.

["Once made . . . be retraced"] Ibid., 204.

["It wasn't . . . only westering"] Ibid., 213.

["the valley . . . the world"] *A Life in Letters*, 73.

["education of the heart"] Warren French, *John Steinbeck*, 95.

["widening of concern"] J. P. Hunter, in John Steinbeck, *The Grapes of Wrath*, Viking Critical Edition, 807.

["from 'I' to 'we' "] Ibid., 206.

["the indomitable . . . the Joads"] Ibid., 733.

["armed with . . . of movement"] Ibid., 20.

["They're just . . . of goin' "] Ibid., 15.

["result . . . cause"] Ibid., 204.

["Folks out . . . of home"] Ibid., 76.

["What the . . . lead 'em"] Ibid., 29.

["A thick-furred . . . home maybe"] Ibid., 29.

["Seems to . . . the way"] Ibid., 173.

["This here . . . to take"] Ibid., 196–7.

["Well, no . . . over there"] Ibid., 396.

["Picking cotton . . . No"] *The Long Valley*, 60.

["Aim to"] *The Grapes of Wrath*, 397.

["get . . . go along"] *The Long Valley*, 60.

["Well, that's . . . of you"] *The Grapes of Wrath*, 398.

["I'll be . . . be there"] Ibid., 572.

["possess . . . happier far"] Milton, *Paradise Lost*, 12:586–7.

["all places thou"] Ibid., 12:618.

["the windows . . . the sun"] *The Grapes of Wrath*, 156.

["Thir place . . . way"] Milton, *Paradise Lost*, 12:647–9.

["the boys . . . easier ways"] *A Life in Letters*, 187.

["in its . . . capitalist society"] *Steinbeck: A Collection of Critical Essays*, 21.

["nice little . . . New York"] *A Life in Letters*, 418.

["It could . . . been ecstatic"] Ibid., 243.

["Where before . . . from John"] Kiernan, 229.

["escape . . . nasty fogs"] *A Life in Letters*, 125.

["the ranch . . . to drink"] Ibid., 183.

["homesick for her garden"] Ibid., 201.

["I'm very . . . visiting it"] Ibid., 212.

["gentleman farmer"] Ibid., 223.

["You know . . . live flesh"] Ibid., 31.

["My garden . . . leave it"] Ibid., 45.

["little house"] Ibid., 223.

["hospitality"] Ibid., 240.

["I was . . . isn't enough"] Ibid., 223.

["Do you . . . one either"] Ibid., 240.

["hospitable house"] Ibid., 240.

["Well there . . . the back"] Ibid., 280.

["security"] Ibid., 239.

["restlessness"] Ibid., 708.

["After four . . . a divorce"] Ibid., 318.

["I have . . . a while"] Ibid., 320.

["how little . . . leave it"] Ibid., 320.

["This whole . . . all yet"] Ibid., 330.

["My little . . . a servant"] Ibid., 343.

["Sometimes it . . . before Carol"] Ibid., 329.

["being alone"] Ibid., 331.

["The lady . . . *first* wife"] *John Steinbeck Papers,* University of Virginia, undated photograph.

["living is . . . not places"] *A Life in Letters,* 280.

["I think . . . work well"] Ibid., 382.

["I have . . . a suitcase"] Ibid., 495.

CHANDLER, MARRIAGE, AND "THE GREAT WRONG PLACE"

["In Los Angeles . . . put together"] Franklin Walker, *A Literary History of Southern California,* 100.

["maze of green"] T. S. Van Dyke, *Millionaires of a Day,* 27.

["a sufficient . . . fine enough"] Ibid., 97.

["exile"] John Gregory Dunne, *True Confessions,* 19.

["the middle . . . goddam sand"] Ibid., 371.

["Whatever man . . . of Eden"] Reyner Banham, *Los Angeles: The Architecture of Four Ecologies,* 31.

["built form"] Ibid., 237.

["sense of . . . to manoeuvre"] Ibid., 242.

["the first . . . all realistically"] Frank McShane, ed., *The Letters of Raymond Chandler,* 68.

["California can . . . in America"] Hinton Rowland Helper, *The Land of Gold: Reality Versus Fiction,* 68.

["I think . . . of art"] W. H. Auden, *The Dyer's Hand,* 151.

["The path . . . a blanket"] Raymond Chandler, *The Big Sleep*, 5.

["exile from . . . he loved"] Frank McShane, *The Life of Raymond Chandler*, 208.

["There are . . . and dismay"] Ibid., 21.

["the flawless . . . the night"] *The Big Sleep*, 170.

["There was . . . the sky"] Raymond Chandler, *Farewell, My Lovely*, 49–50.

["A long . . . slum either"] Raymond Chandler, *The Little Sister*, 202.

["The story . . . hidden truth"] Raymond Chandler, *The Simple Art of Murder*, 21.

["In 1919 . . . as well"] *The Life of Raymond Chandler*, 33.

["This was . . . fifty-three"] Ibid., 34.

["discrepancy"] Ibid., 37.

["In the . . . were enjoying"] Ibid., 39.

["a wild . . . of despair"] Ibid., 39.

["constantly on the move"] Ibid., 59.

["reward"] Ibid., 129.

["I never . . . to it"] Ibid., 59.

["Hollywood's happiest couple"] Ibid., 111.

["smiling, propitiary . . . and defended"] Miriam Gross, ed., *The World of Raymond Chandler*, 87.

["fading eyes . . . of appeal"] Ibid., 87.

["Her unwillingness . . . their children"] *The Life of Raymond Chandler*, 60.

["the light . . . my life"] *The Letters of Raymond Chandler*, 379.

["let the . . . come out"] Raymond Chandler, *The Lady in the Lake*, 212.

["jealous rage"] *The Big Sleep*, 102.

["redemption"] *The Simple Art of Murder*, 20.

["knight in dark armor"] *The Big Sleep*, 1.

["I sure . . . the ground"] *The Letters of Raymond Chandler*, 24.

["Everything is . . . something else"] Ibid., 176.

["The Sternwoods . . . them rich"] *The Big Sleep*, 18.

["Outside, the . . . its light"] Ibid., 215.

["I walked . . . looked in"] *Farewell, My Lovely*, 2.

["Time passes . . . meant less"] Ibid., 54.

["I stopped . . . City Hall"] Ibid., 232.

["Sanctuary"] Ibid., 54.

["I unlocked . . . in living"] Ibid., 161.

["I believe . . . the worst"] *The Letters of Raymond Chandler*, 165.

["forget the whole mess"] *The Big Sleep*, 121.

["hair, eyebrows . . . chin, eyes"] Raymond Chandler, *The High Window*, 5.

["history"] Ibid., 47.

["Look, I . . . ever since"] Ibid., 131.

["It's true . . . very well"] Ibid., 200.

["I had . . . it again"] Ibid., 202.

["waste land"] *The Lady in the Lake*, 137–8.

["We reached . . . at nightfall"] Ibid., 194.

["like paradise"] Ibid., 26.

["Tall yellow . . . blue sky"] Ibid., 26–7.

["A scarlet-topped . . . other one"] Ibid., 27.

["peaceful"] Ibid., 39.

["a voice . . . mountain thunder"] Ibid., 39.

["The depths . . . tangle again"] Ibid., 40.

["Something that . . . a man"] Ibid., 217.

["The Remove"] Philip Durham, *Down These Mean Streets a Man Must Go*, 61.

["was written . . . bad mood"] *The Life of Raymond Chandler*, 154.

["I know . . . chi-chi"] *The Letters of Raymond Chandler*, 405.

["I was . . . waste basket"] *The Little Sister*, 198.

["I opened . . . of ease"] Ibid., 148.

["Civilization had . . . the disgust"] Ibid., 196.

["The most . . . of nothing"] Ibid., 196.

["scathing hatred . . . human race"] *The Life of Raymond Chandler*, 155.

["geographical refuge"] David Smith, "The Public Eye of Raymond Chandler," in *Journal of American Studies* 14 (Dec. 1980), 43.

["frozen star"] *The Little Sister*, 197.

["a hoodlum with sentiment"] Raymond Chandler, *The Long Goodbye,* 62.

["I can't . . . about it"] Ibid., 22.

["Of course . . . open again"] *The Life of Raymond Chandler,* 223.

["gusto: you . . . to give"] *The Letters of Raymond Chandler,* 319.

["I was . . . wrote it"] Ibid., 421.

["intensity of artistic performance"] Ibid., 69.

["It was . . . my life"] Ibid., 422.

["I had . . . in charge"] Raymond Chandler, *Playback,* 76.

["old woman"] Ibid., 128.

["glows every time"] Ibid., 36.

["I've been . . . to you"] Ibid., 167.

["the hard . . . from anyone"] Ibid., 166.

["I left . . . right woman"] *The Letters of Raymond Chandler,* 473.

["idea that . . . quite defeated"] Ibid., 483.

JEFFERS, SNYDER, AND THE ENDED WORLD

["a kind of awakening"] Frederic Carpenter, *Robinson Jeffers,* 35.

["inevitable place"] Lawrence Clark Powell, *Robinson Jeffers,* 15.

["How we go on"] Gary Snyder, *Axe Handles,* 6.

["The August . . . inevitable place"] Carpenter, *Robinson Jeffers,* 32.

["You know . . . our place"] Melba Berry Bennett, *The Stone Mason of Tor House,* 70.

["It was . . . handle stone"] Ibid., 88.

["I'm set . . . in cement"] Ibid., 127.

["slow unchangeability"] Ibid., 99.

["the same . . . six years"] Ibid., 99.

["I will . . . of ours"] Ibid., 91.

["nestled by"] Robinson Jeffers, *The Selected Poetry,* 83.

["Stone-cutters . . . old poems"] Ibid., 84.

["From here . . . ended world"] *The Women at Point Sur,* 55.

["They would . . . more sublime?"] George Sterling, *Robinson Jeffers: The Man and the Artist,* 18.

["the beauty . . . not men"] Robinson Jeffers, *Hungerfield*, 95.

["The old . . . white violence"] *The Selected Poetry*, 358.

["an example . . . western man"] Powell, *Robinson Jeffers*, 143.

["Its progress . . . into space"] Ibid., 143.

["the clapping . . . about here?"] *The Selected Poetry*, 80.

["God attributes . . . No sanctity"] Milton, *Paradise Lost*, 11:836–7.

["sea-brow"] Ibid., 351.

["only the . . . to it"] Ibid., 351.

["The platform . . . of things"] Ibid., 357.

["God is here"] Ibid., 457.

["So without . . . and undesired"] Bennett, 47.

["Kuster's undying . . . to Una"] Ibid., 143.

["co-authored"] *The Selected Poetry*, xv.

["Una has . . . to fall"] *Hungerfield*, 4.

["Mine's empty . . . love died"] Ibid., 115.

["I crawl . . . wear mine"] Ibid., 115.

["This coast . . . the place"] *The Selected Poetry*, 175.

["I imagined . . . the house"] Ibid., 175.

["the closed . . . of things"] Kenneth Rexroth, *Collected Shorter Poems*, 233.

["laboring of . . . pathetic fallacy"] Kenneth Rexroth, *Assays*, 215.

["it is . . . its power"] William Everson, *Archetype West*, 105.

["transposed the . . . unspoliated nature"] William Everson, *Robinson Jeffers: Fragments of an Older Fury*, 5.

["souls"] William Everson, *The Veritable Years*, 75.

["a California odyssey"] Ibid., 11.

["abandoned free . . . traditional meters"] Yvor Winters, *The Collected Poems of Yvor Winters*, 15.

["I might . . . this man"] Ibid., 161.

["the shining land"] Ibid., 158.

["man-made stone . . . living tree"] Ibid., 129.

["As I . . . hand, forever"] *Axe Handles*, 44.

["Faint in . . . the dark"] Ibid., 44.

["I turn . . . pearly water"] Ibid., 44.

["Fifty years . . . on bolts"] Ibid., 45.

["At the . . . the dawn"] Ibid., 45.

["stresses that . . . each instant"] Gary Snyder, *Earth House Hold*, 21.

["It's all . . . or burning"] Gary Snyder, *Myths & Texts*, 46.

["every poem . . . different strategy"] Ekbert Faas, ed., *Towards a New American Poetics*, 132.

["Passing/through"] *Myths & Texts*, 37.

["focal image"] *Towards a New American Poetics*, 135.

["A complex of being"] Thomas Parkinson, "The Theory and Practice of Gary Snyder," in *The Southern Review* 4 (Summer 1968), 452.

["Get a . . . workable territory"] Gary Snyder, *Turtle Island*, 101.

["Down valley . . . still air"] Gary Snyder, *Riprap*, 1.

["All the . . . Drops away"] Ibid., 6.

["I must . . . for work"] Ibid., 3.

["to do"] Ibid., 13.

["At the . . . and sleeps"] Ibid., 15.

["Lay down . . . as things"] Ibid., 30.

["Poetry . . . of metaphysics"] *Myths & Texts*, 43.

["Human tenderness . . . away?–Love"] Ibid., 35.

["the boundless . . . and chipmunks"] Ibid., 44.

["Nature a . . . of play"] *Earth House Hold*, 21.

["Almost had . . . of erosion"] Ibid., 10.

["And I . . . a plan"] Gary Snyder, *The Back Country*, 49.

["I must . . . it alone"] Ibid., 49.

["On a . . . me sane"] Ibid., 31.

["Nothing affects . . . it happens"] S. T. Coleridge, *Anima Poetae*.

["Here I . . . future years"] William Wordsworth, "Tintern Abbey," lines 62–5.

["No paradise, no fall"] *Riprap*, 8.

["turn, turn . . . a-head"] *The Back Country*, 27.

["Remembering how . . . Remembering not"] Wordsworth, *The Prelude* (1850), 2:316–17.

["an obscure . . . possible sublimity"] Ibid., 2:317–18.

["I always . . . my back"] *The Back Country*, 75.

["Descending hillsides . . . and take"] Ibid., 120.

["What my . . . the line"] Ibid., 123.

["vision idly . . . the hills"] Ibid., 123.

["wife . . . wave"] *Earth House Hold*, 125.

["laws of waves"] Gary Snyder, *Regarding Wave*, 42.

["bend and regain"] Ibid., 42.

["Water in . . . frozen moments"] *Earth House Hold*, 14.

["I dream . . . of fox"] Gary Snyder, *Turtle Island*, 40.

["As if . . . were sacred"] *The Poetry of Robert Frost*, 259.

["climax situation . . . the trees"] Gary Snyder, *The Real Work*, 173–4.

["At the . . . is dead"] *Turtle Island*, 107.

["If one . . . like Jeffers?"] *Earth House Hold*, 4.

["best portion . . . and love"] "Tintern Abbey," 33–5.

["Crackly grass . . . little lakes"] *Turtle Island*, 101.

["My sense . . . at home"] *The Real Work*, 59.

["I *love* . . . trucking gravel"] Ibid., 76.

["the tiresome . . . local politics"] *Turtle Island*, 101.

["It is . . . and government"] *The Real Work*, 169.

["I certainly . . . Ponderosa pine"] Ibid., 85–6.

EPILOGUE: FICTIONS OF SPACE

["sensuous poverty"] F. R. Leavis, *Revaluation* (London: Chatto & Windus, 1936), 47.

["a reading . . . the earth"] Carl Sauer, *Land and Life*, 393.

["All the . . . old thinking"] Robert Hass, *Praise*, 4.

["names . . . things"] Robert Hass, *Field Guide*, 5.

["recompense"] Wordsworth, "Tintern Abbey," line 88.

["Life is . . . the trouble"] Wallace Stevens, *Opus Posthumous* (New York: Knopf, 1957), 158.

["They were . . . of reminiscence"] Jack London, *Burning Daylight*, 340.

["Absolutely the . . . is NATURE"] D. H. Lawrence, *Studies in Classic American Literature,* 34.

["The mind . . . of heaven"] R. Edson Lee, *From West to East: Studies in the Literature of the American West,* 72.

["half-create/And what perceive"] "Tintern Abbey," lines 105–6.

["The facts . . . of period"] *Land and Life,* 321.

["I take . . . to now"] Charles Olson, *Call me Ishmael,* 11.

["most us"] *The Poetry of Robert Frost,* 260.

["Longing, we . . . endless distances"] *Praise,* 4–5.

Bibliography

━━━━━━━━━━━━

The following is a list of the books and articles I read in order to write this book. References have been assigned to the chapter in which they are cited or for which they provided background information. Works of general interest about California have been assigned to the Prologue; studies of the American imagination and American space, to the Epilogue. Fiction and history dealing with Southern California have been listed in the Chandler bibliography. Poets read have been listed in the bibliography to Chapter 9. I have endeavored to cite the standard reprint of all books quoted and have provided a brief description for each entry except for those primary works either widely known or discussed at length in the text. All titles in the bibliography have been indexed.

PROLOGUE: THE MYTHOLOGY OF THE REGION

Criticism, history, and reference

Beck, Warren A., and David A. Williams. *California: A History of the Golden State*. Garden City, N.Y.: Doubleday, 1972. A concise, readable history.

Beck, Warren A., and Ynez D. Haase, eds. *Historical Atlas of California*. Norman: Univ. of Oklahoma Press, 1974. Change made visible.

De Voto, Bernard. *The Year of Decision: 1846*. Boston: Little, Brown, 1943. Narrative history of the year that determined the political future of California.

Ernest, Robert, and Robert Granniss Cowan, eds. *A Bibliography of the History of California*. Los Angeles: Torrez Press, 1964. An expanded edition of the classic annotated guide to California history.

Everson, William. *Archetype West: The Pacific Coast as a Literary Region*. Berkeley, Calif.: Oyez, 1976. A poet imposes a strong reading on the literature of the Far West.

Faragher, John Mack. *Women and Men on the Overland Trail*. New Haven, Conn.: Yale Univ. Press, 1979. A sociology of the changing structure of the midwestern family as it travels west.

Hart, James D. *A Companion to California.* New York: Oxford Univ. Press, 1978. A literate and loving guide to Hart's native state.

Holliday, J. S. *The World Rushed In: The California Gold Rush Experience.* New York: Simon & Schuster, 1981. Based on the diary and letters of the William Swain family, this is a superior reconstruction of the Gold Rush through the experience of one man.

Hunt, Rockwell D. *California Firsts.* San Francisco: Fearon, 1957. Precedents.

James, George Wharton. *Heroes of California.* Boston: Little, Brown, 1910. More than fifty stories, with wonderful photographs.

Knoles, George K., ed. *Essays and Assays: California History Reappraised.* San Francisco: California Historical Society, 1973. Valuable articles on periodization and architecture.

McWilliams, Carey. *California: The Great Exception.* 1949; rpt. Westport, Conn.: Greenwood, 1971. Exuberant and knowledgeable but less incisive than *An Island on the Land.*

———. *Southern California: An Island on the Land.* 1946; rpt. Santa Barbara, Calif.: Peregrine Smith, 1973. The most convincing postwar argument that this region has a culture.

Nordhoff, Charles. *Northern California, Oregon, and the Sandwich Islands.* 1874; rpt. Berkeley, Calif.: Ten Speed Press, 1974. Propaganda from the state's premier booster.

Powell, Lawrence Clark. *California Classics: The Creative Literature of the Golden State.* Los Angeles: Ward Ritchie Press, 1971. A useful guide to some forty major careers.

———. *Land of Fiction.* Los Angeles: Glen Dawson, 1952.

Robinson, W. W. *Land in California.* Berkeley: Univ. of California Press, 1948. The best account of the ways in which Californians transform landscape into real estate.

Roc, Margaret Miller, ed. *California: Local History, a Bibliography and Union List of Library Holdings.* 2nd ed., revised and enlarged. Stanford, Calif.: Stanford Univ. Press, 1970. With the *Supplement* of 1976, this authoritative bibliography lists more than twenty thousand items.

Rolle, Andrew F. *California: A History.* New York: Crowell, 1969. The standard state history.

Royce, Josiah. "The Pacific Coast: A Psychological Study of the Relations of Climate and Civilization." In *Race Questions, Provincialism, and Other American Problems.* New York: Macmillan, 1908. The man who went to Harvard speculates on his native state and the spirit of place.

Spies, Werner. *The Running Fence Project/Christo.* New York: Abrams, 1977. Landscape and spectacle in the North Bay counties.

Starr, Kevin. *Americans and the California Dream: 1850–1915.* New York: Oxford Univ. Press, 1973. Winner of the National Book Award, this is the single best book about American beginnings in Northern California.

———. *Inventing the Dream: California Through the Progressive Era.* New York: Oxford Univ. Press, 1985. The second volume in Starr's *Americans and the California Dream* series.

Stewart, George. *The California Trail: An Epic with Many Heroes*. New York: McGraw-Hill, 1962. The story as told by a superior narrative historian. *The Opening of the California Trail*. Berkeley: Univ. of California Press, 1953. A reconstruction of the crossing of the Stevens Party of 1844, with an introduction, notes, maps, and photographs.

Unruh, John D., Jr. *The Plains Across: The Overland Emigrants and the Trans-Mississippi West, 1840–60*. Urbana: University of Illinois Press, 1979. Westering marked the triumph of collective over individual endeavor.

Van Nostrand, Jeanne. *The First Hundred Years of Painting in California: 1775–1875*. San Francisco: John Howell Books, 1980. The emerging visual tradition.

Walker, Franklin. *A Literary History of Southern California*. Berkeley: Univ. of California Press, 1950. Exhaustive and authoritative. *San Francisco's Literary Frontier*. New York: Knopf, 1939. Intelligent biographical emphasis.

Weston, Edward, and Charis Wilson Weston. *California and the West*. New York: Duell, Sloan & Pearce, 1940. The supreme photographic essay on California.

Wilson, Edmund. *The Boys in the Back Room: Notes on California Novelists*. San Francisco: The Colt Press, 1941. A remarkably literal-minded reading of California's sons of Hemingway.

Works Project Administration. *California: A Guide to the Golden State*. New York: Hastings House, 1939. An invaluable survey of the state before the coming of the freeways.

Fiction and first-person response

Atherton, Gertrude. *The Californians*. New York: A. Wessels, 1898. A Jamesian novel about love, race, and land in the San Francisco of the 1880s.

Bidwell, John. *Echoes of the Past*. 1890; rpt. Chicago: Lakeside Press, 1928. Memories of fifty years in California by one of its foremost pioneers. *A Journey to California, 1841: The Journal of John Bidwell*. 1843; rpt. Berkeley, Calif.: Friends of the Bancroft Library, 1964. Diary of the co-leader of the first wagon train to California.

Borthwick, J. D. *Three Years in California*. 1857; rpt. Oakland, Calif.: Biobooks, 1948. Rivals Marryat as an Englishman's picaresque on the phoenix-like culture of the 1850s.

Brewer, William H. *Up and Down California in 1860–1864*. 1930; rpt. Berkeley: Univ. of California Press, 1966. The best field guide before the booms, written by the ramrod on the first California Geological Survey.

Browne, J. Ross. *Crusoe's Island*. New York: Harper Bros., 1864. Tall tales set in an enchanted wasteland.

Chase, J. Smeaton. *California Coast Trails*. Boston: Houghton Mifflin, 1913. An elegiac journey on horseback from San Diego to Crescent City.

Clapp, Louise (Dame Shirley). *The Shirley Letters: 1854–55;* rpt. Salt Lake City: Peregrine Smith, 1970. This sensitive view of life in the mines inspired the early tales of Bret Harte.

Colton, Walter. *Three Years in California*. New York: A. S. Barnes, 1850. The crucial years of the conquest as seen by the Yankee *alcade* of Monterey.

Delano, Alonzo. *Old Block's Sketch-Book; or, Tales of California Life*. 1856; rpt. Santa Ana, Calif.: Fine Arts Press, 1947. A hilarious debunking of myth-making on the Overland Trail.

Farnham, Eliza W. *California, In-doors and Out*. New York: Dix, Edwards, 1856. On a ranch near Santa Cruz two women plant orchards, raise potatoes, and found a garden on their own terms.

Harte, Bret. *The Luck of Roaring Camp and Other Tales*. 1870–76; rpt. Boston: Houghton Mifflin, 1929. The California Edition, this volume contains Harte's first treatment of life in the Mother Lode, "M'liss," as well as the short stories—"The Luck of Roaring Camp," "The Outcasts of Poker Flat," "Miggles," and "Tennessee's Partner"—that were to complete his California Pentateuch.

Jackson, Helen Hunt. *Ramona*. Boston: Roberts Bros., 1884. A still powerful novel about the displacement of the Indian in California.

Jones, Idwal. *The Vineyard*. New York: Duell, Sloan & Pearce, 1942. Viticulture, love, and prohibition in the Napa Valley.

London, Jack. *Burning Daylight*. New York: Macmillan, 1910. The recovery of Sonoma.

    The House of Pride. New York: Macmillan, 1919. Stories of Hawaii.

    Lost Face. New York: Macmillan, 1926. Short stories. Contains "To Build a Fire."

    Martin Eden. New York: Macmillan, 1909. An autobiographical novel of thwarted literary ambition in the East Bay.

    Moon Face. New York: Macmillan, 1906. A book about doubles, this collection contains "All Gold Canyon," the key story about pocket mining in California.

    The Valley of the Moon. New York: Macmillan, 1916. The second recovery of Sonoma.

    When God Laughs. New York: Macmillan, 1911. Short stories.

Manly, William Lewis. *Death Valley in '49*. 1894; rpt. Chicago: Lakeside Press, 1927. A firsthand account of the overland party that gave Death Valley its name.

Marryat, Frank. *Mountains and Molehills*. 1855; rpt. Philadelphia: Lippincott, 1962. An English sportsman endures with good cheer the loss of a Russian River pastoral and the near loss, to Chagres fever, of his life.

Miller, Joaquin. *Life Among the Modocs: Unwritten History*. London: Richard Bentley, 1873. Reports from the last frontier by the performing self.

Nordhoff, Walter (Antonio de Fierro Blanco). *The Journey of the Flame*. Boston: Houghton Mifflin, 1933. Ingenious historical romance about northering from Baja to Monterey.

Powers, Stephen. *Afoot and Alone: A Walk from Sea to Sea*. Hartford: Columbia Book, 1872. An exhausted pedestrian finds California, "bride of mystery," a fair field for projection.

Revere, Joseph Warren. *Naval Duty in California*. 1849; rpt. Oakland, Calif.: Biobooks, 1947. Revere raised the American flag at Sonoma and terminated the Bear Flag revolt; an authority on the changeover from Mexican rule.

Ryan, William Redmond. *Personal Adventures in Upper and Lower California.* London: William Schoberl, 1950. Misery amid "piles of gold."

Rudlain, Charles N., ed. *Early California Travel Series: A Chronological Summary, Index, and Descriptive List.* Los Angeles: Glen Dawson, 1961. A guide to over forty published accounts of various difficult ways west.

Shaw, Reuben Cole. *Across the Plains in Forty-Nine.* 1895; rpt. Chicago: Lakeside Press, 1948. Into California with wagons via Carson Pass.

Stegner, Wallace. *All the Little Live Things.* New York: Viking, 1967. The conflict of generations and the difficulties of retirement in California in the sixties.

Angle of Repose. Garden City, N.Y.: Doubleday, 1971. Based on the life and letters of Mary Hallock Foote, this superb novel is about a life caught between the West and the East.

The Preacher and the Slave. Boston: Houghton Mifflin, 1950. Reissued as *Joe Hill,* this imaginative reconstruction tells the story of IWW organizing in California and the West.

A Shooting Star. New York: Viking, 1961. Although the opening drive from Pasadena to Hillsborough is a tour de force, this novel reads as a runthrough for *Angle of Repose.*

The Spectator Bird. New York: Doubleday, 1976. A sequel to *All the Little Live Things,* in which Joe and Ruth Allston adjust to the past and adapt to the present.

Stevenson, Robert Louis. *From Scotland to Silverado.* ed. James D. Hart. Cambridge, Mass.: Harvard Univ. Press, 1966. An elegant gathering of Stevenson's American travel pieces that culminates in marriage in Monterey and a honeymoon on Mount Saint Helena.

Stewart, George. *Earth Abides.* New York: Random House, 1949. A fantasy of catastrophe and surviving on in the San Francisco Bay.

Fire. New York: Random House, 1948. In California disasters, the disaster becomes the protagonist.

Storm. New York: Random House, 1941. The meteorological sublime.

Swift, John Franklin. *Robert Greathouse.* New York: Carleton, 1870. A Dickensian novel about men buried alive by the ambition to tear riches from the earth. Set in Washoe.

Taylor, Bayard. *El Dorado.* 1850; rpt. New York: Knopf, 1949. A rich portrait of San Francisco and the mines before the fall.

New Pictures from California. 1862; rpt. Oakland, Calif.: Biobooks, 1951. Taylor's subdued return to a place he can no longer find.

Twain, Mark. *Roughing It.* 1871; rpt. Berkeley: Univ. of California Press, 1972. The first book about running away to avoid the draft and find oneself in California.

Upham, Samuel C. *Notes of a Voyage to California via Cape Horn, Together with Scenes in El Dorado in the Years 1849–50.* Philadelphia: Published by the author, 1878. Excellent description of ocean travel to California.

White, Stewart Edward. *Gold.* Garden City, N.Y.: Doubleday, Page, 1913. The first novel in White's trilogy, *The Story of California.*

Williams, James. *Life and Adventures of James Williams: A Fugitive Slave.* San Francisco: Women's Union Print, 1873. A black man's two decades in California.

CHAPTER 1. DANA, LEONARD, AND FRÉMONT: SPECTATORSHIP AND ABANDONMENT

Dana

Adams, Charles Francis. *Richard Henry Dana.* Boston: Houghton Mifflin, 1890. The standard biography.

Dana, Richard Henry. *Two Years Before the Mast.* 1840 and 1969; rpt. New York: Dutton, 1969. The enlarged edition.

    Two Years Before the Mast. 1840; rpt. New York: Penguin, 1981. Contains the important sequel, *Twenty-Four Years After.* Introduction by Thomas Philbrick.

Hart, James D. "New Englanders in Nova Albion: Some 19th Century Views of California." Boston: Trustees of the Public Library of the City of Boston, 1976. These important pages on Dana are amplified by portraits of Colton, Helen Hunt Jackson, Burgess, Robinson, Thomas Starr King, and Clarence King.

Robinson, Alfred. *Life in California.* 1846; rpt. New York: Da Capo, 1969. Robinson lived in Santa Barbara as the agent for Bryant, Sturgis and Company. Dana describes his old California wedding.

Shapiro, Samuel. *Richard Henry Dana, Jr. 1815–1882.* East Lansing: Michigan State Univ. Press, 1961. "My life on land has been a failure," Dana said, and Shapiro sets out to prove it.

Leonard

Clark, William, and Meriwether Lewis. *The Journals of Lewis and Clark.* ed. John Bakeless. New York: New American Library, 1964. A good one-volume edition, with maps.

Clyman, James. *American Frontiersman, 1792–1881.* ed. Charles C. Camp. San Francisco: California Historical Society, 1928. Clyman, eastering as the Donner Party moved west, tried to talk James Reed out of taking Hastings's Cut-off. His journals provide a sardonic and witty commentary on frontier life in California before statehood.

DeVoto, Bernard. *Across the Wide Missouri.* Boston: Houghton Mifflin, 1947. Superb account of the later years of the fur trade.

    The Course of Empire. Boston: Houghton Mifflin, 1952. One of the best books about Lewis and Clark.

Irving, Washington. *The Adventures of Captain Bonneville.* 1837; ed. Edgeley W.

Todd. rpt. Norman: Univ. of Oklahoma Press, 1961. Irving's rendition
   of the journals of the man who sent Walker west toward California.
Leonard, Zenas. *Narrative of the Adventures of Zenas Leonard*. 1839; rpt. Lincoln:
   Univ. of Nebraska Press, 1978.
Pattie, James Ohio. *The Personal Narrative*. 1831; rpt. Philadelphia: Lippincott,
   1962. Pattie reached California via the Colorado River and desert in 1827.
   Edited and perhaps written by Timothy Flint, this is a mythopoeic narra-
   tive of wandering and return.
Smith, Jedediah. *The Ashley–Smith Explorations*. ed. Harrison Dale. Glendale,
   Calif.: Arthur H. Clark, 1941. Standard edition of the travels of the first
   American to reach California by land.

Frémont

Benton, Thomas Hart. *Thirty Years' View*. New York: D. Appleton & Co.,
   1856. Compelling apologetics by Frémont's father-in-law.
Bryant, Edwin. *What I Saw in California*. 1848; rpt. Minneapolis: Ross &
   Haines, 1967. Bryant traveled with the Reeds and the Donners on the
   Overland Trail, met Joseph Walker at Fort Laramie, fought with Frémont, and became the *alcade* of San Francisco.
Burnett, Peter H. *Recollections and Opinions of an Old Pioneer*. 1880; rpt. New
   York: Da Capo Press 1969. One of the most judicious men ever to write
   about California, Burnett became the first elected governor of the state
   after leading the first wagon train from Oregon to California in 1848. He
   met Frémont on the second expedition at Fort Vancouver: "I never travelled with a more pleasant companion than Governor Frémont."
Emory, William H. *Notes of a Military Reconnaissance from Fort Leavenworth, in
   Missouri, to San Diego, in California*. Washington, D.C.: Wendell & Bent-
   huysen, 1848. Written by a hero of the battle of San Pascual, this army
   report opened the Southwest to the American imagination.
Fender, Stephen. *Plotting the Golden West: American Literature and the Rhetoric of
   the California Trail*. Cambridge Univ. Press, 1982. An incisive study of
   the tropes and schema through which writers mediated their experience
   of the West.
Frémont, John Charles. *The Expeditions of John Charles Frémont*. Volume 1:
   Travels from 1838 to 1844. ed. Donald Jackson and Mary Lee Spence.
   Urbana: Univ. of Illinois Press, 1970. A distinguished modern edition.
The Expeditions of John Charles Frémont. Volume 2: *The Bear Flag Revolt and
   the Court-Martial*. Urbana, Ill.: Jackson & Spence, 1973.
Goetzmann, William H. *Army Exploration in the American West, 1803–1863*. 1959;
   rpt. Lincoln: Univ. of Nebraska Press, 1979. An excellent chapter on
   Frémont's vagaries and ambitions.
Hastings, Lansford. *The Emigrant's Guide to Oregon and California*. Cincinnati:
   George Conclin, 1845. The book that led the Donner Party astray.
Nevins, Allan. *Frémont: Pathmarker of the West*. New York: D. Appleton-Cen-
   tury, 1939. The distinguished biography.

Parkman, Francis. *The California and Oregon Trail*. New York: Putnam, 1849.
Beautiful writing by a proto-tourist.

Preuss, Charles. *Exploring with Frémont*. ed. Erwin G. and Elisabeth K. Gudde.
Norman: Univ. of Oklahoma Press, 1958. The journal of a dissenting
voice; Preuss may be the grumpiest explorer on record.

Royce, Josiah. *California; from the Conquest in 1846 to the Second Vigilance Com-
mittee in San Francisco*. 1886; rpt. New York: Knopf, 1948. In this highly
political allegory, California's inception as a state becomes the proving
ground for democratic institutions.

Royce, Sarah. *A Frontier Lady: Recollections of the Gold Rush and Early California*.
ed. Ralph Henry Gabriel. New Haven, Conn.: Yale Univ. Press, 1932.
Seeing God in a burning bush in the deserts of the West.

CHAPTER 2. MUIR AND THE POSSESSION OF LANDSCAPE

Primary sources

Muir, John. *The Cruise of the Corwin; Journal of the Arctic Expedition of 1881 in
Search of de Long and the Jeanette*. ed. William F. Bade. Boston: Houghton
Mifflin, 1917. A dull slog in terrible weather.

Edward Henry Harriman. New York: Doubleday, Page, 1911. A tribute to
the man who financed many of Muir's wanderings.

John of the Mountains: The Unpublished Journals of John Muir. ed. Linnie Marsh
Wolfe. 1938; rpt. Madison: Univ. of Wisconsin Press, 1979. The best access
to Muir's first drafts before the opening of the Muir Papers in the 1970s.

The Mountains of California. 1894; rpt. Berkeley, Calif.: Ten Speed Press,
1977.

My First Summer in the Sierra. 1911; rpt. Dunwoody, Ga.: Norman Berg,
1972.

Our National Parks. 1901; rpt. Madison: Univ. of Wisconsin Press, 1981. Ten
essays written for *The Atlantic Monthly*.

"Rambles of a Botanist Among the Plants and Climates of California."
1872; rpt. Mariposa, Calif.: Rolling K. Press, 1974.

Steep Trails. ed. William F. Bade. Boston: Houghton Mifflin, 1918. Classic
essays on Shasta, the Northwest, and the Grand Canyon.

South of Yosemite: Selected Writings of John Muir. ed. Frederick R. Gunsky.
Garden City, N.Y.: Natural History Press, 1968. Muir's early *San Francisco Bulletin* articles gathered in convenient form.

Stickeen. Boston: Houghton Mifflin, 1909. Exploits of a faithful dog.

The Story of My Boyhood and Youth. 1913; rpt. Madison: Univ. of Wisconsin
Press, 1965.

Studies in the Sierra. ed. William E. Colby. San Francisco: The Sierra Club,
1960. These seven articles on glacial activity appeared originally in the
Overland Magazine in 1874 and 1875.

A Thousand Mile Walk to the Gulf. ed. William F. Bade. Boston: Houghton
Mifflin, 1917. The trip that took Muir to California.

Travels in Alaska. Boston: Houghton Mifflin, 1915. Two trips, in 1879 and
    1880, in pursuit of bigger and better "ice tools."
The Yosemite. 1912; rpt. Garden City, N.Y.: Natural History Press, 1976.
Muir, John, ed. *Picturesque California and the Regions West of the Rocky Mountains
    from Alaska to Mexico.* San Francisco: J. Dewing, 1888. With seven articles
    by Muir, this illustrated two-volume edition is one of the first great
    picture books of the West.

Secondary sources

Brooks, Van Wyck. *The Times of Melville and Whitman.* New York: Dutton,
    1947. Brooks's eleven pages on Muir are the best short introduction to
    the man and his work.
Chase, J. Smeaton. *Yosemite Trails.* Boston: Houghton Mifflin, 1911. Writing
    that rivals Muir's.
Cohen, Michael P. *The Pathless Way: John Muir and the American Wilderness.*
    Madison: Univ. of Wisconsin Press, 1984. Sensitive to the ways in which
    Muir's late books rework his early intentions and principles.
Engberg, Robert, and Donald Wesling. *John Muir: To Yosemite and Beyond,
    Writings from the Years 1863 to 1875.* Madison: Univ. of Wisconsin Press,
    1980. Taking as its theme the growth of the artist's mind, this imagina-
    tive edition of published and unpublished material is a major critical
    statement.
Fox, Stephen. *John Muir and His Legacy: The American Conservation Movement.*
    Boston: Little, Brown, 1981. The first biography to make use of the Muir
    Papers at the University of the Pacific.
Hutchings, James Mason. *In the Heart of the Sierras.* Oakland, Calif.: Pacific
    Press, 1886. Early days in Yosemite as remembered by Muir's employer
    at the sawmill.
Jones, Holway R. *John Muir and the Sierra Club: The Battle of Yosemite.* San
    Francisco: The Sierra Club, 1964. A detailed treatment of the loss of
    Hetch Hetchy.
Le Conte, Joseph. *A Journal of Ramblings through the High Sierra of California.*
    1870; rpt. New York: Ballantine, 1971. Muir in Yosemite as seen by the
    famous professor of geology.
Matthes, François E. *The Incomparable Valley: A Geologic Interpretation of the
    Yosemite.* Berkeley: Univ. of California Press, 1950. Fritioff Fryxell edited
    this nontechnical account by a member of the U.S. Geological Survey.
Nash, Roderick. *Wilderness and the American Mind.* New Haven, Conn.: Yale
    Univ. Press, 1967. The intellectual context for Muir's works and days.
Whitney, Josiah D. *The Yosemite Guide-Book.* Cambridge, Mass.: University
    Press, 1874. The third and pocket edition of the California Geological
    Survey's still useful guide to the Yosemite region.
Wolfe, Linnie Marsh. *Son of the Wilderness: The Life of John Muir.* 1945; rpt.
    Madison: Univ. of Wisconsin Press, 1978. The Pulitzer Prize–winning
    biography.

CHAPTER 3. KING AND CATASTROPHE

Primary sources

The Clarence King Collection. A subcollection of the Hague Collection at the Huntington Library, the King papers include forty-three notebooks based on the California Geological Survey and the Survey of the 40th Parallel, other scientific papers, correspondence, manuscripts, and photographs.

King, Clarence. "Catastrophism and the Evolution of Environment." An address delivered at the Yale Sheffield Scientific School, 1877. Printed in *American Naturalist* 9 (1877) as "Catastrophism and Evolution."

"The Helmet of Mambrino." *Century Magazine* 32 (May 1886).

Mountaineering in the Sierra Nevada. ed. James M. Shebel. 1872; rpt. Lincoln: Univ. of Nebraska Press, 1970. A reprint of the first edition, this text lacks the seventeen pages on Mount Whitney and the preface King added in 1874. Except when referring to this added material, I have quoted from this edition.

Mountaineering in the Sierra Nevada. ed. Francis P. Farquhar. 1874; rpt. New York: Norton, 1935. The most recent edition to contain the account of King's final climb of Mount Whitney. Based on the fourth edition of 1874, this text omits King's preface of that year.

Systematic Geology: Report of the Fortieth Parallel Survey. Washington, D.C.: Government Printing Office, 1878. King's major work as a professional geologist.

Secondary sources

Adams, Henry. *The Education of Henry Adams.* ed. Ernest Samuels. 1907; rpt. Boston: Houghton Mifflin, 1974. King as seen by a best friend.

Atherton, Gertrude. *California: An Intimate History.* New York: Harper Bros., 1914. History as catastrophe.

Bersani, Leo. *Baudelaire and Freud.* Berkeley: Univ. of California Press, 1977. A cogent and brief account of contemporary theories of the decentered (catastrophic) self.

Crosby, Harry Herbert. "So Deep a Trail: A Biography of Clarence King." Ph.D. dissertation, Stanford University, 1953. Inspired by Wallace Stegner, this is the first biography of King.

Farquhar, Francis P. *History of the Sierra Nevada.* Berkeley: Univ. of California Press, 1966. The story of the human encounter with the range by a man who has climbed it.

Lesser, Wayne. "Criticism, Literary History, and the Paradigm: The Education of Henry Adams." *PMLA* 97 (May 1982). A perceptive article on Adams's use of Hay and King.

Levenson, J. C. "Henry Adams and the Art of Politics." *The Southern Review* 4 (Winter 1968). The uses of catastrophe.

Powell, John Wesley. *The Exploration of the Colorado River and Its Canyons.*

1895; rpt. New York: Dover, 1961. The firsthand account of the 1869
expedition led by King's successor on the U.S. Geological Survey.

Smith, Henry Nash. "Clarence King, John Wesley Powell, and the Establishment of the United States Geological Survey." *Mississippi Valley Historical
Review* 34 (June 1947). Powell is the bureaucrat who stayed.

Taylor, Gordon O. "Excursions in the 'Range of Light.' " *The Nature of Identity*. Tulsa: Univ. of Tulsa, 1981. An essay on the tensions and intentions
that shaped King's *Mountaineering*.

Wilkins, Thurman. *Clarence King: A Biography*. New York: Macmillan, 1958.
A superb history of King and the Gilded Age.

CHAPTER 4. MARY AUSTIN: NATURE AND NURTURANCE

Primary sources

Austin, Mary. *The American Rhythm*. Boston: Houghton Mifflin, 1923 and
1930. Speculations on the origins of poetic form in the New World.

Earth Horizon. Boston: Houghton Mifflin, 1932. Austin's autobiography.

Experiences Facing Death. Indianapolis, Ind.: Bobbs-Merrill, 1931. A murky
example of Austin's late mysticism.

The Flock. 1906; rpt. Santa Fe: William Gannon, 1973.

The Ford. Boston: Houghton Mifflin, 1917.

"If I Had a Gifted Daughter." Unpublished manuscript, Huntington Library, Mary Austin Collection, Box 25.

Isidro. Boston: Houghton Mifflin, 1905. A romance of Spanish California.

The Land of Journey's Ending. New York: The Century, 1924.

The Land of Little Rain. 1903; rpt. Albuquerque: Univ. of New Mexico
Press, 1974.

The Lands of the Sun. Boston: Houghton Mifflin, 1927. Reprint of *California, Land of the Sun* (1914). A mythopoeic survey of the topography of
California.

Lost Borders. New York: Harper Bros., 1909.

"The Lost Garden." Unpublished manuscript, Huntington Library, Mary
Austin Collection, Box 41. I have quoted from the second and revised
version.

Mother of Felipe and Other Early Stories. ed. Franklin Walker. Los Angeles:
The Book Club of California, 1950. Contains Austin's first story, about a
mother who refuses to abandon her son to a desert grave.

One Smoke Stories. Boston: Houghton Mifflin, 1934. Tales of procreation
and responsibility on the frontier.

Outland. London: John Murray, 1910. A fantasy of flight and initiation in the
coastal woods near Monterey.

Santa Lucia: A Common Story. New York: Harper Bros., 1908. Repression
and self-discovery in a California university town.

Starry Adventure. Boston: Houghton Mifflin, 1931. Love and architecture in
the Southwest.

"Tejon Notebook." A 7-by-8 1/2-inch notebook with sixty-two handwrit-
ten pages used by Austin in the years 1888–1902. Huntington Library,
Mary Austin Collection, Box 24c.

A Woman of Genius. Garden City, N.Y.: Doubleday, Page, 1912. Austin's
most autobiographical novel.

The Mary Austin Collection. This major holding at the Huntington Library
contains letters and manuscripts by a large number of authors. Included
in the eleven thousand pieces are manuscripts of all of Austin's books
except *The Land of Little Rain,* notebooks and outlines for her novels,
short stories and plays, and more than four hundred photographs.

Secondary sources

Ballard, Rae Galbraith. "Mary Austin's *Earth Horizon*: The Imperfect Circle."
Ph.D. dissertation, Claremont, 1977. The best full-length study of Austin's patterns of self-fashioning.

Cather, Willa. *Death Comes for the Archbishop.* New York: Knopf, 1926.
Cather's unwelcome attempt to appropriate Austin's territory.

Corle, Edwin. *Mojave.* New York: Liveright, 1934. A *Lost Borders* south.

Doyle, Helen MacKnight. *Mary Austin: Woman of Genius.* New York: Gotham
House, 1939. A quirky, intermittent biography by Austin's physician in
Inyo.

Hoagland, Willard, ed. *Mary Austin: A Memorial.* Sante Fe: The Laboratory of
Anthropology, 1944. Essays by various hands.

Pearce, T. M. *The Beloved House.* Caldwell, Idaho: Caxton Printers, 1940. A
brief biography directed toward Austin's New Mexico years.

Mary Hunter Austin. New York: Twayne, 1965.

Ringler, Donald P. "Mary Austin: Kern County Days, 1888–1892." *Southern
California Quarterly* 45 (March 1963). An excellent account, with photographs, of Austin's first years in California.

Van Dyke, John C. *The Desert.* 1901; rpt. Salt Lake City: Peregrine Smith,
1980.

Young, Vernon. "Mary Austin and the Earth Performance." *The Southwest
Review* 35 (Summer 1950). A critical look at Austin's late vision.

CHAPTER 5. NORRIS AND THE VERTICAL

Primary sources

All references to Norris's work except those to *McTeague* are to the ten-volume
edition published by Doubleday, Doran, Garden City, N.Y., in 1928. The
edition contains:

Volumes 1 and 2, *The Octopus,* 1901.
Volume 3, *Blix* and *Moran of the Lady Letty,* 1899.
Volume 4, *The Third Circle* (short stories; 1909) and *A Deal in
Wheat and Other Stories of the New and Old West* (1903).

Volume 5, *Vandover and the Brute,* 1914.
Volume 6, *A Man's Woman,* 1900.
Volume 7, *The Responsibilities of the Novelist* (critical
essays; 1903) and *The Joyous Miracle* (1897).
Volume 8, *McTeague,* 1899.
Volume 9, *The Pit,* 1903.
Volume 10, *Collected Writings* (articles, war reports, short stories), 1928.

Norris, Frank. *McTeague.* ed. Donald Pizer. 1899; rpt. New York: Norton,
1977. I have quoted from this edition not only because of its useful critical
apparatus but because, as Pizer remarks, the text of the novel in the
Complete Edition has no "textual authority."

Secondary sources

Davison, Richard Allan, ed. *Merrill Studies in* The Octopus. Columbus, Ohio:
Charles E. Merrill, 1969. A strong collection of essays.
Dillingham, William B. *Frank Norris: Instinct and Art.* Boston: Houghton Mif-
flin, 1969. Particularly valuable in its discussion of Norris's training and
interest in painting.
French, Warren. *Frank Norris.* New York: Twayne, 1962. A good survey.
McKee, Irving. "Notable Memorials to Mussel Slough." *Pacific Historical Re-
view* 12 (Feb. 1948). McKee details the historical incident on which *The
Octopus* is based, the shoot-out between the ranchers and the agents of the
Southern Pacific on May 11, 1880. Memorials treated here are the novels
by Royce and Norris.
Pizer, Donald. *The Novels of Frank Norris.* Bloomington: Indiana Univ. Press,
1966. The standard critical work.
Royce, Josiah. *The Feud of Oakfield Creek.* Boston: Houghton Mifflin, 1887. A
bad novel by California's foremost philosopher, embroidered around the
events at Mussel Slough.
Walker, Franklin. *Frank Norris: A Biography.* Garden City, N.Y.: Doubleday,
1932. A competent history of a short and mysterious life.

CHAPTER 6. STEINBECK'S LOST GARDENS

Primary sources

All references to Steinbeck's works, unless otherwise indicated, are to the most
recent Penguin reprint, published by Viking–Penguin in New York. Below I
list the original dates of publication along with the date of most recent reprint.

Steinbeck, John. *The Acts of King Arthur and His Noble Knights.* New York:
Farrar, Straus & Giroux, 1976.
Burning Bright. 1950; rpt. 1979.
Cannery Row. 1945; rpt. 1978.
Cup of Gold. 1929; rpt. 1976.

East of Eden. 1952; rpt. 1979.

The Grapes of Wrath. 1939; rpt. The Viking Critical Library. ed. Peter Lisca. New York: Penguin, 1972. An invaluable edition, with maps, essays, a chronology, and a bibliography.

In Dubious Battle. 1936; rpt. 1979.

The Log from the Sea of Cortez. 1951; rpt. 1977.

The Long Valley. 1938; rpt. 1986.

The Moon Is Down. 1942; rpt. 1982.

Of Mice and Men. 1937; rpt. 1978.

The Pastures of Heaven. 1932; rpt., 1982.

The Pearl. 1947; rpt. 1976.

The Short Reign of Pippin IV. 1957; rpt. 1977.

Sweet Thursday. 1954; rpt. 1979.

To a God Unknown. 1933; rpt. 1976.

Tortilla Flat. 1935; rpt. 1977.

Travels with Charley in Search of America. 1962; rpt. 1980.

The Wayward Bus. 1947; rpt. 1979.

The Winter of Our Discontent. 1961; rpt. 1982.

John Steinbeck Papers in the Clifton Waller Barrett Library of the University of Virginia Library. Approximately one hundred items, date range from 1934 to 1964. Letters, galley proofs, and the manuscript of *The Grapes of Wrath*.

Secondary sources

Benson, Jackson. *The True Adventures of John Steinbeck, Writer*. New York: Viking, 1984. The authoritative biography.

Cox, Martha Heasley. "In Search of John Steinbeck: His People and His Land." *San Jose Studies* 1 (1975). A useful guide, with directions and addresses, to Steinbeck's actual California locales.

Davis, Robert Murray, ed. *Steinbeck: A Collection of Critical Essays*. Englewood Cliffs, N.J.: Prentice-Hall, 1972. The introduction is excellent.

French, Warren. *John Steinbeck*. New York: Twayne, 1961. Eloquent on "the education of the heart."

Kiernan, Thomas. *The Intricate Music: A Biography of John Steinbeck*. Boston: Little, Brown, 1979. A sketchy performance.

Levant, Howard. "Tortilla Flat: The Shape of John Steinbeck's Career." *PMLA* 85 (Oct. 1970). A key essay on Steinbeck's ambition to shape his career in accord with mythic schemes.

Lisca, Peter. *The Wide World of John Steinbeck*. New Brunswick, N.J.: Rutgers Univ. Press, 1958. The standard critical work.

Steinbeck, Elaine, and Robert Wallsten, eds. *Steinbeck: A Life in Letters*. New York: Penguin, 1975. This invaluable collection is the closest thing to an autobiography in print.

Stewart, George. *Ordeal By Hunger*. 1936; rpt. New York: Simon & Schuster, 1971. Nothing in the literature of California so resembles the experience of *The Grapes of Wrath* as this classic reconstruction of the westering of the Donner Party.

CHAPTER 7. CHANDLER, MARRIAGE, AND
"THE GREAT WRONG PLACE"

Primary sources

Chandler, Raymond. *The Big Sleep*. 1939; rpt. New York: Random House, 1976.
   Farewell, My Lovely. 1940; rpt. New York: Random House, 1976.
   The High Window. 1942; rpt. New York: Random House, 1976.
   Killer in the Rain. New York: Ballantine, 1972. A collection of eight short stories from which Chandler "cannibalized" his novels. Introduction by Philip Durham.
   The Lady in the Lake. 1943; rpt. New York: Random House, 1976.
   The Little Sister. 1949; rpt. New York: Ballantine, 1971.
   The Long Goodbye. 1953; rpt. New York: Ballantine, 1971.
   Pickup on Noon Street. New York: Ballantine, 1972. Four short stories.
   Playback. 1958; rpt. New York: Ballantine, 1977.
   The Simple Art of Murder. New York: Ballantine, 1972. Chandler's definitive essay about detective fiction, along with four short stories.
   Trouble Is My Business. New York: Ballantine, 1972. Four short stories, with an introduction (1950) by Chandler.

Secondary sources

Auden, W. H. "The Guilty Vicarage." *The Dyer's Hand*. New York: Random House, 1962. A sympathetic and seminal essay on mystery stories.
Banham, Reyner. *Los Angeles: The Architecture of Four Ecologies*. New York: Harper & Row, 1971. A brilliant argument for L.A. as a city that works.
Beekman, E. M. "Raymond Chandler and an American Genre." *Massachusetts Review* 2 (Winter 1973). Locates Chandler within a tradition of "negative romanticism."
Bixby-Smith, Sarah. *Adobe Days*. Cedar Rapids: Torch Press, 1925. A lyrical evocation of Claremont, Long Beach, and Pasadena at the turn of the century.
Burchell, Sidney Herbert. *Jacob Peek, Orange Grower: A Tale of Southern California*. London: Gay & Hancock, 1915. Disaster and renewal in the groves of Redlands.
Byrd, Max. "The Detective Detected." *Yale Review* 64 (Oct. 1974). Marlowe refuses guilt, and so refuses tragedy.
Cleland, Robert Glass. *The Cattle on a Thousand Hills: Southern California 1850–1880*. San Marino, Calif.: The Huntington Library, 1951. A history of the great ranchos.
Didion, Joan. *A Book of Common Prayer*. New York: Simon & Schuster, 1977. The flight from North America.
   Play It As It Lays. New York: Simon & Schuster, 1970. A novel about "freeways" – about endless, pointless desire.

Run River. New York: Simon & Schuster, 1963. Set in the hop farms of the Central Valley, this novel initiates Didion's California cycle about a lost "ceremony of innocence."

Slouching Towards Bethlehem. New York: Dell, 1968. Out of the discontinuous structures of her essays Didion manages to return to an order not afforded by her fictional worlds, to the felt importance, if not the achievement, of "home."

The White Album. New York: Simon & Schuster, 1979. This is the book in which Didion accepts and defends Los Angeles as home.

Dunne, John Gregory. *True Confessions*. New York: Dutton, 1977. "Nothing crossed. And everything did": L.A. as the place where detective stories happen to happen.

Durham, Philip. *Down These Mean Streets a Man Must Go*. Durham: Univ. of North Carolina Press, 1963. Chandler's Knight.

Graham, Margaret Collier. *Stories of the Foot-Hills*. 1895; rpt. Freeport, N.Y.: Books for Libraries Press, 1969. Southern California ranch country.

Gross, Miriam, ed. *The World of Raymond Chandler*. London: Weidenfeld & Nicolson, 1977. Memoirs and criticism.

Helper, Hinton Rowland. *The Land of Gold: Reality Versus Fiction*. Baltimore: Henry Taylor, 1855. Helper sees California as cursed by "mud," "dust," and "vermin," revels in the burning of San Francisco, and lists more than seventy liqueurs obtainable there.

Himes, Chester. *If He Hollers Let Him Go*. Garden City, N.Y.: Doubleday, Doran, 1945. A black man trying to make it in the shipyards of Los Angeles during World War II.

Holder, Charles Frederick. *Life in the Open*. New York: Putnam, 1906. Hunting and fishing from Big Bear to Catalina.

Jameson, Frederic. "On Raymond Chandler." *Southern Review* 6 (Summer 1970). A superior essay on Chandler's vision and style.

Lurie, Alison. *The Nowhere City*. New York: Coward-McCann, 1966. A balanced novel about selves lost and found in the Los Angeles of the Sixties.

McDonald, Ross. *The Chill*. New York: Knopf, 1964. Oedipus in Malibu.

The Underground Man. New York: Knopf, 1971. Forest fire as protagonist.

McShane, Frank. *The Life of Raymond Chandler*. New York: Dutton, 1976.

McShane, Frank, ed. *The Letters of Raymond Chandler*. New York: Columbia Univ. Press, 1981.

Porter, J. C. "End of the Trail: The American West of Hammett and Chandler." *Western Historical Quarterly* 6 (Oct. 1975). Cowboys become detectives.

Pynchon, Thomas. *The Crying of Lot 49*. Philadelphia: Lippincott, 1966. Paranoia in Berkeley and Los Angeles.

Sinclair, Upton. *Oil!* New York: Albert & Charles Boni, 1927. The strike at Signal Hill, the Russian Revolution, and the Harding election interwoven by a mind as capacious and suspicious as Pynchon's.

Smith, David. "The Public Eye of Raymond Chandler." *Journal of American Studies* 14 (Dec. 1980). Chandler's novels advance a coherent and serious social vision.

Speir, Jerry. *Raymond Chandler*. New York: Ungar, 1981. "Chandler the artist is forever rebelling against the restrictions of his chosen genre."

Vachell, Horace Annesley. *Life and Sport on the Pacific Slope*. New York: Dodd, Mead, 1901. Inferior to Holder and Van Dyke as a guidebook to Southern California at the turn of the century.

Van Der Veer, Judy. *Brown Hills*. London: Longmans, 1938. The life of the seasons in the San Diego back country.

Van Dyke, Theodore. *Millionaires of a Day*. New York: Fords, Howard & Hulbert, 1890. The boom of the 1880s.

    Southern California. New York: Fords, Howard & Hulbert, 1886. A wonderfully observant guide.

Viertel, Peter. *The Canyon*. New York: Harcourt Brace, 1940. Wildness at the edge of the city.

Waugh, Evelyn. *The Loved One*. Boston: Little, Brown, 1948. A satire based on Forest Lawn.

West, Jessamyn. *Cress Delahanty*. New York: Harcourt Brace, 1953. The seasons of a girl's life on a ranch in Southern California.

    The Life I Really Lived. New York: Harcourt Brace, 1979. A novelist follows her story to California, "a natural place for endings."

    South of the Angels. New York: Harcourt Brace, 1960. Los Angeles and real estate at the turn of the century.

West, Nathanael. *The Day of the Locust*. New York: Random House, 1939. L.A. + the Midwest = Apocalypse.

CHAPTER 8. JEFFERS, SNYDER, AND THE ENDED WORLD

Jeffers: primary sources

Jeffers, Robinson. *Californians*. New York: Macmillan, 1916.

    Cawdor and Medea. New York: New Directions, 1970. With an introduction by William Everson that sets Jeffers in the Emersonian tradition.

    The Double Axe and Other Poems. New York: Random House, 1948.

    Hungerfield and Other Poems. New York: Random House, 1954.

    The Selected Poetry of Robinson Jeffers. New York: Random House, 1938.

    The Women at Point Sur. New York: Liveright, 1927.

Jeffers: secondary sources

Bennett, Melba Berry. *The Stone Mason of Tor House: The Life and Work of Robinson Jeffers*. Ward Ritchie Press. 1966. An intermittent but useful study.

Carpenter, Frederic I. *Robinson Jeffers*. New York: Twayne, 1962. "His whole poetry may be read as a symbolic exploration and literary description of the meaning of the far West."

Everson, William. *Robinson Jeffers: Fragments of an Older Fury*. Berkeley, Calif.: Oyez, 1968. Passionate.

Powell, Lawrence Clark. *Robinson Jeffers: The Man and His Work*. Pasadena, Calif.: San Pasqual Press, 1934 and 1940. A valuable early study.
Sterling, George. *Robinson Jeffers: The Man and the Artist*. New York: Boni & Liveright, 1926. The appreciation that rescued Jeffers's career.

Snyder: primary sources

Snyder, Gary. *Axe Handles*. San Francisco: North Point Press, 1983.
The Back Country. New York: New Directions, 1968.
Earth House Hold. New York: New Directions, 1969.
The Fudo Trilogy. Berkeley, Calif.: Shaman Drum, 1973. Three further installments of *Mountains and Rivers Without End*.
Myths & Texts. New York: Totem Press, 1960.
The Old Ways: Six Essays. San Francisco: City Lights Books, 1977.
The Real Work: Interviews & Talks, 1964–1979. New York: New Directions, 1980.
Regarding Wave. New York: New Directions, 1970.
Riprap, & Cold Mountain Poems. San Francisco: Four Seasons Foundation, 1965. Translations of Han-shan's "Cold Mountain Poems" added to the 1959 edition of *Riprap*.
Six Sections from Mountains and Rivers Without End Plus One. San Francisco: Four Seasons Foundation, 1970. "The Blue Sky" added to the original six sections published in 1965.
Turtle Island. New York: New Directions, 1974.

Snyder: secondary sources

Bartlett, Lee, ed. *The Beats: Essays in Criticism*. Jefferson, N.C.: McFarland Press, 1981. Important essays on Everson and Snyder.
Faas, Ekbert, ed. *Towards a New American Poetics*. Santa Barbara, Calif.: Black Sparrow Press, 1978. Exemplary interviews with five contemporary poets.
Kerouac, Jack. *The Dharma Bums*. New York: Viking, 1958. Snyder in his early days in Berkeley, disguised as Japhey Ryder.
Kroeber, Theodora. *Ishi in Two Worlds*. Berkeley: Univ. of California Press, 1962. A moving account of the closing years of the last wild native American.
Parkinson, Thomas. "The Poetry of Gary Snyder." *The Southern Review* 4 (Summer 1968). The best article on Snyder's career through *The Back Country*.
"The Theory and Practice of Gary Snyder." *Journal of Modern Literature* 2 (1971–2). A penetrating review of *Earth House Hold* and *Regarding Wave*.
Ramsay, Jarold. *Coyote Was Going Here: Indian Literature of the Oregon Country*. Seattle: Univ. of Washington Press, 1977. Indigenous stories of the kind Snyder heard while growing up.

Steudig, Bob. *Gary Snyder.* New York: Twayne, 1976. First full-length critical study, with important biographical information.

Watts, Alan. *The Way of Zen.* New York: Random House, 1957. A good introduction to some of what Snyder believes, by a man who knew him.

Everson, Rexroth, and others

Allen, Donald M., ed. *The New American Poetry: 1945–1960.* New York: Grove, 1960. The way the San Francisco school looked to an imaginative editor in 1960.

Bidart, Frank. *The Golden State.* New York: Atheneum, 1973. Reasons for moving.

Coolbrith, Ina. *Songs from the Golden Gate.* Boston: Houghton Mifflin, 1895. Lyrics by California's first official poet laureate.

Duncan, Robert. *Bending the Bow.* New York: New Directions, 1969. Poems personal and archetypal by one of California's most eloquent and prolific native sons.

Roots and Branches. New York: New Directions, 1964. With a beautiful poem on Simon Rodia.

Everson, William. *Birth of a Poet: The Santa Cruz Meditations.* ed. Lee Bartlett. Santa Barbara, Calif.: Black Sparrow Press, 1982. Oracular musings that include a section on regionalism and the challenge of California: "To master the art of existence in California is to master it for the world."

Earth Poetry: Selected Essays & Interviews. ed. Lee Bartlett. Berkeley, Calif.: Oyez, 1980.

The Masks of Drought. Santa Barbara, Calif.: Black Sparrow Press, 1980. The second installment of "The Integral Years."

Man-Fate: The Swan Song of Brother Antoninus. New York: New Directions, 1974. First collection of poems from the third phase of Everson's career, "The Integral Years."

The Residual Years: Poems 1934–1948. 1948; rpt. New York: New Directions, 1968. Everson has divided his career into three phases: "The Residual Years" (San Joaquin, marriage, farming); "The Veritable years" (life as a Catholic monk); and "The Integral Years" (life since leaving the order). The trilogy he calls *The Crooked Lines of God.*

The Veritable Years: 1949–1966. Santa Barbara, Calif.: Black Sparrow Press, 1978. Poems written during Everson's years as Brother Antoninus, with a valuable afterword by Albert Gelpi.

Ferlinghetti, Lawrence. *Endless Life: Selected Poems.* New York: New Directions, 1981. By the founder of the City Lights Bookstore.

Hass, Robert. *Field Guide.* New Haven, Conn.: Yale University Press, 1973. Poems of exile and return by a native of the Bay Area.

Praise. New York: Ecco, 1979. Situated poems of the act of the mind.

McMichael, James. *Four Good Things.* Boston: Houghton Mifflin, 1980. Meditative verse autobiography spoken by a boy raised in Pasadena.

Miller, Joaquin. *The Poetical Works of Joaquin Miller.* ed. Stuart P. Sherman.

New York: Putnam, 1923. Barbaric yawping on the Pacific rim, with a
   superb biographical introduction.
Reed, Ishmael, ed. *Calafia: The California Poetry*. Berkeley, Calif.: Y'Bird
   Books, 1979. An anthology of multicultural voices from Zamorano to
   the present.
Rexroth, Kenneth. *American Poetry in the Twentieth Century*. New York: Herder
   & Herder, 1971. An idiosyncratic and exhaustive essay on the politics of
   poetry.
   Assays. New York: New Directions, 1961. Essays on China, France, and
      America, with important comments on "Poets, Old and New."
   The Collected Longer Poems of Kenneth Rexroth. New York: New Directions,
      1968.
   The Collected Shorter Poems of Kenneth Rexroth. New York: New Directions,
      1966.
   New Poems. New York: New Directions, 1974. Further work on the theme
      that love is an art of time.
Soto, Gary. *The Elements of San Joaquin*. Pittsburgh: Univ. of Pittsburgh Press,
   1977. Winner of the United States Award of the International Poetry
   Forum, 1976.
   The Tale of Sunlight. Pittsburgh: Univ. of Pittsburgh Press, 1978. With the
      strong "Manuel Zaragoza Poems."
   Where the Sparrows Work Hard. Pittsburgh: Univ. of Pittsburgh Press, 1981.
      Unemployment, TV, and the sense of being "Brown like us."
Sterling, George. *Selected Poems*. 1923; rpt. St. Clair Shores, Mich.: Scholarly
   Press, 1970. Sterling founded his career on the myth of Atlantis, a long-
   ing for a land below the western horizon where loss is done.
Winters, Yvor. *The Collected Poems of Yvor Winters*. Manchester, England: Car-
   canet, 1978. With an introduction in which Donald Davie claims that
   "one of the strongest impulses behind Winters's poetry is the Virgilian
   pietas – towards a native or adopted (in Winters's case, adopted) terrain."

EPILOGUE: FICTIONS OF SPACE

Billington, Ray. *The Far Western Frontier: 1830–1860*. New York: Harper Bros.,
   1956. A good short history of the years in which America appropriated
   California.
Bush, Clive. *The Dream of Reason*. London: Edward Arnold, 1977. An English-
   man looks at "the relation of the self to a new sociographic space during
   the first 80 or so years of independent American culture."
Flexner, James T. *That Wilder Image: The Painting of America's Native School*.
   Boston: Little, Brown, 1962. A biography of American painting in the
   nineteenth century.
Franklin, Wayne. *Discoverers, Explorers, Settlers: The Diligent Writers of Early
   America*. Chicago: Univ. of Chicago Press, 1979. A perceptive study of
   the ways in which material acts of possession were transformed in the
   New World into modes of imaginative memorial.

Kolodny, Annette. *The Land Before Her: Fantasy and Experience of the American Frontiers, 1630–1860*. Chapel Hill, N.C.: Univ. of North Carolina Press, 1984. Women imagining and encountering the "fact of the west."

The Lay of the Land: Metaphor as Experience and History in American Life and Letters. Chapel Hill, N.C.: Univ. of North Carolina Press, 1975. The literature of male exploration and exploitation carries within itself a pastoral and domesticating impulse.

Lawrence, D. H. *Studies in Classic American Literature*. 1923; rpt. New York: Albert & Charles Boni, 1930. An excellent chapter on Dana.

Lee, Robert Edson. *From West to East: Studies in the Literature of the American West*. Urbana: Univ. of Illinois Press, 1966. Eastern imperatives overcome western ambitions.

Levin, David. *History as Romantic Art: Bancroft, Prescott, Motley, and Parkman*. Stanford, Calif.: Stanford University Press, 1959. History is as written as literature.

Marx, Leo. *The Machine in the Garden: Technology and the Pastoral Ideal in America*. New York: Oxford Univ. Press, 1964. American literature deploys a "complex pastoral" that abhors yet confronts the machine.

Miller, Perry. *Errand into the Wilderness*. Cambridge, Mass.: Harvard Univ. Press, 1956. The transformation of the Puritan spiritual "errand" into a territorial one.

The New England Mind: The Seventeenth Century. Cambridge, Mass.: Harvard Univ. Press, 1939. One of the best studies yet written of the profound regionalism of American minds.

Milton, John R. *The Novel of the American West*. Lincoln: Univ. of Nebraska Press, 1980. Argues a distinction between "the standard western" and "another kind which is a much higher form of art."

Mitchell, Lee Clark. *Witnesses to a Vanishing America: The Nineteenth-Century Response*. Princeton, N.J.: Princeton Univ. Press, 1981. A very useful guide to the writers, painters, and other conservators who recorded the life of the frontier.

Novak, Barbara. *Nature and Culture: American Landscape and Painting 1825–1875*. New York: Oxford Univ. Press, 1980. Luminism and the operatic sublime.

Olson, Charles. *Call Me Ishmael*. New York: Reynal & Hitchcock, 1947. A tribute to "Pacific man."

Poirier, Richard. *A World Elsewhere: The Place of Style in American Literature*. New York: Oxford Univ. Press, 1966. Witty and extravagant close readings.

Sauer, Carl Ortwin. *Land and Life*. ed. John Leighly. Berkeley: Univ. of California Press, 1963. Essays on the pleasures and morphology of landscape by the eminent geographer.

Simpson, Lewis. *The Brazen Face of History: Studies in the Literary Consciousness of America*. Baton Rouge: Louisiana State Univ. Press, 1980. The triumph of "mind" over the particulars of place.

The Man of Letters in New England and the South: Essays on the Literary

Vocation in America. Baton Rouge: Louisiana State Univ. Press, 1973. Regional distinctions of exemplary precision.

Smith, Henry Nash. *Virgin Land: The American West as Symbol and Myth.* Cambridge, Mass.: Harvard Univ. Press, 1950. The book that opened up the field.

Spengemann, William. *The Adventurous Muse: The Poetics of American Fiction.* New Haven, Conn.: Yale Univ. Press, 1977. Travel and discovery as organizing metaphors in American literature.

Slotkin, Richard. *Regeneration Through Violence: The Mythology of the American Frontier, 1600–1860.* Middletown, Conn.: Wesleyan Univ. Press, 1973. "Not the cultivator, but the *conquistadore,* is the American Aeneas."

Turner, Frederick Jackson. *The Frontier in American History.* New York: Holt, 1920. The most debated hypothesis in American historiography.

Williams, William Carlos. *In the American Grain.* 1925; rpt. New York: New Directions, 1956. A poet takes possession of his national past.

Index

Adams, Ansel, iv, 61
Adams, Charles Francis, 252
  Richard Henry Dana, 252
Adams, Clover, 48
Adams, Henry, 34, 48, 65–6, 256
  Democracy, 48
  Education, 65–6, 256
Alcatraz Island, 4
Allen, Donald M., 265
  The New American Poetry: 1945–1960, 265
Anaconda Copper Company, 49
Andes, 24
Angel Island, 2
Arizona, 48, 49
Ashley, William, 24
Atherton, Gertrude, 66, 98, 249, 256
  California: An Intimate History, 66, 256
  The Californians, 249
The Atlantic Monthly, 53
Auden, W. H., 161, 261
  "The Guilty Vicarage," 261
Austin, Mary, xii, xiii, xvii, 67–95, 209,
  257–8
  The American Rhythm, 69, 257
  The Arrow Maker, 69, 257
  Earth Horizon, 67, 72–6, 80, 88, 257
  Experiences Facing Death, 257
  The Flock, 81–3, 86–7, 257
  The Ford, 92, 257
  "If I Had a Gifted Daughter," 74, 257
  Isidro, 257
  The Land of Journey's Ending, 93, 257
  The Land of Little Rain, 69, 75, 81–6,
  257
  The Lands of the Sun, 257

  Lost Borders, 78–82, 87–91, 257
  "The Lost Garden," 94–5, 257
  The Man Jesus, 69, 257
  The Mary Austin Collection, 258
  Mother of Felipe and Other Early Stories,
  257
  One Smoke Stories, 69, 257
  Outland, 257
  Santa Lucia, 257
  Starry Adventure, 257
  "Tejon Notebook," 76, 79, 83, 258
  A Woman of Genius, 69, 72, 258
Austin, Ruth, 68–76
Austin, Stafford Wallace, 67–9, 92
Ayers, Thomas, i

Baja California, 130, 250
Bakeless, John, 252
  The Journals of Lewis and Clark, 252
Balboa, Vasco de, 23
Ballard, Rae, xi, 68, 258
  "Mary Austin's *Earth Horizon*: The Im-
  perfect Circle," 258
Bancroft, Hubert Howe, xvii
Banham, Reyner, 160, 261
  *Los Angeles: The Architecture of Four
  Ecologies*, 160, 261
Bartlett, Lee, 264
  The Beats: Essays in Criticism, 264
Beale, Edward, 69
Bear Valley, 28
Beck, Warren A., 247
  California: A History of the Golden State,
  247
  Historical Atlas of California, 247

Beekman, E. M., 261
"Raymond Chandler and an American Genre," 261
Bennett, Melba Berry, 263
  The Stone Mason of Tor House, 263
Benson, Jackson, xii, 260
  The True Adventures of John Steinbeck, 260
Benton, Thomas Hart, 25, 253
  Thirty Years' View, 25, 30, 253
Bent's Fort, 19
Bergson, Henri, 111, 209, 210
Berkeley, 207, 264
Bersani, Leo, 256
  Baudelaire and Freud, 256
Beskow, Bo, 154
Bidart, Frank, 265
  The Golden State, 265
Bidwell, John, 249
  Echoes of the Past, 249
  A Journey to California, 249
Big Bear, 164
Big Dipper Mine, 103
The Big Sleep (Warner Brothers), iv, 167
Billington, Ray, 266
  The Far Western Frontier: 1830–1860, 266
Bishop, 69
Bixby-Smith, Sarah, 261
  Adobe Days, 261
Black Mountain Glacier, 34
Blackford, Staige, xii
Blake, William, 50, 133, 185, 208
Bloom, Harold, 208
Bogart, Humphrey, 167
Bonneville, Captain B. L. E., iv, 9, 18, 252
  Adventures of Captain Bonneville, 9, 23, 252
  Bonneville's map, iv, 9, 24, 252
Boone, Daniel, 16
Borthwick, J. D., 249
  Three Years in California, 249
Boston, 2
Brewer, William, xv–xvi, 48, 52–4, 249
  Up and Down California, 53, 249
Bridger, James, 18
Broderick, David, 66
Brooks, Van Wyck, 255
  The Times of Melville and Whitman, 255
Browne, J. Ross, 249
  Crusoe's Island, 249

Bryant, Edwin, 15, 253
  What I Saw in California, 253
Buchanan, James, 28
Buenaventura River, 24, 26
Burchell, Sidney Herbert, 261
  Jacob Peek, Orange Grower, 261
Bush, Alfred, xi
Bush, Clive, 266
  The Dream of Reason, 266
Byrd, Max, 261
  "The Detective Detected," 261

Cabrillo, Juan, 5
Cahuenga, capitulation of, 28
Cain, James M., 164
Canada, 43
Cape Horn, 2
Carlinville, 71
Carmel, 69, 75, 92, 135, 174–85
Carpenter, Frederic I., 263
  Robinson Jeffers, 263
Carson, Kit, 20, 21, 26, 28
Carson Lake, 10
Carson Pass, 251
Cascade Range, 27, 190
Castro, José, 26
Cathedral City, 164
Cathedral Rocks, 39
Cather, Willa, 69, 258
  Death Comes for the Archbishop, 69, 258
Cebulski, Frank, xii
Central Valley, 12, 19, 25–6, 116, 185, 262
Cervantes, Miguel de, 66
Champney, Freeman, 151
Chandler, Cissy, 163–73
Chandler, Raymond, xvii, 158–73, 208, 247, 261–3
  The Big Sleep, 161, 164–6, 261
  Farewell, My Lovely, 165–8, 261
  The High Window, 165, 167–9, 261
  Killer in the Rain, 261
  The Lady in the Lake, 165, 169–70, 261
  The Little Sister, 162, 165, 170–1, 261
  The Long Goodbye, 165, 171–3, 261
  Playback, 165, 172, 261
  The Simple Art of Murder, 163, 261
  Trouble Is My Business, 261
Channel Islands, 158
Chase, J. Smeaton, 15, 249, 255
  California Coast Trails, 255
  Yosemite Trails, 255

Chase, Richard, 114
Cheyenne, 48
Chicago, 161
Chiles, Joseph, 18
Clapp, Louise, 249
   The Shirley Letters, 249
Claremont, 261
Clark, William, 1–2, 252
   The Journals, 1–2, 252
Cleland, Robert Glass, 261
   The Cattle on a Thousand Hills, 261
Clyman, James, 252
   American Frontiersman, 1792–1881, 252
Coast Range, 53, 96
Coffin, Tim, xii
Cohen, Michael P., 255
   The Pathless Way: John Muir and the
      American Wilderness, 255
Coleridge, Samuel Taylor, 115, 196
Colfax, 103
Colorado, 19
Colorado River, 69, 93, 253
Colton, Walter, 250
   Three Years in California, 250
Columbia River, 19
Columbus, Christopher, 1
Conrad, Joseph, 69
Coolbrith, Ina, 265
   Songs from the Golden Gate, 265
Cooper, James Fenimore, 56
Core, George, xii
Corle, Edwin, 258
   Mojave, 258
Corral de Tierra, 135
Cotter, Richard, 53–6
Cowan, Robert Granniss, 247
   A Bibliography of the History of Califor-
      nia, 247
Cox, Martha Heasley, 260
   "In Search of John Steinbeck," 260
Crane, Hart, 179
Crescent City, 249
Crosby, Harry Herbert, 256
   "So Deep a Trail: A Biography of Clar-
      ence King," 256
Cuba, 49

Dabney Oil Syndicate, 163
The Dalles, 19, 24
Dana, Richard Henry, Jr., xi, xvii, 2–8,
   11, 209, 252

Twenty-Four Years After, 3–8, 252
Two Years Before the Mast, 3–8, 252
Dana Point, 6
Davie, Donald, 84
Davis, Robert M., 124, 260
   Steinbeck: A Collection of Critical Essays,
      260
Davison, Peter, xi
Davison, Richard Allen, 259
   Merrill Studies in The Octopus, 259
Death Valley, 89, 107, 250
Defoe, Daniel, 18
   Robinson Crusoe, 18
Delano, Alonzo, 250
   Old Block's Sketch-Book, 250
De Niro, Robert, 159
De Quincey, Thomas, 59
De Voto, Bernard, 28, 247, 252
   Across the Wide Missouri, 252
   The Course of Empire, 252
   The Year of Decision: 1846, 247
Didion, Joan, vi, 98, 158–60, 261–2
   A Book of Common Prayer, 261
   Play It As It Lays, 261
   Run River, 261
   Slouching Towards Bethlehem, 261
   The White Album, 261
Diebenkorn, Richard, 108
Dillingham, William, 114, 259
   Frank Norris: Instinct and Art, 259
Donner Party, 149, 252, 253
Donner Pass, 19, 23
Dora, 169
Doré, Paul Gustave, 59
Double Indemnity, 164
Doyle, Helen MacKnight, 75, 258
   Mary Austin: Woman of Genius, 258
Dry Creek, 36
Dulwich College, 161
Duncan, Robert, 265
   Bending the Bow, 265
   Roots and Branches, 265
Dunne, John Gregory, 158, 262
   True Confessions, 158, 262
Durham, Philip, 170, 262
   Down These Mean Streets a Man Must
      Go, 262
Duvall, Robert, 159

Eagle Rock, 153
El Capitan, 39

Emerson, Ralph Waldo, 20, 32–6, 45–6,
    84, 206
    Nature, 32–3, 206
Emory, William H., 22, 253
    Notes of a Military Reconnaissance, 253
Engberg, Robert, xi, 255
    John Muir: To Yosemite and Beyond, 255
England, 69, 161–3, 175
Ernest, Robert, 247
    *A Bibliography of the History of Califor-
    nia*, 247
Estes Park, 65
Everson, William, xvii–xviii, 39, 184–6,
    263–5
    *Archetype West: The Pacific Coast as a
    Literary Region*, xviii, 247
    Birth of a Poet, 265
    Earth Poetry, 265
    The Masks of Drought, 265
    Man-Fate, 265
    The Residual Years, 265
    *Robinson Jeffers: Fragments of an Older
    Fury*, 185, 263
    The Veritable Years, 265

Faas, Ekbert, 196, 264
    Towards a New American Poetics, 264
Farallone Islands, 3
Faragher, John Mack, 247
    Women and Men on the Overland Trail,
    247
Farnham, Eliza W., 250
    California, In-doors and Out, 250
Farquhar, Francis, 256
    A History of the Sierra Nevada, 256
Faulkner, William, 34, 115
Fender, Stephen, 22, 253
    Plotting the Golden West, 22, 253
Ferlinghetti, Lawrence, 265
    Endless Life: Selected Poems, 265
Filreis, Al, xii
Flat River, 49
Flexner, James T., 266
    *That Wilder Image: The Painting of Amer-
    ica's Native School*, 266
Flint, Timothy, 253
Ford, John, 96
Fort Hall, 19
Fort Laramie, 253
Fort Vancouver, 19, 25

Fox, Stephen, 255
    John Muir and His Legacy, 255
Franklin, Wayne, 266
    Discoverers, Explorers, Settlers, 266
Frémont, Jessie Benton, 18
Frémont, John C., iv, xvii, 2, 18–31, 209,
    253
    Memoirs, 20, 26–7, 253
    Reports, 18–31, 253
Frémont Peak, 18–19, 23
French, Warren, 148, 259, 260
    Frank Norris, 259
    John Steinbeck, 260
Freniére, Lorrison, 20
Frost, Robert, 16, 43, 46, 200, 209
Frye, Northrop, 208
Fryxell, Fritioff, xi

Gallatin's map, 24
Gardiner, James, 48, 54
Gass, Alison, 195, 197
Gelpi, Albert, xii
Georges Creek, 85
Gillespie, Lieutenant Archibald, 19, 27–8
Glen Ellen, 208
Godey, Alexis, 20
Goetzmann, William H., 253
    *Army Exploration in the American West,
    1803–1863*, 253
Golden Gate, 4
Goodyear, W. A., 58
Grabo, Norman, xii
Graham, Margaret Collier, 160, 262
    Stories of the Foot-Hills, 160, 262
Grand Canyon, 81
Great Basin, 19, 24
The Great Gatsby, 171
Great Salt Lake, 10, 19, 23
Green River, 2, 8
Greene, Charles and Henry, 175
Greene, Merril, xii
Gross, Miriam, 262
    The World of Raymond Chandler, 262

Haase, Ynez, D., 247
    Historical Atlas of California, 247
Hanford, 96
Hart, James D., xi, xvii, 248, 251–2
    A Companion to California, xvii, 248
    "New Englanders in Nova Albion:

Some 19th Century Views of California," 252
Harte, Bret, 83, 249–50
  The Luck of Roaring Camp and Other Tales, 250
Hass, Robert, xi, 207, 209–10, 265
  Field Guide, 265
  Praise, 265
Hastings's Cut-off, 19, 23, 252
Hastings, Lansford, 23, 253
  Emigrant's Guide, 23, 253
Hawaii, 69, 250
Hawley, Robert, xi–xii
Hay, Clara, 48
Hay, John, 48, 256
Helper, Hinton Rowland, 160, 262
  The Land of Gold: Reality Versus Fiction, 160, 262
Hemingway, Ernest, 33, 146
  "Indian Camp," 146
Heraclitus, 180
Hetch Hetchy Valley, iv, 38–40, 92, 255
Himes, Chester, 262
  If He Hollers Let Him Go, 262
Hoagland, Willard, 258
  Mary Austin: A Memorial, 258
Holder, Charles Frederick, 160, 262–3
  Life in the Open, 160, 262
Holliday, J. S., 248
  The World Rushed In: The California Gold Rush Experience, 248
Hollister, 96–7
Hollywood, 164
Hoover, Herbert, 69
Houston, Sam, 16
Humboldt Lake, 10
Humboldt River, 3, 10
Hunt, Rockwell D., 248
  California Firsts, 248
Hunter, George, 68, 71, 88
Hunter, George, Jr., 75
Hunter, Jennie, 72
Hunter, Jim, 75, 80
Hunter, J. P., 148
Hunter, Mary, 70–6
Hunter, Susannah, 68–78
Huntington, Collis, 120
Huntington Library, 69, 256, 258
Hutchings, J. M., i, iv, 255
  In the Heart of the Sierras, 255

Scenes of Wonder and Curiosity in California, i, iv
Hyde, William, 48

Illinois, 68–9
Independence, 69, 92
India, 197, 205
Inyo, 67, 91–3
Ireland, 176
Irving, Washington, 9, 252
  Adventures of Captain Bonneville, 9, 23, 252
Irwin, John, xii
Italy, 69

Jackson, Donald and Mary Lee Spence, 253
  The Bear Flag Revolt and the Court-Martial, 253
  The Expeditions of John Charles Frémont, I & II, 253
Jackson, Helen Hunt, 250
  Ramona, 250
James, George Wharton, xviii, 248
  Heroes of California, xviii, 248
Jameson, Frederic, 262
  "On Raymond Chandler," 262
Japan, 174, 192, 197, 205
Jeffers, Robinson, xii, xvii, 133, 174–85, 202–3, 263–4
  Californians, 180, 263
  Cawdor and Medea, 263
  The Double Axe and Other Poems, 263
  Hungerfield and Other Poems, 183, 263
  The Selected Poetry of Robinson Jeffers, 178–82, 184–5, 263
  The Women at Point Sur, 179, 263
Jeffers, Una, 174–85
Job's Peak, 47
Jolon Valley, 132
Jones, Holway, 255
  John Muir and the Sierra Club: The Battle of Yosemite, 255
Jones, Idwal, 250
  The Vineyard, 250
Joshua Tree National Monument, 158
Jung, Carl, 120

Kearney, Stephen Watts, 28, 69
Kerouac, Jack, 264
  The Dharma Bums, 264

Kiernan, Thomas, 152, 260
  The Intricate Music: A Biography of John Steinbeck, 260
King, Clarence, xi–xiii, xvii, 34, 47–66, 209, 256–7
  "Catastrophism and the Evolution of Environment," 49–51, 256
  The Clarence King Collection, 256
  "The Helmet of Mambrino," 66, 256
  Mountaineering in the Sierra Nevada (1872), 47–66, 256
  Mountaineering (1874), 60, 62, 256
  Systematic Geology, 49, 50, 256
King, Florence, 48
King, James, 48
King of William, James, 66
Kings County, 96
Kitkitdizze, 174, 202
Klamath Lake, 19
Knoles, George K., 248
  Essays and Assays: California History Reappraised, 248
Kolodny, Annette, 267
  The Land Before Her, 267
  The Lay of the Land, 267
Kuster, Ruth, 183
Kuster, Theodore, 182–4

Lajeunesse, Basil, 28
La Jolla, 164, 170
Larkin, Thomas O., 28
Las Sergas de Esplandián, xviii
Lawrence, D. H., 94, 208, 267
  Studies in Classic American Literature, 267
Le Conte, Joseph, 255
  A Journal of Ramblings Through the High Sierra of California, 255
Lee, Robert Edson, 267
  From West to East: Studies in the Literature of the American West, 267
Leo, John, xi
Leonard, Zenas, xviii, 2–3, 8–15, 26, 253
  Narrative of the Adventures of Zenas Leonard, 8–15, 23, 253
Lesser, Wayne, 256
  "Criticism, Literary History, and the Paradigm: The Education of Henry Adams," 256
Lessing, Gotthold Ephraim, 108, 209

Levant, Howard, 129, 260
  "Tortilla Flat: The Shape of John Steinbeck's Career," 260
Levenson, J.C., 256
  "Henry Adams and the Art of Politics," 256
Levin, David, xii, 267
  History as Romantic Art, 267
Lewis, Meriwether, 1–2, 252
  The Journals, 1–2, 252
Lewis, Wyndham, 209
Lisca, Peter, 148, 260
  The Wide World of John Steinbeck, 260
Lloyd, Warren, 162
London, 161, 164
London, Jack, 98, 208, 250
  Burning Daylight, 208, 250
  The House of Pride, 250
  Lost Face, 250
  Martin Eden, 250
  Moon Face, 250
  The Valley of the Moon, 250
  When God Laughs, 250
Lone Pine, 69
Long Beach, xv, 261
Long Beach Freeway, xv
Los Angeles, 92, 158–73, 175, 261–3
Los Angeles County, 158
Los Angeles River, xv
Los Angeles Water Department, 69, 92
Los Gatos, 124, 152–4
Luhan, Mabel, 183
Lummis, Charles, 69, 74, 175
Lurie, Alison, 262
  The Nowhere City, 262

McDonald, Ross, 262
  The Chill, 262
  The Underground Man, 262
McIntosh, Mavis, 135
McKee, Irving, 259
  "Notable Memorials to Mussel Slough," 259
McMichael, James, 265
  Four Good Things, 265
McShane, Frank, 163, 262
  The Letters of Raymond Chandler, 262
  The Life of Raymond Chandler, 262
McWilliams, Carey, xvii, 248
  California: The Great Exception, 248

Southern California: Island on the Land,
  xvii, 248
Manley, William 15, 250
  Death Valley in '49, 250
Marcosson, Isaac, 117
Marryat, Frank, 249, 250
  Mountains and Molehills, 250
Martinez, 44–5
Marvell, Andrew, 142, 185
Marx, Leo, 267
  The Machine in the Garden, 267
Matthes, Francois E., 255
  The Incomparable Valley, 255
Melville, Herman, 56
Memphis and El Paso Railroad, 29
Merced River, 11–12
Mexico, 49
Miller, Joaquin, 15, 18, 250, 265
  Life Among the Modocs, 250
  The Poetical Works of Joaquin Miller, 265
Miller, Perry, xvi, 267
  Errand into the Wilderness, 267
  *The New England Mind: The Seventeenth
    Century,* 267
Millet, Jean, 108
Milton, John, 43, 126, 130, 151, 182, 185,
  196, 206, 208
  Paradise Lost, 151
Milton, John R., 267
  The Novel of the American West, 267
Mississippi River, 20
Mitchell, Lee Clark, 267
  Witnesses to a Vanishing America, 267
Monterey, 3, 25–6, 75, 124, 137, 153–4,
  175, 250–1
Monument Valley, 96
Moore, Harry, 133
Mother Lode, 64, 250
Mount Dana, xii
Mount Langley, 58
Mount Picacho, 69
Mount Ritter, 35
Mount Saint Helena, 251
Mount Shasta, 47, 51–3
Mount Snowdon, 60
Mount Tyndall, 53–62
Mount Whitney, 45, 53, 56–62, 256
Muir, John, iv, xi, xii, xvii, 32–46, 50,
  92, 186, 203, 210, 254–5
  Cruise of the Corwin, 254

Edward Henry Harriman, 254
John of the Mountains, 254
The Mountains of California, 34–46, 254
My First Summer in the Sierra, 41–2, 45,
  254
Our National Parks, 254
Picturesque California, 255
"Rambles of a Botanist," 39, 254
South of Yosemite, 254
Steep Trails, 254
Stickeen, 254
Story of My Boyhood and Youth, 42–3,
  254
Studies in the Sierra, 254.
Thousand Mile Walk, 254
Travels in Alaska, 255
Yosemite, 32–7, 39, 254
Mullholland, William, 92
Munich, 161
Mussel Slough, 96, 259

Nash, Roderick, 255
  Wilderness and the American Mind, 255
Nebraska, 161
Nevada, 10, 19, 25
Nevada City, 202
Nevins, Allan, 25, 253
  Frémont: Pathmarker of the West, 253
New Directions Publishing Corporation,
  204
New England, 133
New Mexico, 69, 92–4
New York, 69, 152–4
Nicolet, Joseph Nicolas, 20
Nordhoff, Charles, 248
  *Northern California, Oregon, and the
    Sandwich Islands,* 248
Nordhoff, Walter, 250
  The Journey of the Flame, 250
Norris, Frank, iv, xii, xvii, 96–123, 179,
  210, 258–9
  Blix, 101, 258
  Collected Writings, 259
  A Deal In Wheat, 258
  "Dying Fires," 102
  "Grettir at Drangey," 102
  The Joyous Miracle, 259
  "Little Dramas of the Curbstone," 102
  McTeague, 98, 103–8, 114, 258–9
  A Man's Woman, 101, 259

Norris, Frank (*cont.*)
  "The Mechanics of Fiction," 115–7
  "A Memorandum of Sudden Death,"
    100–1
  Moran of the Lady Letty, 258
  The Octopus, 96–8, 107–123, 258–9
  The Pit, 259
  The Responsibilities of the Novelist, 259
  "A Reversion to Type," 103
  "The Ship That Saw a Ghost," 100–1
  The Third Circle, 258
  Vandover and the Brute, 98–100, 259
Novak, Barbara, 267
  *Nature and Culture: American Landscape
    and Painting 1825–1875,* 267

Odyssey, 115
Oklahoma, 148
Olson, Charles, 209, 267
  Call Me Ishmael, 267
Oregon, 19, 20, 25–6, 203
Oregon Trail, 18, 25
Orinoco River, 1
Overland Monthly, 69
Owens Valley, 69, 91–3, 106
Oxford English Dictionary, 126

Pacheco Pass, 38
Pacific Grove, 124–5, 152–7
Pacific Ocean, 2–8, 12, 14, 24
Pacific Palisades, 164
Palm Springs, 173
Paris, 161
Parkinson, Thomas, 188, 264
  "The Poetry of Gary Snyder," 264
  "The Theory and Practice of Gary
    Snyder," 264
Parkman, Francis, 208, 254
  The California and Oregon Trail, 254
Pasadena, xv, 69, 176, 186, 261, 265
Pascal, Julian, 163
Patchen, Mary, 70–6
Pater, Walter, 209
Pattie, James Ohio, 18, 253
  The Personal Narrative, 253
Pearce, T. M., 258
  The Beloved House, 258
Phoenix, 49
Pizer, Donald, 103, 259
  The Novels of Frank Norris, 259
Placer County, 106

Platte River, 2, 19
Point Concepcion, 2, 5
Point Reyes, xii
Poirier, Richard, 267
  A World Elsewhere, 267
Polanski, Roman, 92
  Chinatown, 92
Pomona, 169
Porter, J. C., 262
  "End of the Trail: The American West
    of Hammett and Chandler," 262
Pound, Ezra, 188
  Cantos, 188
Powell, Dilys, 164
Powell, John Wesley, 256–7
  *The Exploration of the Colorado River and
    Its Canyons,* 256
Powell, Lawrence Clark, 180–1, 248, 264
  *California Classics: The Creative Litera-
    ture of the Golden State,* 248
  Land of Fiction, 248
  Robinson Jeffers: The Man and His Work,
    264
Powers, Stephen, 250
  Afoot and Alone, 250
Preuss, Charles, 25, 254
  Exploring with Frémont, 254
Pynchon, Thomas, 160, 262
  The Crying of Lot 49, 262
Pyramid Lake, 19

Ralston, William, 66
Ramsay, Jarold, 264
  *Coyote Was Going Here: Indian Literature
    of the Oregon Country,* 264
Reed, Ishmael, 266
  Calafia: The California Poetry, 266
Reed, James, 252
Renner, Virginia, xiii
Reno, 48
Resaca de la Palma, battle of, 27
Revere, Joseph Warren, 250
  Naval Duty in California, 250
Rexroth, Kenneth, 185–6, 266
  American Poetry in the Twentieth Century,
    266
  Assays, 266
  The Collected Longer Poems, 266
  The Collected Shorter Poems, 266
  New Poems, 266
Rhodia, Simon, 176

Ricketts, Ed, 131
Ridge, Martin, xiii
Ringler, Donald P., 258
  "Mary Austin: Kern County Days,"
  258
Rio Grande, 93
Rivera, Diego, 69
Riverside, 164
Robinson, Alfred, 252
  Life in California, 252
Robinson, W. W., 248
  Land in California, 248
Roc, Margaret Miller, 248
  California: Local History, a Bibliography
  and Union List of Library Holdings, 248
Rocky Mountains, 1, 2, 10, 18, 25
Rolle, Andrew F., 248
  California: A History, 248
Royce, Josiah, 19, 29–30, 248, 254, 259
  California, 30, 254
  The Feud of Oakfield Creek, 259
  "The Pacific Coast: A Psychological
  Study of the Relations of Climate and
  Civilization,", 248
Royce, Sarah, 30, 254
  A Frontier Lady, 254
Rudlain, Charles N., 251
  Early California Travel Series, 251
Ruskin, John, 49
Russian, River, 250
Ryan, William Redmond, 251
  Personal Adventures in Upper and Lower
  California, 251

Sag Harbor, 124
Sagan, Carl, 181
  Cosmos, 181
St. Louis, 2, 11, 23
Salinas, 128, 153
Salinas Valley, 133, 139
San Bernardino Mountains, 169
San Diego, 2–5, 7, 14, 70–1, 249
San Dimas, 169
San Emigdio Ranch, iv, 76–7
San Francisco, xvi, 2, 5, 28, 38, 69, 185,
  253
San Francisco Bay, 25
San Gorgonio Wilderness Area, 158
San Joaquin Valley, 12, 69, 77, 116
San Jose, 26
San Juan Bautista, iv, xii, 97, 110

San Juan Bautista, Mission, 97, 110
San Juan Capistrano, 4, 6
San Juan Mountains, 28
San Juan Ridge, 188
San Mateo, 75
San Pasqual, battle of, 69, 253
San Pedro, 4, 7
Santa Anita Rancho, 96
Santa Barbara, 2, 4, 5
Santa Clara, 73, 75
Santa Clara County, 151
Santa Cruz, 250
Santa Fe, 2, 25, 69, 75, 183
Santa Monica, 160
Sauer, Carl, 206, 209, 267
  Land and Life, 267
Schultz, Bob, xii
Seattle, 190
Shakespeare, William, 115
Shapiro, Samuel, 252
  Richard Henry Dana, Jr. 1815–1882, 252
Shaw, Reuben Cole, 251
  Across the Plains in Forty-Nine, 251
Shebl, James, xi
Sheehy, Don, xii
Sheep Rock, 58
Shenandoah Valley, 28
Sidney, Sir Phillip, 186
Sierra Madre, 81
Sierra Madre (Mexico), 49
Sierra Nevada, 10–12, 14, 19–26, 32–46,
  47–66, 87, 103, 152, 174, 186, 202–5
Silver Lake, 164
Simplon Pass, 36, 58, 60
Simpson, Lewis, xii, xvi, 267–8
  The Brazen Face of History, 267
  The Man of Letters in New England and
  the South, 267
Sinclair, Upton, 262
  Oil!, 262
Slotkin, Richard, 268
  Regeneration Through Violence, 268
Smith, Bob, xi
Smith, David, 170, 262
  "The Public Eye of Raymond Chandler,"
  262
Smith, Henry Nash, 257, 268
  "Clarence King, John Wesley Powell,
  and the Establishment of the United
  States Geological Survey," 257
  Virgin Land, 268

Smith, Jedediah, 18, 253
   The Ashley-Smith Explorations, 253
Snyder, Gary, iv, xvii, 35, 174–5, 186–
   205, 208, 264–5
   Axe Handles, 186–8, 204, 264
   The Back Country, 188–9, 195–9, 264
   Earth House Hold, 194, 199, 264
   The Fudo Trilogy, 264
   Myths & Texts, 35, 188, 192–4, 197, 264
   The Old Ways, 264
   The Real Work, 264
   Regarding Wave, 188, 199, 264
   Riprap, and Cold Mountain Poems, 188–
   93, 201, 264
   *Six Sections from Mountains and Rivers
     Without End Plus One,* 188, 264
   Turtle Island, 188, 200, 204, 264
Snyder, Gen, 202
Snyder, Kai, 202
Somerset, 124
Sonoma, 250
Soto, Gary, 266
   The Elements of San Joaquin, 266
   The Tale of Sunlight, 266
   Where the Sparrows Work Hard, 266
South Pass, 19–20, 23
Southern Pacific Railroad, 96, 116
Speir, Jerry, 263
   Raymond Chandler, 263
Spengemann, William, 268
   *The Adventurous Muse: The Poetics of
     American Fiction,* 268
Spengler, Oswald, 180
Spies, Werner, 248
   The Running Fence Project/Christo, 248
Stanford University, 185
Starr, Kevin, xi–xii, xvii, 30, 248
   Americans and the California Dream, xvii,
   30, 248
   *Inventing the Dream: California Through
     the Progressive Era,* xvii, 248
Stegner, Wallace, 98, 251, 256
   All the Little Live Things, 251
   Angle of Repose, 251
   The Preacher and the Slave, 251
   A Shooting Star, 251
   The Spectator Bird, 251
Steinbeck, Carol, 128, 130–1, 152–6
Steinbeck, Elaine, iv, 124, 153–7, 260
   Steinbeck: A Life in Letters, 260
Steinbeck, Gwyndolyn, 153–7

Steinbeck, John, iv, xii, xvii, 124–57, 179,
   208, 259–60
   *The Acts of King Arthur and His Noble
     Knights,* 259
   Burning Bright, 259
   Cannery Row, 128, 131, 259
   Cup of Gold, 127–8, 259
   East of Eden, 127, 131–2, 260
   The Grapes of Wrath, 126, 128, 130,
   147–51, 260
   In Dubious Battle, 129, 260
   The Log from the Sea of Cortez, 130–1,
   260
   The Long Valley, 137–47, 150, 155, 260
   The Moon Is Down, 260
   Of Mice and Men, 128, 129–30, 260
   Papers, 260
   The Pastures of Heaven, 128, 135–7, 260
   The Pearl, 260
   The Short Reign of Pippin IV, 260
   Sweet Thursday, 128, 260
   To a God Unknown, 132–7, 260
   Tortilla Flat, 128–9, 260
   *Travels with Charley in Search of Amer-
     ica,* 260
   The Wayward Bus, 260
   The Winter of Our Discontent, 127, 260
Stephen, Leslie, 56
   "A Bad Five Minutes in the Alps," 56
Sterling, George, 180, 264, 266
   Robinson Jeffers: The Man and the Artist,
   264
   Selected Poems, 266
Steudig, Bob, 265
   Gary Snyder, 265
Stevens, Elisha, 249
Stevens, Wallace, xvi, 36, 107, 207
Stevenson, Robert Louis, 15, 251
   From Scotland to Silverado, 251
Stewart, George, 149, 249, 251, 260
   The California Trail, 249
   Earth Abides, 251
   Fire, 251
   The Opening of the California Trail, 249
   Ordeal by Hunger, 149, 260
   Storm, 251
Stockton, Robert Field, 28
Suez, 192
Sunset, 176
Sutter, John Augustus, 25, 186
Swain, William, 248

Swift, John Franklin, 251
  Robert Greathouse, 251

Taylor, Bayard, xvi, 15, 251
  El Dorado, xvi, 251
  New Pictures from California, xvi, 251
Taylor, Gordon O., 257
  "Excursions in the 'Range of Light,' "
  257
Tehachapi, 78, 158
Tejon, 69, 74, 87, 92–3
Tennyson, Alfred Lord, 128–9
  Idylls of the King, 128–9
Thoreau, Henry David, 16–18, 35, 41, 46,
  73, 84, 112, 176
  Walden, 16–18, 35, 84, 176
Tor House, iv, 174, 176–8, 183
Truckee Valley, 25
True Confessions (United Artists), iv, 159
Tulare County, 96–7
Tuolomne Meadows, 41
Turner, Frederick Jackson, 268
  The Frontier in American History, 268
Turner, J. M. W., 49
Twain, Mark, 56, 251
  Roughing It, 251

Uehara, Masa, iv, 174, 192, 201, 204
University of Southern California, 182
University of Washington, 182
University of Wisconsin, 43
Unruh, John D., Jr., 249
  The Plains Across, 249
Upham, Samuel C., 251
  Notes of a Voyage to California, 251
U.S. Bureau of Reclamation, 91–2
U.S. Geological Survey, 48–9, 257
Utah, 19

Vachell, Horace Annesley, 263
  Life and Sport on the Pacific Slope, 263
Van Der Veer, Judy, 263
  Brown Hills, 263
Van Dyke, John, 93–4, 258
  The Desert, 93–4, 258
Van Dyke, T. S., 158, 263
  Millionaires of a Day, 158, 263
  Southern California, 263
Van Nostrand, Jeanne, 249
  The First Hundred Years of Painting in
  California: 1775–1875, 249

Velázquez, Diego, 175
  Las Meninas, 175
Vernal Falls, 42
Viertel, Peter, 160, 263
  The Canyon, 160, 263

Walker, Franklin, xvii, 103, 158, 249, 259
  Frank Norris, 259
  A Literary History of Southern California,
  xvii, 249
  San Francisco's Literary Frontier, xvii, 249
Walker, Captain Joseph, 2–3, 8, 9, 11, 14,
  18, 252–3
Walker Pass, 14
Walla Walla River, 19
Wallsten, Robert, 260
  Steinbeck: A Life in Letters, 260
Warren, Robert Penn, 209
Washington, 191, 203
Waterloo, 115
Watkins, Carleton, iv, 77
Watts, Alan, 265
  The Way of Zen, 265
Waugh, Evelyn, 160, 263
  The Loved One, 263
Wells, H. G., 69
Wesling, Donald, xi, 255
  John Muir: To Yosemite and Beyond, 255
West, Jessamyn, 263
  Cress Delahanty, 263
  The Life I Really Lived, 263
  South of the Angels, 263
West, Nathaniel, 160, 175, 263
  The Day of the Locust, 175, 263
Weston, Edward and Charis, 249
  California and the West, 249
Whipple, T. K., 136
White, Stewart Edward, 252
  Gold, 252
Whitman, Walt, 179
Whitney, Josiah, 34, 39, 48, 50, 255
  The Yosemite Guide-Book, 255
Wilhelmson, Carl, 153
Wilkins, Thurman, xi, 257
  Clarence King, 257
Williams, David A., 247
  California: A History of the Golden State,
  247
Williams, James, 252
  Life and Adventures of James Williams: A
  Fugitive Slave, 252

Williams, William Carlos, xviii, 15–17, 33, 268
 In the American Grain, 15–17, 268
Wilson, Edmund, 249
 The Boys in the Back Room: Notes on California Novelists, 249
Wind River Mountains, 19–20
Winter, Ella, 176
Winters, Yvor, 185–6, 266
 The Collected Poems, 266
Wisconsin, 42
Wolfe, Linnie Marsh, 254–5
 Son of the Wilderness: The Life of John Muir, 255
Wordsworth, William, 5, 36, 41, 58–60, 84, 186, 196–7, 202–3, 207–8

The Prelude, 43
Works Project Administration, 93, 249
 California: A Guide to the Golden State, 249

Yale University, 48
Yeats, William Butler, 146, 181, 203
Yerba Buena, 2
Yosemite Falls, 32–4, 37, 39
Yosemite National Park, 38
Yosemite Valley, i, 10, 12, 28, 32–46, 50, 254–5
Young, Vernon, 93, 258
 "Mary Austin and the Earth Performance," 258